BLACK LEGACY PRESS™
WWW.BLACKLEGACYPRESS.ORG

SLAVE NARRATIVES

VOLUME II
ARKANSAS NARRATIVES
PART 4

By
United States.
Work Projects Administration

Copyright © 2024 by BLACKLEGACYPRESS.ORG

All rights reserved. No part of this publication may be reproduced or transmitted in any form or by any means electronic or mechanical, including information storage and retrieval systems without permission in writing from the publisher, except for student research using the appropriate citations.

ISBN: 978-1-63652-221-0

SLAVE NARRATIVES

A Folk History of Slavery in the United States.
From Interviews with Former Slaves

**UNITED STATES.
WORK PROJECTS ADMINISTRATION**

TYPEWRITTEN RECORDS PREPARED BY
THE FEDERAL WRITERS' PROJECT
1936-1938
ASSEMBLED BY
THE LIBRARY OF CONGRESS PROJECT
WORK PROJECTS ADMINISTRATION
FOR THE DISTRICT OF COLUMBIA
SPONSORED BY THE LIBRARY OF
CONGRESS

WASHINGTON 1941

VOLUME II
ARKANSAS NARRATIVES
PART 4

Prepared by
The Federal Writers' Project of
The Works Progress Administration
For the State of Arkansas

CONTENTS

CLARICE JACKSON 1
CLARICE JACKSON 5
ISRAEL JACKSON 7
LULA JACKSON 11
LULA JACKSON 23
MARY JACKSON 27
TAYLOR JACKSON 29
VIRGINIA JACKSON 35
WILLIAM JACKSON 37
LAWSON JAMAR 39
NELLIE JAMES 41
ROBERT JAMES 43
ELLIS JEFFERSON 47
MOSES E. JEFFRIES 49
ELLIS JEFSON 55
ABSOLOM JENKINS 59
DORA JERMAN 63
ADALINE JOHNSON 65
ALICE JOHNSON 73
ALLEN JOHNSON 79
ANNIE JOHNSON 85
BEN JOHNSON 89
BEN JOHNSON 91

BETTY JOHNSON	93
CINDA JOHNSON	97
ELLA JOHNSON	99
FANNY JOHNSON	107
GEORGE JOHNSON	113
JOHN JOHNSON	117
LETHA JOHNSON	121
LEWIS JOHNSON	123
LIZZIE JOHNSON	127
LOUIS JOHNSON	131
MAG JOHNSON	135
MANDY JOHNSON	139
MARION JOHNSON	143
MARION JOHNSON	147
MARION JOHNSON	153
MARTHA JOHNSON	157
MILLIE JOHNSON	159
ROSIE JOHNSON	161
SAINT JOHNSON	163
WILLIE JOHNSON	165
ANGELINE JONES	169
CHARLIE JONES	171
CYNTHA JONES	173
EDMOND JONES	177
ELIZA JONES	181

EVELYN JONES	183
JOHN JONES	187
JOHN JONES	189
LIDIA JONES	193
LYDIA JONES	195
LIZA JONES	197
LUCY JONES	201
MARY JONES	203
MARY JONES	209
NANNIE JONES	211
REUBEN JONES	213
VERGIL JONES	217
WALTER JONES	221
OSCAR FELIX JUNELL	223
SAM KEATON	227
TINES KENDRICKS	229
TINES KENDRICKS	239
FRANK KENNEDY	243
KERNS ADRIANNA	245
GEORGE KEY	251
LUCY KEY	253
ANNA KING	257
ANNA KING	261
MOSE KING	263
SUSIE KING	267

WILLIAM KIRK	273
BETTY KRUMP	275
PRESTON KYLES	279
PRESTON KYLES	281
SUSA LAGRONE	283
BARNEY A. LAIRD	287
AREY LAMAR	291
SOLOMON LAMBERT	293
FRANK LARKIN	301
FRANK LARKIN	303
FRANK LARKIN	307
WILLIAM LATTIMORE	311
BESSIE LAWSOM	315
HENRY LEE	319
MANDY LEE	323
MARY LEE	325
TALITHA LEWIS	327
ABBIE LINDSAY	331
ROSA LINDSEY	337
WILLIAM LITTLE	339
MINERVA LOFTON	341
ROBERT LOFTON	345
JOHN H. LOGAN	353
ELVIE LOMACK	359
HENRY LONG	363

ANNIE LOVE	369
NEEDHAM LOVE	371
LOUIS LUCAS	377
LIZZIE LUCKADO	385
JOHN LUCKETT	387
JOHN LYNCH	389
JOSEPHINE SCOTT LYNCH	393

Interviewer: Mrs. Bernice Bowden
Person interviewed: Clarice Jackson
Eighteenth and Virginia, Pine Bluff, Arkansas
Age: 82

CLARICE JACKSON

"I was six or seven when they begin goin' to the Civil War. We had a big old pasture opposite and I know they would bring the soldiers there and drill 'em.

"Oh my God, don't talk about slavery. They kept us in so you know we couldn't go around.

"But if they kept 'em a little closer now, the world would be a better place. I'm so glad I raised my children when they was raisin' children. If I told 'em to do a thing, they did it 'cause I would always know what was best. I got here first you know.

"People now'days is just shortening their lives. The Lord is pressin' us now tryin' to press us back. But thank God I'm saved.

"Did you ever see things like they is now?

"I looks at the young folks and it seems like they is all in a hurry—looks like they is on the last round.

"These here seabirds, (a music machine called seaburg—ed.) is ruinin' the young folks.

"I feels my age now, but I thank the Lord I got a home and got a little income.

"My children can't help me—ain't got nothin' to help with but a little washin'. My daughter been bustin' the suds for a livin' 'bout thirty-two years now.

"I never went to school. My dad put me to work after freedom and then when schools got so numerous, I got too big. Ain't but one thing I want to learn this side of the River, is to read the Bible. I wants to confirm Jesus' words.

"The fus' place we went after we left the home place durin' of the war, we went to Wolf Creek. And then they pressed 'em so close we went to Red River. And they pressed 'em so close again we went to Texas and that's where we was when freedom come.

"That was in July and they closed the crap (crop) and then six weeks 'fore Christmas they loaded the wagons and started back to Arkansas. We come back to the Johnson place and stayed there three years, then my father rented the Alexander place on the Tamo.

"I stayed right there till I married. I married quite young, but I had a good husband. I ain't sayin' this just 'cause he's sleepin' but ever'body will tell you he was good to me. Made a good livin' and I wore what I wanted to.

"He come from South Carolina way before the war. Come from Abbeville. They was emigratin' the folks.

"I tell you all I can, but I won't tell you nothin' but the truth."

Interviewer's Comment

Owns her home and lives on the income from rental property.

United States. Work Projects Administration

Interviewer: Mrs. Bernice Bowden
Person interviewed: Clarice Jackson
1738 Virginia Street, Pine Bluff, Arkansas
Age: 84

CLARICE JACKSON

"Was I here in slavery days? Well, I remember when the soldiers went to war. Oh, I'm old—I ain't no baby. But I been well taken care of—I been treated well.

"I was bred and born right here in Arkansas and been livin' here all the time 'cept when they said the Yankees was comin'. I know we was just closin' up a crop. They put us in wagons and carried us to Wolf Creek in Texas and then they carried us to Red River. That was because it would be longer 'fore we found out we was free and they would get more work out a us.

"Old master's name was Robert Johnson and they called him Bob.

"After freedom they brought us back to Arkansas and put the colored folks to workin' on the shares. Yes'm they said they got their share. They looked like they was well contented. They stayed three or four years. We was treated more kinder and them that was not big enough to work was let go to school. I went to school awhile and then I had a hard spell of sickness—it was this slow fever. I was sick five or six weeks and it was a long time 'fore

I could get my health so I didn't try to go to school no more. Seemed like I forgot everything I knowed.

"When I was fifteen I got tired of workin' so hard so I got married, but I found out things was wusser. But my husband was good to me. Yes ma'm, he was a good man and nice to me. He was a good worker. He was deputy assessor under Mr. Triplett and he was a deputy sheriff and then he was a magistrate. Oh, he was a up-to-date man. He went to school after we was married and wanted me to go but I thought too much of my childun. When he died, 'bout two years ago, he left me this house and two rent houses. Yes ma'm, he was a good man.

"They ain't nothin' to this here younger generation. Did you ever see 'em goin' so fast? They won't take time to let you tell 'em anything. They is in a hurry. The world is too fast for me, but thank the Lord my childun is all settled. I got some nieces and nephews though that is goin' too fast.

"Yes'm, I'm gettin' along all right. I ain't got nothin' to complain of."

Interviewer: Mrs. Bernice Bowden
Person interviewed: Israel Jackson
3505 Short Second, Pine Bluff, Arkansas
Age: 78

ISRAEL JACKSON

"My name's Israel Jackson. No ma'am, I wasn't born in Arkansas—born in Yaller Bush County, Mississippi August de third, 1860.

"My old master? Called him General—General Bradford. I don't know where he was but he was gone somewhere. Don't know her name—just called her missis.

"Yas'm, I was big enough to work. Dey had me to lead out my young master's horse on de grass. I had a halter on it and one time I laid down and went to sleep. I had de rope tied to my leg and when it come twelve o'clock de horse drag me clear to de house. No ma'am, I didn't wake up till I got to de house. It was my young master's saddle horse.

"Yas'm, I knowed dey was a war 'cause de men come past just as thick. No'm, I wasn't afraid. I kept out of de way. Old missis wouldn't let us get in de way. I 'member dey stopped dere and told us we was free. Lots of de folks went off but my mother kept workin' in de field, and my father didn't leave.

"Old master had us go by his name. Dat's what dey called 'em—all de hands on de place.

"I thought from boyhood he was awful cruel. Didn't 'low us chillun in de white folks' house at all. Had one woman dat cooked. Dey was fifty or a hundred chillun on de place and dey had a big long trough dug out of a log and each chile had a spoon and he'd eat out of dat trough. Yas'm, I 'member dat. Eat greens and milk. As for meat, we didn't know what dat was. My mother would go huntin' at night and get a 'possum to feed us and sometimes old master would ketch her and take it away from her and give her a piece of salt meat. But sometimes she'd bury a 'possum till she had a chance to cook it. And dey'd take sackin' like you make cotton sacks and dye it and make us clothes.

"When de conch would blow at four o'clock every mornin' everybody got up and got ready for de field. Dey'd take dere chillun up to dat big long house. When mother went to de field I'd go along and lead de horse till I got to where dey was workin', then I'd sit down and let the horse eat. I was young and it's been so long.

"No ma'am, I never went to school. No ma'am, can't read or write. Never had no schools as I remember.

"Dey stayed on de place after freedom. No ma'am, dey did not pay 'em. I'se old but I ain't forgot dat. Dey fed theirselves by stealin' and gettin' things in de woods.

"After dem Blue Jackets come in dere General Bradford never did come back and our folks stayed dere and when dey did leave dey went to Sunflower County. After dat we got along better.

"How many brothers and sisters? I b'lieve I had five.

"I stayed with my parents till I was grown. No ma'am, dey didn't 'low us to marry. When we was twenty we was neither man nor boy; we was considered a hobble-de-hoy. And when we got to be twenty-one we was considered a man and your parents turned you loose, a man. So I left home and went to Louisiana. I stayed dere a year, then I went back to Mississippi and worked. I come here to Arkansas twenty-six years ago. Is dis Jefferson? Well, I come here to de west end.

"Since I been here I been workin' at de foundry—Dilley's foundry.

"'Bout two years ago I got sick and broke up and not able to work and Mr. Dilley give me a pension—ten dollars a month. But de wages and hour got here now and I don't know what he's gwine do. When de next pay-day comes he might give me somethin' and he might not.

"Miss, de white folks has done so bad here dat I don't know what dey's gwine a do. Mr. Ed and his father been takin' care of me for twenty years. Dey sure has been takin' care of me. Miss, I can't find no fault of Mr. Ed Dilley at all.

"I can do a little light work but when I work half a day I get nervous and can't do nothin'.

"No ma'am, I never did vote. Dey didn't 'low us to vote. Well, if dey did I didn't know it and I didn't vote.

"Well, Miss, I think de young folks is near to de dogs and de dogs ought to have 'em and bury 'em. Miss, I don't 'cept none of 'em. I wouldn't want to go on and tell you how dey has treated me. Dey ain't no use to ask 'cause I ain't gwine tell you. The people is more wicked and more wuss and ever'thing. I don't think nothin' of 'em.

"Miss, let me tell you de only folks dat showed me any friendly is Mr. Ed Dilley. I worked out dere night and day, Sunday and Monday—any time he called.

"Miss, I ain't never seen any jail house; I ain't never been to police headquarters; I ain't never been called a witness in my life. I try to live right, all I know, and if I do wrong it's somethin' I don't know. I ain't had dat much trouble in my life.

"I went up here to Judge Brewster to see about de pension and he said, 'Got a home?' I said, 'Yes.' 'Got it paid for?' 'Yes.' 'Got a deed?' 'Yes.' 'Got a abstract?' 'Yes.' 'Well, bring it up here and sign it and go get de pension.'

"But I wouldn't do it. Miss, I would starve till I was as stiff as a peckerwood peckin' at a hole 'fore I'd sign anything on my deed. Miss, I wouldn't put a scratch on my deed. I wouldn't trust 'em, wouldn't trust 'em if dey was behind a Winchester."

Interviewer: Samuel S. Taylor
Person interviewed: Lula Jackson
1808 Valentine Street, Little Rock, Arkansas
Age: 79?

LULA JACKSON

"I was born in Alabama, Russell County, on a place called Sand Ridge, about seven miles out from Columbus, Georgia. Bred and born in Alabama. Come out here a young gal. Wasn't married when I come out here. Married when a boy from Alabama met me though. Got his picture. Lula Williams! That was my name before I married. How many sisters do you have? That's another question they ask all the time; I suppose you want to know, too. Two. Where are they? That's another one of them questions they always askin' me. You want to know it, too? I got one in Clarksdale, Mississippi. And the other one is in Philadelphia; no, I mean in Philipp city, Tallahatchie (county). Her name is Bertha Owens and she lives in Philipp city. What state is Philipp city in? That'll be the next question. It is in Mississippi, sir. Now is thar anything else you'd like to know?

"My mother's name was Bertha Williams and my father's name was Fred Williams. I don't know nothing 'bout mama's mother. Yes, her name was Crecie. My father's mother was named Sarah. She got killed by lightning. Crecie's husband was named John Oliver. Sarah's husband was named William Daniel. Early Hurt was mama's master. He had an awful name and he was an awful man. He whipped you till he'd bloodied you and blistered you. Then he would cut open the blisters and drop sealing-wax in them and in the open wounds made by the whips.

"When the Yankees come in, his wife run in and got in the bed between the mattresses. I don't see why it didn't kill her. I don't know how she stood it. Early died when the Yankees come in. He was already sick. The Yankees come in and said, 'Did you know you are on the Yankee line?'

"He said, 'No, by God, when did that happen?'

"They said, 'It happened tonight, G——D—— you.'

"And he turned right on over and done everything on hisself and died. He had a eatin' cancer on his shoulder.

Schooling, Etc.

"My mother had so many children that I didn't get to go to school much. She had nineteen children, and I had to stay home and work to help take care of them. I can't write at all.

"I went to school in Alabama, 'round on a colored man's place—Mr. Winters. That was near a little town called Fort Mitchell and Silver Rim where they put the men in jail. I was a child. Mrs. Smith, a white woman from the North, was the second teacher that I had. The first was Mr. Croler. My third teacher was a man named Mr. Nelson. All of these was white. They wasn't colored teachers. After the War, that was. I have the book I used when I went to school. Here is the little Arithmetic I used.

Here is the Blue Back Speller. I have a McGuffy's Primer too. I didn't use that. I got that out of the trash basket at the white people's house where I work. One day they throwed it out. That is what they use now, ain't it?

"Here is a book my husband give me. He bought it for me because I told him I wanted a second reader. He said, 'Well, I'll go up to the store and git you one.' Plantation store, you know. He had that charged to his account.

"I used to study my lesson. I turned the whole class down once. It was a class in spelling. I turned the class down on 'Publication'—p-u-b-l-i-c-a-t-i-o-n. They couldn't spell that. But I'll tell the world they could spell it the next day.

"My teacher had a great big crocus sack, and when she got tired of whipping them, she would put them in the sack. She never did put me in that sack one time. I got a whipping mos' every day. I used to fight, and when I wasn't fightin' for myself, I'd be fighting for other children that would be scared to fight for theirselves, and I'd do their fighting for them.

"That whippin' in your hand is the worst thing you ever got. Brother, it hurts. I put a teacher in jail that'd whip one of my children in the hand.

Occupational History and Family

"My mama said I was six years old when the War ended and that I was born on the first day of October. During the War, I run up and down the yard and played, and run up and down the street and played; and when I would make too much noise, they'd whip me and send me back to my mother and tell her not to whip me no more, because they had already done it. I would help look after my mother's children. There were five children younger than I was. Everywhere she went, the white people would want me to nurse their children, because they said, 'That little rawboneded one is goin' to be the smartest one you got. I want her.' And my ma would say:

"'You ain't goin' to git 'er.' She had two other girls—Martha and Sarah. They was older than me, and she would hire them out to do nursing. They worked for their master during slave time, and they worked for money after slavery.

"My mama's first husband was killed in a rasslin' (wrestling) match. It used to be that one man would walk up to another and say, 'You ain't no good.' And the other one would say, 'All right, le's see.' And they would rassle.

"My mother's first husband was pretty old. His name was Myers. A young man come up to him one Sunday morning when they were gettin' commodities. They got sorghum, meat, meal, and flour; if what they got wasn't enough, then they would go out and steal a hog. Sometime they'd steal it anyhow; they got tired of eatin' the same thing all the time. Hurt would whip them for it. Wouldn't let the overseer whip them. Whip them hisself. 'Fraid the overseer wouldn't give them enough. They never could find my grandfather's meat. That was Grandfather William Down. They couldn't find his meat because he kept it hidden in a hole in the ground. It was under the floor of the cabin.

"Old Myers made this young man rassle with him. The young fellow didn't want to rassle with him; he said Myers was too old. Myers wasn't my father; he was my mother's first husband. The young man threw him. Myers wasn't satisfied with that. He wanted to rassle again. The young man didn't want to rassle again. But Myers made him. And the second time, the young man threw him so hard that he broke his collar-bone. My mother was in a family way at the time. He lived about a week after that, and died before the baby was born.

"My mother's second husband was named Fred Williams, and he was my father. All this was in slavery times. I am his oldest child. He raised all his children and all his stepchildren too. He and my mother lived together for over forty years, until she was more than seventy. He was much younger than she was—just eighteen years old when he married her. And she was a woman with five children. But she was a real wife to him. Him and her would fight, too. She was jealous of him. Wouldn't be none of that with me. Honey, when you hit me once, I'm gone. Ain't no beatin' on me and then sleepin' in the same bed with you. But they fit and then they lived together right on. No matter what happened, his clean clothes were ready whenever he got ready to go out of the house—even if it was just to go to work. His meals were ready whenever he got ready to eat. They were happy together till she died.

"But when she died, he killed hisself courtin'. He was

a young preacher. He died of pneumonia. He was visiting his daughter and got exposed to the weather and didn't take care of hisself.

"Right after the War, I was hired as a half-a-hand. After that I got larger and was hired as a whole hand, me and the oldest girl. I worked on one farm and then another for years. I married the first time when I was fifteen years old. That was almost right after slave time. Four couples of us were married at the same time. They lived close to me. I didn't want my husband to git in the bed with me when I married the first time. I didn't have no sense. I was a Christian girl.

"Frank Sampson was his name. It rained the day we married. I got my feet wet. My husband brought me home and then he turned 'round and went back to where the wedding was. They had a reception, and they danced and had a good time. Sampson could dance, too, but I didn't. A little before day, he come back and said to me—I was layin' in the middle of the bed—'Git over.' I called to mother and told her he wanted to git in the bed with me. She said, 'Well, let him git in. He's yo'r husband now.'

"Frank Sampson and me lived together about twenty years before he got killed, and then I married Andrew Jackson. He had children and grandchildren. I don't know what was the matter with old man Jackson. He was head deacon of the church. We only stayed together a year or more.

"I have been single ever since 1923, jus' bumming 'round white folks and tryin' to work for them and makin' them give me somethin' to eat. I ain't been tryin' to fin' no man. When I can't fin' no cookin' and washin' and ironin' to do, I used to farm. I can't farm now, and 'course I can't git no work to do to amount to nothin'. They say I'm too old to work.

"The Welfare helps me. Don't know what I'd do if it wasn't for them. I git some commodities too, but I don't git any wood. Some people says they pay house rent, but they never paid none of mine. I had to go to Marianna and git my application straight before I could git any help. They charged me half a dollar to fix out the application. The Welfare wanted to know how I got the money to pay for the application if I didn't have money to live on. I had to git it, and I had to git the money to go to Marianna, too. If I hadn't, I never would have got no help.

Husband's Death

"I told you my first husband got killed. The mule run away with his plow and throwed him a summerset. His head was where his heels should have been, he said, and the mule dragged him. His chest was crushed, and mashed. His face was cut and dirtied. He lived nine days and a half after he was hurt and couldn't eat one grain of rice. I never left his bedside 'cept to cook a little broth for him. That's all he would eat—just a little broth.

"He said to his friend, 'See this little woman of mine? I hate to leave her. She's just such a good little woman. She ain't got no business in this world without a husband.'

"And his friend said to him, 'Well, you might as well make up your mind you got to leave her, 'cause you goin' to do it.'

"He got hurt on Thursday and I couldn't git a doctor till Friday. Dr. Harper, the plantation doctor, had got his house burned and his hands hurt. So he couldn't come out to help us. Finally Dr. Hodges come. He come from Sunnyside, Mississippi, and he charge me fourteen dollars. He just made two trips and he didn't do nothin'.

"Bowls and pitchers were in style then. And I always kept a pitcher of clean water in the house. I looked up and there was a bunch of men comin' in the house. It was near dark then. They brought Sampson in and carried him to the bed and put him down. I said, 'What's the matter with Frank?' And they said, 'The mule drug him.' And they put him on the bed and went on out. I dipped a handkerchief in the water and wet it and put it in his mouth and took out great gobs of dust where the mule had drug him in the dirt. They didn't nobody help me with him then; I was there alone with him.

"I started to go for the doctor but he called me back and said it wasn't no use for me to go. Couldn't git the doctor then, and if I could, he'd charge too much and wouldn't be able to help him none nohow. So we wasn't able to git the doctor till the next day, and then it wasn't the plantation doctor. We had planted fifteen acres in cotton, and we had ordered five hundred pounds of meat for our winter supply and laid it up. But Frank never got to eat none of it. They sent three or four hands over to git their meals with me, and they et up all the meat and all the other supplies we had. I didn't want it. It wasn't no use to me when Frank was gone. After they paid the doctor's bill and took out for the supplies we was supposed to git, they handed me thirty-three dollars and thirty-five cents. That was all I got out of fifteen acres of cotton.

Ravelings

"I sew with rav'lin's. Here is some rav'lin's I use. I pull that out of tobacco sacks, flour sacks, anything, when I don't have the money to buy a spool of thread. I sew right on just as good with the rav'lin's as if it was thread. Tobacco sacks make the best rav'lin's. I got two bags full of tobacco sacks that I ain't unraveled yet. There is a man down town who saves them for me. When a man pulls out a sack he says, 'Save that sack for me, I got an old colored lady that makes thread out of tobacco sacks.' These is what he has give me. (She showed the interviewer a sack which had fully a gallon of little tobacco sacks in it—ed.)

"They didn't use rav'lin's in slave time. They spun the thread. Then they balled it. Then they twisted it, and then they sew with it. They didn't use rav'lin's then, but they used them right after the War.

"My mama used to say, 'Come here, Lugenia.' She and me would work together. She wanted me to reel for her. Ain't you never seen these reels? They turn like a spinning-wheel, but it is made indifferent. You turn till the thing pops, then you tie it; then it's ready to go to the loom. It is in hanks after it leaves the reel and it is pretty, too.

Present Condition

"I used to live in a four-room house. They charged me seven dollars and a half a month for it. They fixed it all up and then they wanted to charge ten dollars, and it wouldn't have been long before they went up to fifteen. So I moved. This place ain't so much. I pays five dollars and a half for it. When it rains, I have to go outside to keep from gittin' too wet. But I cut down the weeds all around the place. I planted some flowers in the front yard, and some vegetables in the back. That all helps me out. When I go to git commodities, I walk to the place. I can't stand the way these people act on the cars. Of course, when I have a bundle, I have to use the car to come back. I just put it on my head and walk down to the car line and git on. Lord, my mother used to carry some bundles on her head."

Interviewer's Comment

According to the marriage license issued at the time of her last marriage in 1922, Andrew Jackson was sixty years old, and sister Jackson was fifty-two. But Andrew Jackson was eighty when sister Jackson married him, she says. Who can blame him for saying sixty to the clerk? Sister Jackson admits that she was six years old during the War and states freely and accurately details of those times, but what wife whose husband puts only sixty in writing would be willing to write down more than fifty-two for herself?

Right now at more than seventy-nine, she is spry and

jaunty and witty and good humored. Her house is as clean as a pin, and her yard is the same.

The McGuffy's Primer which she thinks is used now is a modernized McGuffy printed in 1908. The book bought for her by her first husband is an original McGuffy's Second Reader.

United States. Work Projects Administration

Interviewer: Samuel S. Taylor
Person interviewed: Lula Jackson (supplement) [HW: cf. 30600]
1808 Valentine Street, Little Rock, Arkansas
Age: 79
Occupation: Field hand

LULA JACKSON

Whippings

"Early Hurt had an overseer named Sanders. He tied my sister Crecie to a stump to whip her. Crecie was stout and heavy. She was a grown young woman and big and strong. Sanders had two dogs with him in case he would have trouble with anyone. When he started layin' that lash on Crecie's back, she pulled up that stump and whipped him and the dogs both.

"Old Early Hurt came up and whipped her hisself. Said, 'Oh, you're too bad for the overseer to whip, huh?'

"Wasn't no such things as lamps in them days. Jus' used pine knots. When we quilted, we jus' got a good knot and lighted it. And when that one was nearly burnt out, we would light another one from it.

"We had a old lady named 'Aunt' Charlotte; she wasn't my aunt, we jus' called her that. She used to keep the children when the hands were working. If she liked you she would treat your children well. If she didn't like you, she wouldn't treat them so good. Her name was

Charlotte Marley. She was too old to do any good in the field; and she had to take care of the babies. If she didn't like the people, she would leave the babies' napkins on all day long, wet and filthy.

"My papa's mama, Sarah, was killed by lightning. She was ironing and was in a hurry to get through and get the supper on for her master, Early Hurt. I was the oldest child, and I always was scared of lightning. A dreadful storm was goin' on. I was under the bed and I heard the thunder bolt and the crash and the fall. I heard mama scream. I crawled out from under the bed and they had grandma laid out in the middle of the floor. Mama said, 'Child, all the friend you got in the world is dead.' Early Hurt was standin' over her and pouring buckets of water on her. When the doctor come, he said, 'You done killed her now. If you had jus' laid her out on the ground and let the rain fall on her, she would have come to, but you done drownded her now.' She wouldn't have died if it hadn't been for them buckets of water that Early Hurt throwed in her face.

"Honey, they ain't nothin' as sweet to drink out of as a gourd. Take the seeds out. Boil the gourd. Scrape it and sun it. There ain't no taste left. They don't use gourds now."

Interviewer's Comment

Violent death followed Lula Jackson's family like an implacable avenger. Her father's mother was struck and killed by lightning. Her mother's first husband was thrown to his death in a wrestling match. Her own husband was dragged and kicked to death by a mule. Her brother-in-law, Jerry Jackson, was killed by a horse. But Sister Jackson is bright and cheery and full of faith in God and man, and utterly without bitterness.

United States. Work Projects Administration

Interviewer: Thomas Elmore Lucy
Person interviewed: Mary Jackson,
Russellville, Arkansas
Age: 75?

MARY JACKSON

"My name is Mary Jackson, and I was born in Miller Grove, Hunt County, Texas during the War. No sir, I do not know the year. Our master's name was Dixon, and he was a wealthy plantation owner, had lots of property in Hunt County.

"The days after the War—called the Reconstruction days, I believe—were sure exciting, and I can 'mind' a lot of things the people did, one of them a big barbecue celebration commemoratin' the return of peace. They had speeches, and music by the band—and there were a lot of soldiers carrying guns and wearing some kind of big breastplates. The white children tried to scare us by telling us the soldiers were coming to kill us little colored children. The band played 'Dixie' and other familiar tunes that the people played and sang in those days.

"Yes sir, I remember the Klu Klux Klan. They sure kept us frightened and we would always run and hide when we heard they were comin'. I don't know of any special harm they done but we were afraid of em.

"I have been a member of the A. M. E. Church for forty years, and my children belong to the same church.

"No sir, I don't know if the government ever promised our folks anything—money, or land, or anything else.

"Don't ask me anything about this 'new generation' business. They're simply too much for me; I cannot understand em at all. Don't know whether they are coming or going. In our day the parents were not near so lenient as they are today. I think much of the waywardness of the youth today should be blamed on the parents for being too slack in their training."

NOTE: Mrs. Jackson and her son live in a lovely cottage, and her taste in dress and general deportment are a credit to the race.

Interviewer: Miss Irene Robertson
Person interviewed: Taylor Jackson,
Edmondson, Arkansas
Age: 88?
[Date Stamp: MAY 11 1938]

TAYLOR JACKSON

"I was born two miles from Baltimore, Maryland. I was a good size boy. My father carried me to see the war flag go up. There was an awful crowd, one thousand people, there. I had two masters in this country besides in Virginia. When war was declared there was ten boats of niggers loaded at Washington and shipped to New Orleans. We stayed in the 'Nigger Traders Yard' there about three months. But we was not to be sold. Master Cupps [Culps?] owned father, mother and all of us. If they gained the victory he was to take us back to Virginia. I never knowed my grandparents. The yard had a tall brick wall around it. We had a bunk room, good cotton pads to sleep on and blankets. On one side they had a wall fixed to go up on from the inside and twelve platforms. You could see them being sold on the inside and the crowd on the outside. When they auctioned them off they would come, pick out what they wanted to sell next and fill them blocks again. They sold niggers all day long. They come in another drove they had, had men out buying over the country. They come in thick wood doors with iron nails bradded through, fastened on big hinges, fastened it with chains and iron bars. The house was a big red brick house. We didn't get none too much to eat at that place. I reckon one side was three hundred yard long of the wall and the house was that long. Some of them in there cut their hands off with a knife or ax. Well, they couldn't sell them. Nobody would buy them. I don't know what they ever done with them. Plenty of them would cut their hand off if they could get something to cut with to keep from being sold.

"We stayed in that place till Wyley Lions [Lyons?] come and got us in wagons. He kept us for Master Cupps. Mother was a house girl in Virginia. She was one more good cook. I started hoeing and picking cotton in Virginia for master. When I was fourteen years old I done the same in Mississippi with Wiley Lyons in Mississippi close to Canton. In Canton, Mississippi Wiley Lyons had the biggest finest brick house in that country. He had two farms. In Bolivar County was the biggest. I could hear big shooting from Canton fifteen miles away. He wasn't mean and he didn't allow the overseers to be mean.

"Hilliard Christmas [a neighbor] was mean to his folks. My father hired his own time. He raised several ten acre gardens and watermelons. He paid Mr. Cupp in Virginia. He come to see our folks how they was getting along.

"A Negro on a joining farm run off. They hunted him with the dogs and they found him at a log. Heap his legs froze, so the white doctor had to cut them off. He was on Solomon's farms. After that he got to be a cooper. He made barrels and baskets—things he could do sittin' in his chair. They picked him up and made stumps for him. Some folks was mean.

"My mother was Rachel and my father was Andrew

Jackson. I had three brothers fought in the War. I was too young. They talked of taking me in a drummer boy the year it ceased. My nephew give me this uniform. It is warm and it is good. My breeches needs some repairs reason I ain't got them on. [He has worn a blue uniform for years and years—ed.]

"There was nine of us children. I got one girl very low now. She's in Memphis. I been in Arkansas 45 years. I come here jes' drifting looking out a good location. I never had no dealings with the Ku Klux. I been farming all my life. Yes, I did like it. I never owned a home nor no land. I never voted in my life. I had nine children of my own but only my girl living now.

"Nine or ten years ago I could work every minute. Times was good! good! Could get plenty work—wood to cut and ditching. It is not that way now. I can't do a day's work now. I'm failing fast. I feel it.

"Young folks can make a living if they work and try. Some works too hard and some don't hardly work. Work is scarcer than it ever was to my knowledge. Times changed and changed the young folks. Mother died two or three years after the War. My father died first year we come to Mississippi.

[We went by and took the old Negro to West Memphis. From there he could take a jitney to Memphis to see his daughter—ed.]

"I ain't never been 'rested. I ain't been to jail. Nearly well be as so confined with the mud. [We assured him it was nicer to ride in the car than be in jail—ed.]

"I couldn't tell how many I ever seen sold. I seen

some sold in Virginia, I reckon, or Maryland—one off the boats. They kept them tied. They was so scared they might do anything, jump in the big waters. They couldn't talk but to some and he would tell white folks what he said. [They used an interpreter.] Some couldn't understand one another if they come from far apart in the foreign country. Slavery wasn't never bad on me. I never was sold off from my folks and I had warmer, better clothes 'an I have now. I had plenty to eat, more'an I has now generally. I had better in slavery than I have now. That is the truth. I'm telling the truth, I did. Some didn't. One neighbor got mad and give each hand one ear of corn nine or ten o'clock. They take it to the cook house and get it made up in hominy. Some would be so hungry they would parch the corn rather 'an wait. He'd give 'em meal to make a big kettle of mush. When he was good he done better. Give 'em more for supper.

"Freedom—soldiers come by two miles long look like. We followed them. There was a crowd following. Wiley Lyons had no children; he adopted a boy and a girl. Me and the boy was growing up together. Me and the white boy (fifteen or sixteen years old, I reckon we was) followed them. They said that was Grant's army. I don't know. 'That made us free' they told us. The white boy was free, he just went to see what was happening. We sure did see! We went by Canton to Vicksburg when fighting quit. Folks rejoiced, and then went back wild. Smart ones soon got work. Some got furnished a little provisions to help keep them from starving. Mr. Wiley Lyons come got us after five months. We hung around my brother that had been in the War. I don't know if he was a soldier or a waiter. We worked around Master Lyons' house at Canton till he died. I started farming again with him.

"I get $8 a month pension and high as things is that is a powerful blessing but it ain't enough to feed me good. It cost more to go after the commodities up at Marion than they come to [amount to in value]."

United States. Work Projects Administration

Interviewer: Miss Irene Robertson
Person interviewed: Virginia Jackson,
Helena, Arkansas
Age: 74
[Date Stamp: MAY 31 1938]

VIRGINIA JACKSON

"Mother said I was born the same year peace was declared. I was born before the Civil War close, I reckon. I was born in Tunica, Mississippi. Mother belong to Mistress Cornelia and Master John Hood. He come from Alabama in wagons and brought mother and whole lot of 'em, she said, to Tunica, Mississippi. My mother and father never sold. They told me that. She said she was with the master and he give her to father. He ask her did she want him and ask him if he want her. They lived on joint places. They slept together on Wednesday and Saturday nights. He stayed at Hood's place on Sunday. They was owned by different masters. They didn't never say 'bout stepping over no broom. He was a Prince. When he died she married a man named Russell. I never heard her say what his name was. My father was Mathew Prince. They was both field hands. I never knowed my father. I called my stepfather popper. I always did say mother.

"Mother said her master didn't tell them it was freedom. Other folks got told in August. They passed it 'round secretly. Some Yankees come asked if they was getting paid for picking cotton in September. They told their master. They told the Yankees 'yes' 'cause they was afraid they would be run off and no place to go. They said Master Hood paid them well for their work at cotton selling time. He never promised them nothing. She said he never told one of them to leave or to stay. He let 'em be. I reckon they got fed. I wore cotton sack dresses. It wasn't bagging. It was heavy stiff cloth.

"Mother and her second husband come to Forrest City. They hoped they could do better. I come too. I worked in the field all my whole life 'cepting six years I worked in a laundry. I washed and ironed. I am a fine ironer. If I was younger I could get all the mens' shirts I could do now. I do a few but I got neuralgia in my arms and shoulders.

"I don't believe in talking 'bout my race. They always been lazy folks and smart folks, and they still is. The present times is good for me. I'm so thankful. I get ten dollars and some help, not much. I don't go after it. I let some that don't get much as I get have it. I told 'em to do that way."

Interviewer: Mrs. Bernice Bowden
Person interviewed: William Jackson
Route 6, Box 81, Pine Bluff, Arkansas
Age: 84

WILLIAM JACKSON

"Me? Well, I was born July 12, 1853. Now you can figure that up.

"I was sold four times in slavery times. I was sold through the nigger traders and you know they didn't keep you long.

"I was born in Tennessee, raised in Mississippi, and been here in Arkansas up and down the Arkansas River ever since I was fifteen.

"A fellow bought me in Tennessee and sold me to a fellow named Abe Collins in Mississippi. He sold me to Dr. Maloney and then Winn and Trimble in Hempstead County bought me. They run a tanyard.

"I went to school one day in my life. My third master's children learned me my ABC's in slavery times. I'm not educated but I can read. Read the Bible and something like that.

"The Ku Klux run me one night. They come to the door and I went out the window. They went to my master's tanyard in broad open day and took leather. Oh, I been all through the roughness. But the Lord has blessed me ever since I been in this world. I can see good and hear good and get about.

"I come here to Arkansas with some refugees, and I been up and down the river ever since.

"In slavery times I had plenty to eat, such as 'twas. Had biscuits on Sunday made out of shorts.

"I lived with one man, Dr. Maloney, who was pretty cruel. I run away from him once, but he caught me fore night. Put me in a little house on bread and water for three or four days and then he sold me. Said he wouldn't have a nigger that would run away. Otherwise I been treated pretty well.

"I come to Pine Bluff in '82. Last place I farmed was at what they call the Nichol place.

"I used to vote Republican—wouldn't let us vote nothin' else. In this country they won't let niggers vote in the primary 'cause they can vote in the presidential election. I held one office—justice of the peace.

"If the younger generation don't change, the Lord goin' to put curses on em. That's just what's goin' to come of em. More you do for em the worse they is. Don't think about the future—just today."

Interviewer: Miss Irene Robertson
Person interviewed: Lawson Jamar,
Edmondson, Arkansas
Age: 66
[Date Stamp: MAY 11 1938]

LAWSON JAMAR

"Papa had twelve children and when he died he lef' two and now I am all the big family left.

"Mama was born in Huntsville, Alabama. I was born there too. She was Liza, b'long to Tom and Unis Martin. Papa b'long to Mistress Sarah and Jack Jamar. They had to work hard. They had to do good work. They had to not slight their work. Papa's main job was to carry water to the hands. He said it kept him on the go. They had more than one water boy. They had to go to the wash hole before they went to bed and wash clean. The men had a place and the women had their place. They didn't have to get in if it was cold but they had to wash off.

"They hauled a wagon load of axes or hoes and lef' 'em in the field so they could get 'em. Then they would haul plows, hoes or axes to the shop to be fixed up. They had two or three sets. They worked from early till late. They had a cook house. They cooked at their own houses when the work wasn't pushing. When they got behind they would work in the moonlight. If they got through they all went and help some neighbor two or three nights and have a big supper sometimes. They done that on Saturday nights, go home and sleep all day Sunday.

"If they didn't have time to wash and clean the houses and the beds some older women would do that and tend to the babies. They had a hard time during the War. It was hard after the War. Papa brought me to this country to farm. He farmed till he started sawmilling for Chappman Dewy at Marked Tree. Then he swept out and was in the office to help about. He never owned nothing. He come and I farmed. He helped a little. He was so old. He talked more about the War and slavery. I always have farmed. Farmed all my life.

"I don't farm now. I got asthma and cripple with rheumatism. What my wife and children can't do ain't done now. [Three children.] I don't get no help but I applied for it.

"Present times is all right where a man can work. The present generation rather do on heap less and do less work. They ain't got manners and raisin' like I had. They don't know how to be polite. We tries to learn 'em [their children] how to do."

NOTE: The woman was black and so was the cripple Negro man; their house was clean, floors, bed, tables, chairs. Very good warm house. They couldn't remember the old tales the father told to tell them to me.

Interviewer: Thomas Elmore Lucy
Person interviewed: Nellie James,
Russellville, Arkansas
Age: 72

NELLIE JAMES

"Nellie James is my name. Yes, Mr. D. B. James was my husband, and he remembered you very kindly. They call me 'Aunt Nellie.' I was born in Starkville, Ouachita County, Mississippi the twenty-ninth of March, in 1866, just a year after the War closed. My parents were both owned by a plantation farmer in Ouachita County, Mississippi, but we came to Arkansas a good many years ago.

"My husband was principal of the colored school here at Russellville for thirty-five years, and people, both white and black, thought a great deal of him. We raised a family of six children, five boys and a girl, and they now live in different states, some of them in California. One of my sons is a doctor in Chicago and is doing well. They were all well educated. Mr. James saw to that of course.

"So far as I remember from what my parents said, the master was reasonably kind to all his slaves, and my husband said the same thing about his own master although he was quite young at the time they were freed. (Yes sir, you see he was born in slavery.)

"I was too young to remember much about the Ku Klux Klan, but I remember we used to be afraid of them and we children would run and hide when we heard they were coming.

"No sir, I have never voted, because we always had to pay a dollar for the privilege—and I never seemed to have the dollar (laughingly) to spare at election time. Mr. James voted the Republican ticket regularly though.

"All our family were Missionary Baptists. I united with the Baptist church when I [HW: was] thirteen years old.

"I think the young people of both races are growing wilder and wilder. The parents today are too slack in raising them—too lenient. I don't know where they are headed, what they mean, what they want to do, or what to expect of them. And I'm too busy and have too hard a time trying to make ends meet to keep up with their carryings-on."

NOTE: Mrs. Nellie James, widow of Prof. D. B. James, one of the most successful Negro teachers who ever served in Russellville, is a quiet, refined woman, a good housekeeper, and has reared a large and successful family. She speaks with good, clear diction, and has none of the brogue that is characteristic of the colored race of the South.

Interviewer: Samuel S. Taylor
Person interviewed: Robert James
4325 W. Eighth Street, Little Rock, Arkansas
Age: 66, or older
Occupation: Cook

ROBERT JAMES

"I was born in Lexington, Mississippi, in the year 1872. My mother's name was Florida Hawkins. Florida James was her slavery name. David Jones was her old master. That was in Mississippi—the good old country! People hate it because they don't like the name but it was a mighty good country when I was there. The white people there were better to the colored people when I was there than they are here. But there is a whole lots of places that is worse than Arkansas.

"I have been here forty-eight years and I haven't had any trouble with nobody, and I have owned three homes in my time. My nephew and my brother happened to meet up with each other in France. They thought about me and wrote and told me about it. And I writ to my sister in Chicago following up their information and got in touch with my people. Didn't find them out till the great war started. Had to go to Europe to find my relatives. My sister's people and mine too were born in Illinois, but my mother and two sisters and another brother were born in Mississippi. Their kin born in Illinois were half-brothers and so on.

Refugeeing—Ghosts

"I heard my mother say that her master and them had to refugee them to keep them from the Yankees. She told a ghost tale on that. I guess it must have been true.

"She said they all hitched up and put them in the wagon and went to driving down the road. Night fell and they came to a big two-story house. They went to bed. The house was empty, and they couldn't raise nobody; so they just camped there for the night. After they went to bed, big balls of fire came rolling down the stairs. They all got scared and run out of the house and camped outside for the night. There wasn't no more sleeping in that house.

"Some people believe in ghosts and some don't. What do you believe? This is what I have seen myself. Mules and horses were running 'round screaming and hollering every night. One day, I was walking along when I saw a mule big as an elephant with ears at least three feet long and eyes as big as auto lamps. He was standing right in the middle of the road looking at me and making no motion to move. I was scared to death, but I stooped down to pick up a stone. It wasn't but a second. But when I raised up, he had vanished. He didn't make a sound. He just disappeared in a second. That was in the broad open daylight. That was what had been causing all the confusion with the mules and horses.

"When I first married I used to room with an old lady named Johnson. Time we went to bed and put the light out, something would open the doors. Finally I got scared and used to tell my wife to get up and close the doors. Finally she got skittish about it. There used to be the biggest storms around there and yet you couldn't see nothin'. There wasn't no rain nor nothin'. Just sounds and noises like storms. My wife comes to visit me sometimes now.

"My mother says there wasn't any such thing as marriage in slave times. Old master jus' said, 'There's your husband, Florida.'"

United States. Work Projects Administration

Little Rock District
FOLKLORE SUBJECTS

Name of Interviewer: Irene Robertson
Subject: HISTORY OF ELLIS JEFFERSON—(NEGRO)
Story—Information (If not enough space on this page add page.)

This Information given by: Ellis Jefferson (Uncle Jeff) (C)
Place of Residence: Hazen, Arkansas
Occupation: Superanuated Minister of the M. E. Church
Age: 77

ELLIS JEFFERSON

[TR: Personal information moved from bottom of form.]

He has his second eyesight and his hair is short and white. He is a black skinned, bright-eyed old man. "Uncle Jeff" said he remembered when the Civil War had ended they passed by where he lived with teams, wagons filled, and especially the artillery wagon. They were carrying them back to Washington. His mother was freed from Mrs. Nancy Marshall of Roanoke, Va. She moved and brought his mother, he and his sister, Ann, to Holly Springs, Miss. The county was named for his mistress: Marshall County, Mississippi.

In 1868 they moved to [HW: within] 4 miles of De-Witt and 10 miles of Arkansas Post. Later they moved to Kansas and near Wichita then back to Marshall, Texas. His sister has four sons down there. He thinks she is still living. His Mistress went back to Roanoke, Va., and his mother died at Marshall. Tom Marshall was his Master's name, but he seems to have died in the Civil War. This old Uncle Jeff lived in Alabama and has preached there and in northern Mississippi and near Helena, Arkansas. He helped cook at Helena in a hotel. He preaches some but the WPA supports him now. Uncle Jeff can't remember his dreams he said "The Bible says, young men dream dreams and old men see visions."

He had a real vision once, he was going late one afternoon to get his mules up and he heard a voice "I have a voice I want you to complete. Carry my word." He was a member of the church but he made a profession and a year later was ordained into the ministry. He believes in dreams. Says they are warnings.

Uncle Jeff says he has written some poetry but it has all been lost.

When anyone dies the sexton goes to the church and tolls the bell as many times as the dead person is old. They take the body to the church for the night and they gather there and watch. He believes the soul rises from the ground on the Resurrection Day. He believes some people can put a "spell" on other people. He said that was witchery.

[HW: Marshall County, Miss., named for John Marshall of Virginia, Chief Justice of the U. S. Supreme Court, 1801-35. History of Marshall (County), Mississippi, by Clayton M. Alexander.]

FOLKLORE SUBJECTS

Name of Interviewer: S. S. Taylor
Subject: [HW: Moses Jeffries]
Story—Information (If not enough space on this page add page.)

This information given by: Moses E. Jeffries
Place of Residence: 1110 Izard Street, Little Rock, Arkansas
Occupation: Plasterer
Age: 81

MOSES E. JEFFRIES

[TR: Age: 75 on 4th page of form.]
[TR: Personal information moved from bottom of form.]

"I was born in 1856. My age was kept with the cattle. As a rule, you know, slaves were chattels. There was a fire and the Bible in which the ages were kept was lost. The man who owned me couldn't remember what month I was born in. Out of thirteen children, my mother could only remember the age of one. I had twelve brothers and sisters—Bob Lacy, William Henry, Cain Cecil, Jessie, Charles, Harvey, Johnnie, Anna, Rose, Hannah, Lucy, and Thomas. I am the only one living now. My parents were both slaves. My father has been dead about fifty-nine years and my mother about sixty or sixty-one years. She died before I married and I have been married fifty years. I have them in my Bible.

I remember when Lincoln was elected president and they said there was going to be war. I remember when they had [HW: a] slave market in New Orleans. I was living betweeen [TR: between] Pine Bluff and New Orleans (living in Arkansas) and saw the slaves chained together as they were brought through my place and located somewhere on some of the big farms or plantations.

I never saw any of the fighting but I did see some of the Confederate armies when they were retreating near the end of the war. I was just about ten years old at the time and was in Marshall, Texas.

The man that owned me said to the old people that they were free, that they didn't belong to him any more, that Abraham Lincoln had set them free. Of course, I didn't know what freedom was. They brought the news to them one evening, and them niggers danced nearly all night.

I remember also seeing a runaway slave. We saw the slaves first, and the dogs came behind chasing them. They passed through our field about half an hour ahead of the hounds, but the dogs would be trailing them. The hunters didn't bother to stop and question us because they knew the hounds were on the trail. I have known slaves to run away and stay three years at a time. Master would whip them and they would run away. They wouldn't have no place to go or stay so they would come back after a while. Then they would be punished again. They wouldn't punish them much, however, because they might run off again.

MARRIAGE

If I went on a plantation and saw a girl I wanted to marry, I would ask my master to buy her for me. It wouldn't matter if she were somebody else's wife; she would become mine. The master would pay for her and bring her home and say, "John, there's your wife. That is all the marriage there would be. Yellow women used to be a novelty then. You wouldn't see one-tenth as many then as now. In some cases, however, a man would retain his wife even after she had been sold away from him and would have permission to visit her from time to time.

INHERITANCE OF SLAVES

If a man died, he often stated in his will which slaves should go to each child he had. Some men had more than a hundred slaves and they divided them up just as you would cattle. Some times there were certain slaves that certain children liked, and they were granted those slaves.

WHAT THE FREEDMEN RECEIVED

Nothing was given to my parents at freedom. None of the niggers got anything. They didn't give them anything. The slaves were hired and allowed to work the farms on shares. That is where the system of share cropping came from. I was hired for fifty dollars a year, but was paid only five. The boss said he owed me fourteen dollars but five was all I got. I went down town and bought some candy. It was the first time I had had that much money.

I couldn't do anything about the pay. They didn't give me any land. They hired me to work around the house and I ate what the boss ate. But the general run of slaves got pickled pork, molasses, cornmeal and sometimes flour (about once a week for Sunday). The food came out of the share of the share cropper.

You can tell what they did by what they do now. It (share cropping) hasn't changed a particle since. About Christmas was the time they usually settled up. Nobody was forced to remain as a servant. I know one thing,— Negroes did not go to jail and penitentiary like they do now.

KU KLUX KLAN

The Ku Klux Klan to the best of my knowledge went into action about the time shortly after the war when the amendments to the Constitution gave the Negroes the right to vote. I have seen them at night dressed up in their uniform. They would visit every Negro's house in the comunity [TR: community]. Some they would take out and whip, some they would scare to death. They would ask for a drink of water and they had some way of drinking a whole bucketful to impress the Negroes that they were supernatural. Negroes were very superstitious then. Colonel Patterson who was a Republican and a colonel or general of the militia, white and colored, under the governorship of Powell Clayton, stopped the operation of the Klan in this state. After his work, they ceased terrorizing the people.

POLITICAL OFFICIALS

Many an ex-slave was elected sheriff, county clerk, probate clerk, Pinchback[A] was elected governor in Louisiana. The first Negro congressman was from Mississippi and a Methodist preacher Hiram Revells[B]. We had a Nigger superintendent of schools of the state of Arkansas, J. C. Corbin[C]—I don't remember just when, but it was in the early seventies. He was also president of the state school in Pine Bluff—organized it.

SUFFRAGE

The ex-slave voted like fire directly after the war. That was about all that did vote then. If the Niggers hadn't voted they never would have been able to elect Negroes to office.

I was elected Alderman once in Little Rock under the administration of Mayer Kemer. We had Nigger coroner, Chief of Police, Police Judge, Policemen. Ike Gillam's father was coroner. Sam Garrett was Chief of Police; Judge M. W. Gibbs was Police Judge. He was also a receiver of public lands. So was J. E. Bush, who founded the Mosaics [HW: (Modern Mosaic Templars of America)]. James W. Thompson, Bryant Luster, Marion H. Henderson, Acy L. Richardson, Childress' father-in-law, were all aldermen. James P. Noyer Jones was County Clerk of Chicot County, S. H. Holland, a teacher of mine, a little black nigger about five feet high, as black as ink, but well educated was sheriff of Desha County. Augusta had a Negro who was sheriff. A Negro used to hold good offices in this state.

I charge the change to Grant. The Baxter-Brooks matter caused it. Baxter was a Southern Republican from the Northeastern part of the state, Batesville, a Southern man who took sides with the North in the war. Brooks was a Methodist preacher from the North somewheres. When Grant recognized the Baxter faction whom the old ex-slaveholders supported because he was a Southerner and sided with Baxter against Brooks, it put the present Democratic party in power, and they passed the Grandfather law barring Negroes from voting.

Negroes were intimidated by the Ku Klux. They were counted out. Ballot boxes were burned and ballots were destroyed. Finally, Negroes got discouraged and quit trying to vote."

Footnotes:

[A] [HW: P. B. S. Pinchback, elected Lieutenant-Governor of La. Held office 43 days.]

[B] [HW: Hiram Revells, elected to fill the unexpired term of Jefferson Davis.]

[C] [HW: J. C. Corbin appointed state superintendent of public instruction in 1873—served until the end of 1875.]

Interviewer: Miss Irene Robertson
Person interviewed: Ellis Jefson (M. E. Preacher),
Hazen, Ark.
Age: 77

ELLIS JEFSON

"My father was a full blood African. His parents come from there and he couldn't talk plain.

"My great grandma was an Indian squaw. Mother was crossed with a white man. He was a Scotchman.

"My mother belong to old man John Marshall. He died before I left Virginia.

"Old Miss Nancy Marshall and the boys and their wives, three of em was married, and slaves set out in three covered wagons and come to Holly Springs, Mississippi in 1867.

"Blunt Marshall was a Baptist preacher. In 1869 my grandma died at Holly Springs.

"I had two sisters Ann and Mariah. Old Miss Nancy Marshall had kin folks at Marshall, Texas. She took Ann with her and I have never seen her since.

"In 1878 we immigrated to Kansas. We soon got back to Helena. Mariah died there and in 1881 mother died.

"Old Miss Nancy's boys named Blunt, John, Bill, Harp. I don't know where they scattered out to finally.

"All my folks ever expected was freedom. We was nicely taken care of till the family split up. My father was suppressed. He belong to Master Ernman. He run off and went on with the Yankees when they come down from Virginia. We think he got killed. We never heard from him after 1863.

"In 1882 my white folks went to Padukah, Kentucky. They was on the run from Yellow Fever. They had kin up there. I stayed in Memphis and nursed. They put up flags. Negroes didn't have it. They put coffins on the porches before the people died. Carried wagons loads of dead bodies wrapped in sheets. White folks would meet and pray the disease be lifted. When they started vomiting black, there was no more hopes. Had to hold them on bed when they was dying. When they have Yellow Fever white folks turn yellow. I never heard of a case of Yellow Fever in Memphis mong my race. Dr. Stone of New Orleans had better luck with the disease than any other doctor. I was busy from June till October in Memphis. They buried the dead in long trenches. Nearly all the business houses was closed. The boats couldn't stop in towns where Yellow Fever had broke out.

"I never seen the Ku Klux.

"I never seen no one sold. My father still held a wild animal instinct up in Virginia; they couldn't keep him out of the woods. He would spend two or three days back in there. Then the Patty Rollers would run him out and back home. He was a quill blower and a banjo picker. They had two corn piles and for prizes they give them whiskey.

They had dances and regular figure callers. This has been told to me at night time around the hearth understand. I can recollect when round dancing come in. It was in 1880. Here's a song they sung back in Virginia: 'Moster and mistress both gone away. Gone down to Charleston/ to spend the summer day. I'm off to Charleston/early in the mornin'/ to spend nother day.'

"I used to help old Miss Nancy make candles for her little brass lamp. We boiled down maple sap and made sugar. We made turpentine.

"I don't know about the Nat Turner Rebellion in Virginia. We had rebellions at Helena in 1875. The white folks put the Negroes out of office. They put J. T. White in the river at Helena but I think he got out. Several was killed. J. T. White was a colored sheriff in Phillips County. In Lee County it was the same way. The Republican party would lect them and the Democratic party roust them out of office.

"In 1872 I went to school 2-1/2 miles to Arkansas Post to a white teacher. I went four months. Her name was Mrs. Rolling. My white folks started me and I could spell to 'Baker' in the Blue Book Speller before I started to school. That is the only book I ever had at school. I learned to read in the Bible next.

"In 1872 locust was numerous. We had four diseases to break out: whooping cough, measles, smallpox; and cholera broke out again. They vaccinated for smallpox, first I ever heard of it. They took matter out of one persons arm and put it in two dozen peoples arms. It killed out the smallpox.

"In 1873 I saw a big forest fire. It seemed like prairie and forest fires broke out often.

"When I growed up and run with boys my color I got wicked. We gambled and drunk whiskey, then I seen how I was departing from good raising. I changed. I stopped sociating with bad company. The Lord hailed me in wide open day time and told me my better life was pleasing in his sight. I heard him. I didn't see nuthin'. I was called upon to teach a Sunday School class. Three months I was Sunday School leader. Three months more I was a licensed preacher. Ordained under Bishop Lee, Johnson, Copeland—all colored bishops at Topeka, Kansas. Then I attended conference at Bereah, Kentucky. Bishop Dizney presided. I preached in Kentucky, Missouri, Kansas, Alabama, Tennessee, Mississippi, and Arkansas. I am now what they call a superannuated minister.

"One criticism on my color. They will never progress till they become more harmonious in spirit with the desires of the white people in the home land of the white man. I mean when a white person come want some work or a favor and he not go help him without too much pay."

Interviewer: Miss Irene Robertson
Person interviewed: Absolom Jenkins,
R.F.D., Helena, Arkansas
Age: 80
[Date Stamp: MAY 31 1938]

ABSOLOM JENKINS

"I was born a few years before the break out of the old war (Civil War). I had a boy fit in this last war (World War). He gets a pension and he sends me part of it every month. He don't send me no amount whatever he can spare me. He never do send me less than ten dollars. I pick cotton some last year. I pick twenty or thirty pounds and it got to raining and so cold my granddaughter said it would make me sick.

"I was born durin' slavery. I was born 'bout twenty-five miles from Nolan, Tennessee. They call me Ab Jenkins for my old master. He was A. B. Jenkins. I don't know if his name was Absolom or not. Mother was name Liddy Strum. They was both sold on the block. They both come to Tennessee from Virginia in a drove and was sold to men lived less than ten miles apart. Then they got consent and got married. I don't know how they struck up together.

"They had three families of us. We lived up close to A. B. Jenkins' house. He had been married. He was old man when I knowed him. His daughter lived with him. She was married. Her husband was brought home from the war dead. I don't know if he got sick and died or shot. The only little children on the place was me and Jake Jenkins. We was no kin but jus' like twins. Master would call us up and stick his finger in biscuits and pour molasses in the hole. That was sure good eating. The 'lasses wouldn't spill till we done et it up. He'd fix us up another one. He give us biscuits oftener than the grown folks got them. We had plenty wheat bread till the old war come on. My mother beat biscuits with a paddle. She cooked over at Strum's. I lived over at Jenkins. Grandma Kizzy done my cooking. Master's girl cooked us biscuits. Master Jenkins loose his hat, his stick, his specks, and call us to find 'em. He could see. He called us to keep us outer badness. We had a big business of throwing at things. He threatened to whoop us. We slacked up on it. I never heard them say but I believe from what I seen it was agreed to divide the children. Pa would take me over to see mama every Sunday morning. We leave soon as I could get my clean long shirt and a little to eat. We walked four miles. He'd tote me. She had a girl with her. I never stayed over there much and the girl never come to my place 'cepting when mama come. They let her stand on the surrey and Eloweise stand inside when they went to preaching. She'd ride Master Jenkins' mare home and turn her loose to come home. Me and papa always walked.

"When freedom come on, the country was tore to pieces. Folks don't know what hard times is now. Some folks said do one thing for the best, somebody said do another way. Folks roved around for five or six years trying to do as well as they had done in slavery. It was years 'fore they got back to it. I was grown 'fore they ever got to doing well again. My folks got off to Nashville. We lived there by the hardest—eight in family. We moved to Mississippi bottoms not far from Meridian. We started picking up. We all got fat as hogs. We farmed and done well. We got to own forty acres of ground and lost two of the girls with malaria fever. Then we sold out and come to Helena. We boys, four of us, farmed, hauled wood, sawmilled, worked on the boats about till our parents died. They died close to Marion on a farm we rented. I had two boys. One got drowned. The other helps me out a heap. He got some little children now and got one grown and married.

"The Ku Klux was hot in Tennessee. They whooped a heap of people. The main thing was to make the colored folks go to work and not steal, but it was carpet-baggers stealing and go pack it on colored folks. They'd tell colored folks not to do this and that and it would get them in trouble. The Ku Klux would whoop the colored folks. Some colored folks thought 'cause they was free they ought not work. They got to rambling and scattered out.

"I voted a long time. The voting has caused trouble all along. I voted different ways—sometimes Republican and sometimes Independent. I don't believe women ought to vote somehow. I don't vote. I voted for Cleveland years ago and I voted for Wilson. I ain't voted since the last war. I don't believe in war.

"Times have changed so much it is lack living in another world now. Folks living in too much hurry. They getting too fast. They are restless. I see a heaps of overbearing folks now. Folks after I got grown looked so fresh and happy. Young folks look tired, mad, worried now. They fixes up their face but it still show it. Folks quicker than they used to be. They acts before they have time to think now. Times is good for me but I see old folks need things. I see young folks wasteful—both black and white.

White folks setting the pace for us colored folks. It's mighty fast and mighty hard."

Interviewer: Miss Irene Robertson
Person interviewed: Dora Jerman,
Forrest City, Arkansas
Age: 60?

DORA JERMAN

"I was born at Bow-and-arrow, Arkansas. Sid McDaniel owned my father. Mother was Mary Miller and she married Pete Williams from Tennessee. Grandma lived with us till she died. She used to have us sit around handy to thread her needles. She was a great hand to piece quilts. Her and Aunt Polly both. Aunt Polly was a friend that was sold with her every time. They was like sisters and the most pleasure to each other in old age.

"My great-great-grandma said to grandma, 'Hurry back wid that pitcher of water, honey, so you will have time to run by and see your mama and the children and tell them good-bye. Old master says you going to be sold early in the morning.' The water was for supper. That was the last time she ever seen or heard of any of her own kin folks. Grandma said a gang of them was sold next morning. Aunt Polly was no kin but they was sold together. Whitfield bought one and Strum bought the other.

"They come on a boat from Virginia to Aberdeen, Mississippi. They wouldn't sell her mother because she brought fine children. I think she said they had a regular stock man. She and Aunt Polly was sold several times and together till freedom. When they got off the boat they had to walk a right smart ways and grandma's feet cracked open and bled. 'Black Mammy' wrapped her feet up in rags and greased them with hot tallow or mutton suet and told her not to cry no more, be a good girl and mind master and mistress.

"Grandma said she had a hard time all her life. She was my mother's mother and she lived to be way over a hundred years old. Aunt Polly lived with her daughter when she got old. Grandma died first. Then Aunt Polly grieved so. She was old, old when she died. They still lived close together, mostly together. Aunt Polly was real black; mama was lighter. I called grandma 'mama' a right smart too. They called each other 'sis'. Grandma said, 'I love sis so good.' Aunt Polly lessened her days grieving for sis. They was both field hands. They would tell us girls about how they lived when they was girls. We'd cry.

"We lived in the country and we listened to what they said to us. If it had been times then like now I wouldn't know to tell you. Folks is in such a hurry somehow. Gone or going somewhere all the time.

"All my folks is most all full-blood African. I don't believe in races mixing up. It is a sin. Grandma was the brightest one of any of us. She was ginger-cake color.

"No, I don't vote. I don't believe in that neither.

"Times is too fast. Fast folks makes fast times. They all fast. Coming to destruction."

Interviewer: Miss Irene Robertson
Person interviewed: Adaline Johnson
Joining the Plunkett farms
Eight miles from Biscoe, Arkansas
Age: 96

ADALINE JOHNSON

"I was born twelve miles from the capital, Jackson, Mississippi, on Strickland's place. My mother was born in Edgecombe County, North Carolina. Master Jim Battle was old man. He owned three big plantations, full of niggers. They took me to Edgecombe County where my mother was born. Battles was rich set of white folks. They lived at Tarbry, North Carolina and some at Rocky Mount. Joe Battle was my old master. There was Hue Battle too. Master Joe Battle and Master Marmaduke was bosses of the whole country. They told Mars Joe not to whoop that crazy nigger man. He undertook it. He hit him seven licks with the hoe and killed him. Killed him in Mississippi.

"Master Marmaduke fell at the hotel at Greensboro, North Carolina. He was a hard drinker and they didn't tell them about it at the hotel. He got up in the night, fell down the steps and killed hisself. Tom Williams didn't drink. He went to war and got shot. He professed religion when he was twelve years old and kept the faith. Had his Testament in his pocket and blood run on it. That was when he was shot in the Civil War.

"They took that crazy nigger man to several places,

found there was no law to kill a crazy man. They took him to North Carolina where was all white folks at that place in Edgecombe County. They hung the poor crazy nigger. They was 'fraid of uprisings the reason they took him to place all white folks lived.

"My papa and Brutten (Brittain) Williams same age. Old Mistress Frankie (Tom Williams', Sr. wife) say, 'Let 'em be, he ain't goiner whoop Fenna, he's kin to him. He ain't goiner lay his hand on Fenna.' They whoop niggers black as me. Fenna waited on Master Brutten Williams. Fenna was half white. He was John Williams' boy. John was Brutten's brother. John Williams went to Mississippi and overseed for Mr. Bass. Mars Brutten got crazy. He'd shoot at anything and call it a hawk.

"Mother was a field woman. When she got in ill health, they put her to sew. Miss Evaline Perry in Mississippi learned her how to sew. She sewed up bolts of cloth into clothes for the niggers.

"Brutten Williams bought her from Joe Battle and he willed her to Joe Williams. She cooked and wove some in her young life. Rich white folks didn't sell niggers unless they got mad about them. Like mother, they changed her about. We never was cried off and put up in front of the public.

"Mars Joe Battle wasn't good. He ruled 'em all. He was Mars Marmaduke Battle's uncle. They went 'round to big towns and had a good time. Miss Polly Henry married Mars Brutten. He moved back (from Mississippi) to North Carolina. They had a big orchard. They give it all away soon as it ripen. He had a barrel of apple and peach brandy. He give some of it out in cups. They said there was some double rectifying in that barrel of brandy. He died.

"Master Tom was killed in war. When he had a ferlough he give all the men on his place five dollars and every woman a sow pig to raise from. Tole us all good-bye, said he'd never get back alive. He give me one and my mother one too. We prized them hogs 'bove everything we ever had. He got killed. Master Tom was so good to his niggers. He never whooped them. His wife ruled him, made him do like she wanted everything but mean to his niggers. Her folks slashed their niggers and she tried to make him do that too. He wouldn't. They said she wore the breeches 'cause she ruled him.

"She was Mistress Helland Harris Williams. She took our big hogs away from every one of us. We raised 'em up fine big hogs. She took them away from us. Took all the hogs Master Tom give us back. She had plenty land he left her and cows, some hogs. She married Allen Hopkins. They had a boy. He sent him to Texas, then he left her. She was so mean. Followed the boy to Texas. They all said she couldn't rule Allen Hopkins like she did Tom Williams. She didn't.

"When freedom come on, mother and me both left her 'cause I seen she wouldn't do. My papa left too and he had raised a little half white boy. 'Cause he was same age of Brutten Williams, Tom took Brutten's little nigger child and give him to papa to raise. His name Wilks. His own black mama beat him. When freedom come on, we went to Cal Pierce's place. They kept Wilks. He used to run off and come to us. They give him to somebody else 'way off. Tom had a brother in Georgia. It was Tom's wife wouldn't let Wilks go on living with us.

"Old mistress just did rave about her boys mixing up with them niggers but she was better than any other white women to Wilks and Fenna and George.

"'Big Will' could do much as any two other niggers. When they bought him a axe, it was a great big axe. They bought him a great big hoe. They got a new overseer. Overseer said he use a hoe and axe like everybody else. 'Big Will' killed the overseer with his big axe. Jim Battle was gone off. His son Marmaduke Battle put him in jail. When Jim Battle come back he said Marmaduke ought to sent for him, not put him in jail. Jim Battle sold 'Big Will'. We never heard or seen him no more. His family stayed on the plantation and worked. 'Big Will' could split as many more rails as anybody else on the place.

"I seen people sell babies out of the cradle. Poor white people buy babies and raise them.

"The Battles had gins and stores in North Carolina and Williams had farms, nothing but farms.

"When I was a girl I nursed the nigger women's babies and seen after the children. I nursed Tom Williams' boy, Johnny Williams. He run to me, said, 'Them killed my papa.' I took him up in my arms. Then was when the Yankee soldiers come on the place. Sid Williams went to war. I cooked when the regular cook was weaving. Mother carded and spun then. I had a ounce of cotton to card every night from September till March. When I'd be dancing around, Miss Helland Harris Williams say, 'You better be studying your pewter days.' Meant for me to stop dancing.

"Mistress Polly married a Perry, then Right Hendrick.

Perrys was rich folks. When Marmaduke Battle died all the niggers cried and cried and bellowed because they thought they would be sold and get a mean master.

"They had a mean master right then—Right Hendrick. Mean a man as ever God ever wattled a gut in I reckon. That was in Mississippi. They took us back and forth when it suited them. We went in hacks, surreys and stage-coaches, wagons, horseback, and all sorts er ways. We went on big river boats sometimes. They sold off a lot of niggers to settle up the estate. What I want to know is how they settle up estates now.

"They parched persimmon seed and wheat during the war to make coffee. I ploughed during the Civil War. Strange people come through, took our snuff and tobacco. Master Tom said for us not have no light at night so the robbers couldn't find us so easy. He was a good man. The Yankees said they had to subdue our country. They took everything they could find. Times was hard. That was in North Carolina.

"When Brutten Williams bought me and mama—mama was Liza Williams—Master Brutten bought her sister three or four years after that and they took us to (Zeblin or) Sutton in Franklin County. Now they call it Wakefield Post Office. Brutten willed us to Tom. Sid, Henry, John was Tom Williams' boys, and his girls were Pink and Tish.

"Master John and Marmaduke Battle was rich as they could be. They was Joe Battle's uncles. Jesse Ford was Marmaduke's half-brother in Texas. He come to Mississippi to get his part of the niggers and the rest was put on a block and sold. Master Marmaduke broke his neck when he fell downstairs. I never heard such crying before nor since as I heard that day. Said they lost their best master. They knowed how bad they got whooped on Ozoo River.

"Master Marmaduke walked and bossed his overseers. He went to the big towns. He never did marry. My last master was Tom Williams. He was so nice to us all. He confessed religion. He worked us hard, then hard times come when he went to war. He knowed our tracks—foot tracks and finger tracks both.

"Somebody busted a choice watermelon, plugged it out with his fingers and eat it. Master Tom said, 'Fenna, them your finger marks.' Then he scolded him good fashioned. Old Mistress Frankie say, 'Don't get scared, he ain't go to whoop him, they kin. Fenna kin to him, he not goiner hurt him.'

"At the crossroads there was a hat shop. White man brought a lot of white free niggers to work in the hat shop. Way they come free niggers. Some poor woman had no living. Nigger men steal flour or a hog, take it and give it to her. She be hungry. Pretty soon a mulatto baby turned up. Then folks want to run her out the country. Sometimes they did.

"Old man Stinson (Stenson?) left and went to Ohio. They wrote back to George to come after them to Ohio. Bill Harris had a baltimore trotter. The letter lay about in the post office. They broke it open, read it, give it to his owner. He got mad and sold George. He was Sam Harrises carriage driver. Dick and him was half-brothers. Dick learned him about reading and writing. When the war was over George come through on the train. Sam Harris run up there, cracked his heels together, hugged him, and give him ten dollars. He sold him when he was so mad. I don't know if he went to Ohio to Stinson's or not.

"We stayed in the old country twenty-five or thirty years after freedom.

"When we left Miss Helland Harris Williams', Tim Terrel come by there with his leg shot off and was there till he could get on to his folks.

"When I come here I was expecting to go to California. There was cars going different places. We got on Mr. Boyd's car. He paid our way out here. Mr. Jones brought his car to Memphis and stopped. Mr. Boyd brought us right here. That was in 1892. We got on the train at Raleigh, North Carolina.

"Papa bought forty acres land from the Boyd estate. Our children scattered and we sold some of it. We got twenty acres. Some of it in woods. I had to sell my cow to bury my granddaughter what lived with me—taking care of me. Papa tole my son to take care of me and since he died my son gone stone blind. I ain't got no chickens hardly. I go hungry nigh all the time. I gets eight dollars for me and my blind son both. If I could get a cow. We tries to have a garden. They ain't making nothing on my land this year. I'm having the hardest time I ever seen in my life. I got a toothpick in my ear and it's rising. The doctor put some medicine in my ears—both of them.

"When I was in slavery I wore peg shoes. I'd be working and not time to take off my shoes and fix the tacks—beat 'em down. They made holes in bottoms of my feet; now they got to be corns and I can't walk and stand."

Interviewer's Comment

This is another one of those terrible cases. This old woman is on starvation. She had a cow and can't get another one. The son is blind but feels about and did milk. The bedbugs are nearly eating her up. They scald but can't get rid of them. They have a fairly good house to live in. But the old woman is on starvation and away back eight miles from Biscoe. I hate to see good old Negroes want for something to eat. She acts like a small child. Pitiful, so feeble. The second time I went out there I took her daughter who walks out there every week. We fixed her up an iron bedstead so she can sleep better. I took her a small cake. That was her dinner. She had eaten one egg that morning. She was a clean, kind old woman. Very much like a child. Has a rising in her head and said she was afraid her head would kill her. She gave me a gallon of nice figs her daughter picked, so I paid her twenty-five cents for them. She had plenty figs and no sugar.

Interviewer: Samuel S. Taylor
Person interviewed: Alice Johnson
601 W. Eighth Street, Little Rock, Arkansas
Age: 77

ALICE JOHNSON

"You want to know what they did in slavery times! They were doin' jus' what they do now. The white folks was beatin' the niggers, burning 'em and boilin' 'em, workin' 'em and doin' any other thing they wanted to do with them. 'Course you wasn't here then to know about nigger dogs and bull whips, were you? The same thing is goin' on right now. They got the same bull whips and the same old nigger dogs. If you don't believe it, go right out here to the county farm and you find 'em still whippin' the niggers and tearing them up and sometimes lettin' the dogs bite them to save the bull whips.

"I was here in slavery time but I was small and I don't know much about it 'cept what they told me. But you don't need to go no further to hear all you want to know. They sont you to the right place. They all know me and they call me Mother Johnson. So many folks been here long as me, but don't want to admit it. They black their hair and whiten their faces, and powder and paint. 'Course it's good to look good all right. But when you start that stuff, you got to keep it up. Tain't no use to start and stop. After a while you got that same color hair and them same splotches again. Folks say, 'What's the matter, you gittin so dark?' Then you say, 'Uh, my liver is bad.' You got to keep that thing up, baby.

"I thank God for my age. I thank God He's brought me safe all the way. That is the matter with this world now. It ain't got enough religion.

"I was born in Mississippi way below Jackson in Crystal Springs. That is on the I. C. Road near New Orleans. The train that goes there goes to New Orleans. I was bred and born and married there in Crystal Springs. I don't know just when I was born but I know it was in the month of December.

"I remember when the slaves were freed. I remember the War 'cause I used to hear them talking about the Yankees and I didn't know whether they were mules or horses or what not. I didn't know if they was varmints or folks or what not. I can't remember whether I seen any soldiers or not. I heard them talking about soldiers, but I didn't see none right 'round where we was.

"Now what good's that all goin' to do me? It ain't goin' to do me no good to have my name in Washington. Didn't do me no good if he stuck my name up on a stick in Washington. Some of them wouldn't know me. Those that did would jus' say, 'That's old Alice Johnson.'

"Us old folks, they don't count us. They jus' kick us out of the way. They give me 'modities and a mite to spend. Time you go and get lard, sugar, meat, and flour, and pay rent and buy wood, you don't have 'nough to go 'round. Now that might do you some good if you didn't have to pay rent and buy wood and oil and water. I'll tell you something so you can earn a living. Your mama give you a education so you can earn a living and you earnin' it jus' like she meant you to. But most of us don't earn it that way, and most of these educated folks not earnin' a livin' with their education. They're in jail somewheres. They're walkin' up and down Ninth Street and runnin' in and out of these here low dives. You go down there to the penitentiary and count those prisoners and I'll bet you don't find nary one that don't know how to read and write. They're all educated. Most of these educated niggers don't have no feeling for common niggers. 'They just walk on them like they wasn't living. And don't come to 'em tellin' them that you wanting to use them!

"The people et the same thing in slavery time that they eat now. Et better then 'n they do now. Chickens, cows, mules died then, they throw 'em to the buzzards. Die now, they sell 'em to you to eat. Didn't eat that in slavery time. Things they would give to the dogs then, they sell to the people to eat now. People et pure stuff in slavery. Don't eat pure stuff now. Got pure food law, but that's all that is pure.

"My mother's name was Diana Benson and my father's name was Joe Brown. That's what folks say, I don't know. I have seen them but I wasn't brought up with no mother and father. Come up with the white folks and colored folks fust one and then the other. I think my mother and father died before freedom. I don't know what the name of their master was. All my folks died early.

"The fus' white folks I knowed anything about was Rays. They said that they were my old slave-time masters. They were nice to me. Treated me like they would their own children. Et and slept with them. They treated me jus' like they own. Heap of people say they didn't have no owners, but they got owners yet now out there on that government farm.

"The fus' work I done in my life was nussing. I was a child then and I stayed with the white folks' children. Was raised up in the house with 'em. I was well taken care of too. I was jus' like their children. That was at Crystal Springs.

"I left them before I got grown and went off with other folks. I never had no reason. Jus' went on off. I didn't go for better because I was doing better. They jus' told me to come and I went.

"I been living now in Arkansas ever since 1911. My husband and I stayed on to work and make a living. I take care of myself. I'm not looking for nothin' now but a better home over yonder—better home than this. Thank the Lawd, I gits along all right. The government gives me a check to buy me a little meat and bread with. Maybe the government will give me back that what they took off after a while. I don't know. It takes a heap of money to feed thousands and millions of people. When the check comes, I am glad to git it no matter how little it is. Twarn't for it, I would be in a sufferin' condition.

"I belong to the Arch Street Baptist Church. I been for about twenty years. I was married sixteen years to my first husband and twenty-eight to my second. The last one has been dead five years and the other one thirty-six years. I ain't got none walkin' 'round. All my husbands is dead. There ain't nothin' in this quitin' and goin' and breakin' up and bustin' up. I don't tell no woman to quit and don't tell no man to quit. Go over there and git 'nother woman and she will be wuss than the one you got.

When you fall out, reason and git together. Do right. I stayed with both of my husbands till they died. I ain't bothered 'bout another one. Times is so hard no man can take care of a woman now. Come time to pay rent, 'What you waiting for me to pay rent for? You been payin' it, ain't you?' Come time to buy clothes, 'What you waitin' for me to buy clothes for? Where you gittin' 'um from before you mai'd me?' Come time to pay the grocery bill, 'How come you got to wait for me to pay the grocery bill? Who been payin' it?' No Lawd, I don't want no man unless he works. What could I do with him? I don't want no man with a home and bank account. You can't git along with 'im. You can't git along with him and you can't git along with her."

United States. Work Projects Administration

Interviewer: Samuel S. Taylor
Person interviewed: Allen Johnson
718 Arch Street, Little Rock, Arkansas
Age: About 82

ALLEN JOHNSON

"I was born in Georgia about twelve miles from Cartersville, in Cass County, and about the same distance from Cassville. I was a boy about eight or nine years old when I come from there. But I have a very good memory. Then I have seed the distance and everything in the Geography. My folks were dead long ago now. My oldest brother is dead too. He was just large enough to go to the mills. In them times, they had mills. They would fix him on the horse and he would go ahead.

"My father's name was Clem Johnson, and my mother's name was Mandy. Her madam's name I don't know. I was small. I remember my grandma. She's dead long long ago. Long time ago! I think her name was Rachel. Yes, I'm positive it was Rachel. That is what I believe. I was a little bitty fellow then. I think she was my mother's mother. I know one of my mother's sisters. Her name was Lucinda. I don't know how many she had nor nothin'.

"Johnsons was the name of the masters my mother and father had. They go by the name of Johnson yet. Before that I don't know who they had for masters. The pastor's name was Lindsay Johnson and the old missis was Mary Johnson. People long time ago used to send boys big enough to ride to the mill. My brother used to go. It ran by water-power. They had a big mill pond. They dammed that up. When they'd get ready to run the mill, they'd open that dam and it would turn the wheel. My oldest brother went to the mill and played with old master's son and me.

"They used to throw balls over the house and see which could catch them first. There would be three or four on a side of the house and they would throw the ball over the house to see which side would be quickest and aptest.

"My mother and father both belonged to the same man, Lindsay Johnson. I was a small boy. I can't tell you how he was to his folks. Seems like though he was pretty good to us. Seemed like he was a pretty good master. He didn't overwork his niggers. He didn't beat and 'buse them. He gave them plenty to eat and drink. You see the better a Negro looked and the finer he was the more money he would bring if they wanted to sell them. I have heard my mother and father talk about it plenty of times.

"My father worked in the field during slavery. My mother didn't do much of no kind of work much. She was a woman that had lots of children to take care of. She had four children during slavery and twelve altogether. Her children were all small when freedom was declared. My oldest brother, I don't remember much about slavery except playing 'round with him and with the other little boys, the white boys and the nigger boys. They were very nice to me.

"I was a great big boy when I heard them talking about

the pateroles catching them or whipping them. At that time when they would go off they would have to have a pass. When they went off if they didn't have a pass they would whip and report them to their owners. And they would be likely to get another brushing from the owners. The pateroles never bothered the children any. The children couldn't go anywhere without the consent of the mother and father. And there wasn't any danger of them running off. If they caught a little child between plantations, they would probably just run them home. It was all right for a child to go in the different quarters and play with one another during daytime just so they got back before night. I was a small boy but I have very good recollections about these things. I couldn't tell you whether the pateroles ever bothered my father or not. Never heard him say. But he was a careful man and he always knew the best time and way to go and come. Them old fellows had a way to git by as well as we do now.

"They fed the slaves about what they wanted to. They would give them meat and flour and meal. I used to hear my father say the old boss fed him well. Then again they would have hog killln' time 'long about Christmas. The heads, lights, chittlings and fats would be given to the slaves. 'Course I didn't know much about that only what I heard from the old folks talking about it. They lived in the way of eating, I suppose, better than they do now. Had no expense whatever.

"As to amusements, I'll tell you I don't know. They'd have little dances about like they do now. And they give quiltings and they'd have a ring play. My mother never knew anything about dances and fiddling and such things; she was a Christian. They had churches you know.

My white folks didn't object to the niggers goin' to meetin'. 'Course they had to have a pass to go anywhere. If they didn't they'd git a brushin' from the pateroles if they got caught and the masters were likely to give them another light brushin' when they got home.

"I think that was a pretty good system. They gave a pass to those that were allowed to be out and the ones that were supposed to be out were protected. Of course, now you are your own free agent and you can go and come as you please. Now the police take the place of the pateroles. If they find you out at the wrong time and place they are likely to ask you about it.

"A slave was supposed to pick a certain amount of cotton I have heard. They had tasks. But we didn't pick cotton. Way back in Georgia that ain't no cotton country. Wheat, corn, potatoes, and things like that. But in Louisiana and Mississippi, there was plenty of cotton. Arkansas wasn't much of a cotton state itself. It was called a 'Hoojer' state when I was a boy. That is a reference to the poor white man. He was a 'Hoojer'. He wasn't rich enough to own no slaves and they called him a 'Hoojer'.

"The owners would hire them to take care of the niggers and as overseers and pateroles. They was hired and paid a little salary jus' like the police is now. If we didn't have killing and murderin', there wouldn't be no need for the police. The scoundrel who robs and kills folks ought to be highly prosecuted.

"I reckon I was along eight or nine years old when freedom came. My oldest brother was twelve, and I was next to him. I must have been eight or nine—or maybe ten.

"My occupation since freedom has been farming and doing a little job work—anything I could git. Work by the day for mechanic and one thing and another. I know nothin' about no trade 'ceptin' what I have picked up. Never took no contracts 'ceptin' for building a fence or somethin' small like that. Mechanic's work I suppose calls for license."

United States. Work Projects Administration

Interviewer: Samuel S. Taylor
Person interviewed: Annie Johnson
804 Izard Street, Little Rock, Arkansas
Age: 78

ANNIE JOHNSON

"I was born in Holly Springs, Mississippi, and I was four years old when the Civil War closed. My parents died when I was a baby and a white lady named Mrs. Mary Peters took me and raised me. They moved from there to Champaign, Illinois when I was about six years old. My mother died when I was born. Them white people only had two slaves, my mother and my father, and my father had run off with the Yankees. Mrs. Peters was their mistress. She died when I was eight years old and then I stayed with her sister. That was when I was up in Champaign.

"The sister's name was Mrs. Mary Smith. She just taught school here and there and around in different places, and I went around with her to take care of her children. That kept up until I was twenty years old. All of her traveling was in Illinois.

"I didn't get much schooling. I went to school a while and taken sore eyes. The doctor said if I continued to go to school, I would strain my eyes. After he told me that I quit. I learned enough to read the Bible and the newspaper and a little something like that, but I can't do much. My eyes is very weak yet.

"When I was twenty years old I married Henry Johnson, who was from Virginia. I met him in Champaign. We stayed in Champaign about two years. Then we came on down to St. Louis. He was just traveling 'round looking for work and staying wherever there was a job. Didn't have no home nor nothing. He was a candy maker by trade, but he did anything he could get to do. He's been dead for forty years now. He came down here, then went back to Champaign and died in Springfield, Illinois while I was here.

"I don't get no pension, don't get nothing. I get along by taking in a little washing now and then.

"My mother's name was Eliza Johnson and my father's name was Joe Johnson. I don't know a thing about none of my grandparents. And I don't know what my mother's name was before she married.

"A gentleman what worked on the place where I lived said that if you didn't have a pass during slave times, that if the pateroles caught you, they would whip you and make you run back home. He said he had to run through the woods every which way once to keep them from catching him.

"I have heard the old folks talk about being put on the block. The colored woman I lived with in Champaign told me that they put her on the block and sold her down into Ripley, Mississippi.

"She said that the way freedom came was this. The boss man told her she was free. Some of the slaves lived with him and some of them picked up and went on off somewhere.

"The Ku Klux never bothered me. I have heard some of the colored people say how they used to come 'round and bother the church services looking for this one and that one.

"I don't know what to say about these young folks. I declare, they have just gone wild. They are almost getting like brutes. A woman come by here the other day without more 'n a spoonful of things on and stopped and struck a match and lit her cigarette. You can't talk to them neither. I don't know what we ought to do about it. They let these white men run around with them. I see 'em doing anything. I think times are bad and getting worse. Just as that shooting they had over in North Little Rock." (Shooting and robbing of Rev. Sherman, an A. M. E. minister, by Negro robbers.)

United States. Work Projects Administration

Interviewer: Miss Irene Robertson
Person interviewed: Ben Johnson
Near Holly Grove and Clarendon, Arkansas
Age: 73

BEN JOHNSON

"My master was Wort Garland. My papa's master was Steve Johnson. Papa went off to Louisiana and I never seen him since. I guess he got killed. I was born in Madison County, Tennessee. I come to Arkansas 1889. Mother was here. She come on a transient ticket. My papa come wid her to Holly Grove. They both field hands. I worked on the section—railroad section. I cut and hauled timber and farms. I never own no land, no home. I have two boys went off and a grown girl in Phillips County. I don't get no help. I works bout all I able and can get to do.

"I have voted. I votes a Republican ticket. I like this President. If the men don't know how to vote recken the women will show em how.

"The present conditions is very good. The present generation is beyond me.

"I heard my folks set around the fireplace at night and talk about olden times but I couldn't tell it straight and I was too little to know bout it.

"We looked all year for Christmas to get some good things in our stockings. They was knit at night. Now we has oranges and bananas all the time, peppermint candy—in sticks—best candy I ever et. Folks have more now that sort than we had when I was growing up. We was raised on meat and corn bread, milk, and garden stuff. Had plenty apples, few peaches, sorghum molasses, and peanuts. Times is better now than when I come on far as money goes. Wood is scarce and folks can't have hogs no more. No place to run and feed cost so much. Can't buy it. Feed cost more 'en the hog. Times change what makes the folks change so much I recken."

Interviewer: Miss Irene Robertson
Person interviewed: Ben Johnson (deaf),
Clarendon, Arkansas
Age: 84
Black

BEN JOHNSON

"Steve Johnson was my owner. Way he come by me was dat he married in the Ward family and heired him and my mother too. Louis Johnson was my father's name. At one time Wort Garland owned my mother, and she was sold. Her name was Mariah.

"My father went to war twice. Once he was gone three weeks and next time three or four months. He come home sound. I stayed on Johnson's farm till I was a big boy."

United States. Work Projects Administration

Interviewer: Samuel S. Taylor
Person interviewed: Betty Johnson
1920 Dennison Street, Little Rock, Arkansas
Age: 83
[Date Stamp: MAY 11 1938]

BETTY JOHNSON

"I was born in Montgomery, Alabama, within a block of the statehouse. We were the only colored people in the neighborhood. I am eighty-three years old. I was born free. I have never been a slave. I never met any slaves when I was small, and never talked to any. I didn't live near them and didn't have any contacts with them.

"My father carried my mother to Pennsylvania before I was born and set her free. Then he carried her back to Montgomery, Alabama, and all her children were born free there.

"We had everything that life needed. He was one of the biggest planters around in that part of the country and did the shipping for everybody.

"My mother's name was Josephine Hassell. She had nine children. All of them are dead except three. One is in Washington, D. C.; another is in Chicago, Illinois, and then I am here. One of my brothers was a mail clerk for the government for fifty years, and then he went to Washington and worked in the dead letter office.

"My father taken my oldest brother just before the

Civil War and entered him in Yale and he stayed there till he finished. Later he became a freight conductor and lost his life when his train was caught in a cyclone. That's been years ago.

"My sisters in Washington and Chicago are the only two living besides myself. All the others are dead. All of them were government workers. My sister in Washington has four boys and five girls. My sister in Chicago has two children—one in Detroit and one in Washington. I am the oldest living.

"We never had any kind of trouble with white people in slave time, and we never had any since. Everybody in town knowed us, and they never bothered us. The editor of the paper in Montgomery got up all our history and sent the paper to my brother in Washington. If I had saved the paper, I would have had it now. I don't know the name of the paper. It was a white paper. I can't even remember the name of the editor.

"We were always supported by my father. My mother did [HW: ?] do nothing at all except stay home and take care of her children. I had a father that cared for us. He didn't leave that part undone. He did his part in every respect. He sent every child away to school. He sent two to Talladega, one to Yale, three to Fiske, and one to Howard University.

"I don't remember much about how freedom came to the slaves. You see, we didn't live near any of them and would not notice, and I was young anyway. All I remember is that when the army came in, everybody had a stick with a white handkerchief on it. The white handkerchief represented peace. I don't know just how they announced that the slaves were free.

"We lived in as good a house as this one here. It had eight rooms in it. I was married sixty years ago. My husband died two years ago. We were married fifty-eight years. Were the only colored people here to celebrate the fiftieth anniversary. (She is mistaken in this; Waters McIntosh has been married for fifty-six years and he and his wife are still making it together in an ideal manner—ed.) I am the mother of eight children; three girls are living and two boys. The rest are dead.

"I married a good man. Guess there was never a better. We lived happily together for a long time and he gave me everything I needed. He gave me and my children whatever we asked for.

"I was sick for three years. Then my husband took down and was sick for seven years before he died.

"I belong to the Holiness Church down on Izard Street, and Brother Jeeter is my pastor."

INTERVIEWER'S COMMENT

Betty Johnson's memory is accurate, and she tells whatever she wishes to tell without hesitation and clearly. She leaves out details which she does not wish to mention evidently, and there is a reserve in her manner which makes questioning beyond a certain point impertinent. However, just what she tells presents a picture into which the details may easily be fitted.

Her husband is dead, but he was evidently of the

same type she is. She lives in a beautiful and well kept cottage. Her husband left a similar house for each of her three children. The husband, of course, was colored. It is equally evident that the father was white.

Although my questions traveled into corners where they evidently did not wish to follow, the mother and son, who was from time to time with her, answered courteously and showed no irritation.

Interviewer: Mrs. Bernice Bowden
Person interviewed: Cinda Johnson
506 E. Twenty, Pine Bluff, Arkansas
Age: 83

CINDA JOHNSON

"Yes ma'm, this is Cinda. Yes'm, I remember seein' the soldiers but I didn't know what they was doin'. You know old folks didn't talk in front of chilluns like they does now—but I been here. I got great grand chillun—boy big enuf to chop cotton. That's my daughter's daughter's chile. Now you know I been here.

"I heered em talkin' bout freedom. My mother emigrated here drectly after freedom. I was born in Alabama. When we come here, I know I was big enuf to clean house and milk cows. My mother died when I was bout fifteen. She called me to the bed and tole me who to stay with. I been treated bad, but I'm still here and I thank the Lord He let me stay.

"I been married twice. My first husband died, but I didn't have no graveyard love. I'm the mother of ten whole chillun. All dead but two and only one of them of any service to me. That's my son. He's good to me and does what he can but he's got a family. My daughter-in-law—all she does is straighten her hair and look cute.

"One of my sons what died belonged to the Odd Fellows and I bought this place with insurance. I lives here alone in peace. Yes, honey, I been here a long time."

Interviewer: Samuel S. Taylor
Person interviewed: Ella Johnson
913-1/2 Victory Street, Little Rock, Arkansas
Age: About 85

ELLA JOHNSON

"I was born in Helena, Arkansas. Not exactly in the town but in hardly not more than three blocks from the town. Have you heard about the Grissoms down there? Well, them is my white folks. My maiden name was Burke. But we never called ourselves any name 'cept Grissom.

"My mother's name was Sylvia Grissom. Her husband was named Jack Burkes. He went to the Civil War. That was a long time ago. When they got up the war, they sold out a lot of the colored folks. But they didn't get a chance to sell my mother. She left. They tell me one of them Grissom boys has been down here looking for me. He didn't find me and he went on back.

My mother's mistress was named Sylvia Grissom too. All of us was named after the white folks. All the old folks is dead, but the young ones is living. I think my mother's master was named John. They had so many of them that I forgit which is which. But they had all mama's children named after them. My mother had three girls and three boys.

"When the war began and my father went to war, my mother left Helena and came here. She run off from the

Grissoms. They whipped her too much, those white folks did. She got tired of all that beating. She took all of us with her. All six of us children were born before the war. I was the fourth.

"There is a place down here where the white folks used to whip and hang the niggers. Baskin Lake they call it. Mother got that far. I don't know how. I think that she came in a wagon. She stayed there a little while and then she went to Churchill's place. Churchill's place and John Addison's place is close together down there. That is old time. Them folks is dead, dead, dead. Churchill's and Addison's places joined near Horse Shoe Lake. They had hung and burnt people—killed 'em and destroyed 'em at Baskin Lake. We stayed there about four days before we went on to Churchill's place. We couldn't stay there long.

"The ha'nts—the spirits—bothered us so we couldn't sleep. All them people that had been killed there used to come back. We could hear them tipping 'round in the house all the night long. They would blow out the light. You would kiver up and they would git on top of the kiver. Mama couldn't stand it; so she come down to General Churchill's place and made arrangements to stay there. Then she came back and got us children. She had an old man to stay there with us until she come back and got us. We couldn't stay there with them ha'nts dancing 'round and carryin' us a merry gait.

"At Churchill's place my mother made cotton and corn. I don't know what they give her for the work, but I know they paid her. She was a hustling old lady. The war was still goin' on. Churchill was a Yankee. He went off and left the plantation in the hands of his oldest son. His son was named Jim Churchill. That is the old war; that is the first war ever got up—the Civil War. Ma stayed at Churchill's long enough to make two or three crops. I don't know just how long. Churchill and them wanted to own her—them and John Addison.

"There was three of us big enough to work and help her in the field. Three—I made four. There was my oldest sister, my brother, and my next to my oldest sister, and myself—Annie, John, Martha, and me. I chopped cotton and corn. I used to tote the leadin' row. Me and my company walked out ahead. I was young then, but my company helped me pick that cotton. That nigger could pick cotton too. None of the res' of them could pick anything for looking at him.

"Mother stayed at Churchill's till plumb after the war. My father died before the war was over. They paid my mother some money and said she would get the balance. That means there was more to come, doesn't it? But they didn't no more come. They all died and none of them got the balance. I ain't never got nothin' either. I gave my papers to Adams and Singfield. I give them to Adams; Adams is a Negro that one-legged Wash Jordan sent to me. They all say he's a big crook, but I didn't know it. Adams kept coming to my house until he got my papers and then when he got the papers he didn't come no more.

"After Adams got the papers, he carried me down to Lawyer Singfield's. He said I had to be sworn in and it would cost me one dollar. Singfield wrote down every child's name and everybody's age. When he got through writing, he said that was all and me and Pearl made up one dollar between us and give it to him. And then we come on away. We left Mr. Adams and Mr. Singfield in Singfield's office and we left the papers there in the office with them. They didn't give me no receipt for the papers and they didn't give me no receipt for the dollar. Singfield's wife has been to see me several times to sell me something. She wanted to git me to buy a grave, but she ain't never said nothin' about those papers. You think she doesn't know 'bout 'em? I have seen Adams once down to Jim Perry's funeral on Arch Street. I asked him about my papers and he said the Government hadn't answered him. He said, 'Who is you?' I said, 'This is Mrs. Johnson.' Then he went on out. He told me when he got a answer, it will come right to my door.

"I never did no work before goin' on Churchill's plantation. Some of the oldest ones did, but I didn't. I learned how to plow at John Addison's place. The war was goin' on then. I milked cows for him and churned and cleaned up. I cooked some for him. Are you acquainted with Blass? I nursed Julian Blass. I didn't nurse him on Addison's place; I nursed him at his father's house up on Main Street, after I come here. I nursed him and Essie both. I nursed her too. I used to have a time with them chillen. They weren't nothin' but babies. The gal was about three months old and Julian was walkin' 'round. That was after I come to Little Rock.

"My mother come to Little Rock right after the war. She brought all of us with her but the oldest. He come later.

"She want to work and cooked and washed and ironed here. I don't remember the names of the people she worked for. They all dead—the old man and the old ladies.

"She sent me to school. I went to school at Philander

[HW: (Philander Smith College?)] and down to the end of town and in the country. We had a white man first and then we had a colored woman teacher. The white man was rough. He would fight all the time. I would read and spell without opening my book. They would have them blue-back spellers and McGuffy's reader. They got more education then than they do now. Now they is busy fighting one another and killin' one another. When you see anything in the paper, you don't know whether it is true or not. Florence Lacy's sister was one of my teachers. I went to Union school once. [HW: —— insert from P. 5]

"You remember Reuben White? They tried to bury him and he came to before they got him in the grave. He used to own the First Baptist Church. He used to pastor it too. He sent for J. P. Robinson by me. He told Robinson he wanted him to take the Church and keep it as long as he lived. Robinson said he would keep it. Reuben White went to his brother's and died. They brought him back here and kept his body in the First Baptist Church a whole week. J. P. carried on the meetin', and them sisters was fightin' him. They went on terrible. He started out of the church and me and 'nother woman stopped him. At last they voted twice, and finally they elected J. P. He was a good pastor, but he hurrahed the people and they didn't like that.

"Reuben White didn't come back when they buried him the second time. They were letting the coffin down in the grave when they buried him the first time, and he knocked at it on the inside, knock, knock. (Here the old lady rapped on the doorsill with her knuckles—ed.) They drew that coffin up and opened it. How do I know? I was there. I heard it and seen it. They took him out of the coffin and carried him back to his home in the ambulance. He lived about three or four years after that.

"I had a member to die in my order and they sent for the undertaker and he found that she wasn't dead. They took her down to the undertaker's shop, and found that she wasn't dead. They said she died after they embalmed her. That lodge work ran my nerves down. I was in the Tabernacle then. Goodrich and Dubisson was the undertakers that had the body. Lucy Tucker was the woman. I guess she died when they got her to the shop. They say the undertaker cut on her before he found that she was dead.

"I don't know how many grades I finished in school. I guess it was about three altogether. I had to git up and go to work then. [TR: This paragraph was marked with a line on the right; possibly it is the paragraph to be inserted on the previous page.]

"After I quit school, I nursed mighty nigh all the time. I cooked for Governor Rector part of the time. I cooked for Dr. Lincoln Woodruff. I cooked for a whole lot of white folks. I washed and ironed for them Anthonys down here. She like to had a fit over me the last time she saw me. She wanted me to come back, but my hand couldn't stand it. I cooked for Governor Rose's wife. That's been a long time back. I wouldn't 'low nobody to come in the kitchen when I was working. I would say, 'You goin' to come in this kitchen, I'll have to git out.' The Governor was awful good to me. They say he kicked the res' of them out. I scalded his little grandson once. I picked up the teakettle. Didn't know it had water in it and it slipped and splashed water over the little boy's hand. If'n it had been hot as it ought to have been, it would have burnt him bad. He went out of that kitchen hollerin'. The Governor didn't say nothin' 'cept, 'Ella, please don't do it again.' I said, 'I guess that'll teach him to stay out of that kitchen now.' I was boss of that kitchen when I worked there.

"We took the lock off the door once so the Governor couldn't git in it.

"I dressed up and come out once and somebody called the Governor and said, 'Look at your cook.' And he said, 'That ain't my cook.' That was Governor Rector. I went in and put on my rags and come in the kitchen to cook and he said, 'That is my cook.' He sure wanted me to keep on cookin' for him, but I just got sick and couldn't stay.

"I hurt my hand over three years ago. My arm swelled and folks rubbed it and got all the swelling down in one place in my hand. They told me to put fat meat on it. I put it on and the meat hurt so I had to take it off. Then they said put the white of an egg on it. I did that too and it was a little better. Then they rubbed the place until it busted. But it never did cure up. I poisoned it by goin' out pulling up greens in the garden. They tell me I got dew poisoning.

"I don't git no help from the Welfare or from the Government. My husband works on the relief sometimes. He's on the relief now.

"I married—oh, Lordy, lemme see when I did marry. It's been a long time ago, more 'n thirty years it's been. It's been longer than that. We married up here on Twelfth and State Street, right here in Little Rock. I had a big wedding. I had to go to Thompson's hall. That was on Tenth and State Street. They had to go to git all them people in. They had a big time that night.

"I lived in J. P. Robinson's house twenty-two years. And then I lived in front of Dunbar School. It wasn't Dunbar then. I know all the people that worked at the school. I been living here about six months."

Interviewer's Comment

Ella Johnson is about eighty-five years old. Her father went to war when the War first broke out. Her mother ran away then and went to Churchill's farm not later than 1862. Ella Johnson learned to plow then and she was at least nine years old she says and perhaps older when she learned to plow. So she must be at least eighty-five.

Interviewer: Mary D. Hudgins
Person interviewed: Fanny Johnson
Aged: 76
Home: Palmetto (lives with daughter who owns a comfortable, well furnished home)

As told by: Mrs. Fanny Johnson

FANNY JOHNSON

"Yes ma'am. I remembers the days of slavery. I was turned five years old when the war started rushing. No ma'am, I didn't see much of the Yankees. They didn't come thru but twice. Was I afraid? No ma'am. I was too busy to be scared. I was too busy looking at the buttons they wore. Until they went in Master's smoke house. Then I quit looking and started hollering. But, I'll tell you all about that later.

My folks all come from Maryland. They was sold to a man named Woodfork and brought to Nashville. The Woodfork colored folks was always treated good. Master used to buy up lots of plantations. Once he bought one in Virginia with all the slaves on the place. He didn't believe in separating families. He didn't believe in dividing mother from her baby.

But they did take them away from their babies. I remember my grandmother telling about it. The wagon would drive down into the field and pick up a woman. Then somebody would meet her at the gate and she would nurse her baby for the last time. Then she'd have to go on. Leastwise, if they hadn't sold her baby too.

It was pretty awful. But I don't hold no grudge against anybody. White or black, there's good folks in all kinds. I don't hold nothing against nobody. The good Lord knows what he is about. Most of the time it was just fine on any Woodfork place. Master had so many places he couldn't be at 'em all. We lived down on the border, on the Arkansas-Louisiana line sort of joining to Grand Lake. Master was up at Nashville, Tennessee. Most of the time the overseers was good to us.

But it wasn't that way on all the plantations. On the next one they was mean. Why you could hear the sound of the strap for two blocks. No there wasn't any blocks. But you could hear it that far. The "niggah drivah" would stand and hit them with a wide strap. The overseer would stand off and split the blisters with a bull whip. Some they whipped so hard they had to carry them in. Just once did anybody on the Woodfork place get whipped that way.

We never knew quite what happened. But my grandmother thought that the colored man what took down the ages of the children so they'd know when to send them to the field must have wrote Master. Anybody else couldn't have done it. Anyhow, Master wrote back a letter and said, 'I bought my black folks to work, not to be killed.' And the overseer didn't dare do so any more.

No ma'am, I never worked in the field. I wasn't old enough. You see I helped my grandmother, she is the one who took care of the babies. All the women from the lower end would bring their babies to the upper end for her to look after while they was in the field. When I got old enough, I used to help rock the cradles. We used to have lots of babies to tend. The women used to slip in and nurse their babies. If the overseer thought they stayed too long he used to come in and whip them out—out to the fields. But they was good to us, just the same. We had plenty to wear and lots to eat and good cabins to live in. All of them wasn't that way though.

I remember the women on the next plantation used to slip over and get somthing to eat from us. The Woodfork colored folks was always well took care of. Our white folks was good to us. During the week there was somebody to cook for us. On Sunday all of them cooked in their cabins and they had plenty. The women on the next plantation, even when they was getting ready to have babies didn't seem to get enough to eat. They used to slip off at night and come over to our place. The Woodfork people never had to go nowhere for food. Our white folks treated us real good.

Didn't make much difference when the war started rushing. We didn't see any fighting. I told you the Yankees come thru twice——let me go back a spell.

We had lots of barrels of Louisiana molasses. We could eat all we wanted. When the barrels was empty, we children was let scrape them. Lawsey, I used to get inside the barrel and scrape and scrape and scrape until there wasn't any sweetness left.

We was allowed to do all sorts of other things too. Like there was lots of pecans down in the swamps. The boys, and girls too for that matter, was allowed to pick them and sell them to the river boats what come along. The men was let cut cord wood and sell it to the boats.

Flat boats they was. There was regular stores on them. You could buy gloves and hats and lots of things. They would burn the wood on the boat and carry the nuts up North to sell. But me, I liked the sugar barrel best.

When the Yankees come thru, I wasn't scared. I was too busy looking at the bright buttons on their coats. I edged closer and closer. All they did was laugh. But I kept looking at them. Until they went into the smoke house. Then I turned loose and hollered. I hollered because I thought they was going to take all Master's sirup. I didn't want that to happen. No ma'am they didn't take nothing. Neither time they came.

After the war was over they took us down the river to The Bend. It was near Vicksburg——an all day's ride. There they put us on a plantation and took care of us. It was the most beautifulest place I ever see. All the cabins was whitewashed good. The trees was big and the whole place was just lovely. It was old man Jeff Davis' place.

They fed us good, gave us lots to eat. They sent up north, the Yankees did, and got a young white lady to come down and teach us. I didn't learn nothing. They had our school near what was the grave yard. I didn't learn cause I was too busy looking around at the tombstones. They was beautiful. They looked just like folks to me. Looks like I ought have learned. They was mighty good to send somebody down to learn us that way. I ought have learned, it looks ungrateful, but I didn't.

My mother died on that place. It was a mighty nice place. Later on we come to Arkansas. We farmed. Looked like it was all we knowed how to do. We worked at lots of places. One time we worked for a man named Thomas E.

Allen. He was at Rob Roy on the Arkansas near Pine Bluff. Then we worked for a man named Kimbroo. He had a big plantation in Jefferson county. For forty years we worked first one place, then another.

After that I went out to Oklahoma. I went as a cook. Then I got the idea of following the resort towns about. In the summer I'd to [TR: go?] to Eureka.[D] In the winter I'd come down to Hot Springs.[E] That was the way to make the best money. Folks what had money moved about like that. I done cooking at other resorts too. I cooked at the hotel at Winslow.[F] I done that several summers.

Somehow I always come back to Hot Springs. Good people in Eureka. Finest man I ever worked for—for a rich man was Mr. Rigley, [TR: Wrigley] you know. He was the man who made chewing gum. We didn't have no gas in Eureka. Had to cook by wood. I remember lots of times Mr. Wrigley would come out in the yard where I was splitting kindling. He'd laugh and he'd take the ax away from me and split it hisself. Finest man——for a rich man I ever see.

Cooking at the hotel at Winslow was nice. There was lots of fine ladies what wanted to take me home with them when they went home. But I told them, 'No thank you, Hot Springs is my home. I'm going there this winter.'

I'm getting sort of old now. My feet ain't so sure as they used to be. But I can get about. I can get around to cook and I can still see to thread a needle. My daughter has a good home for me." (I was conducted into a large living room, comfortably furnished and with a degree of taste—caught glimpses of a well furnished dining room and a kitchen equipment which appeared thoroughly modern—Interviewer)

"People in Hot Springs is good people. They seem sort of friendly. Folks in Eureka did too, even more so. But maybe it was cause I was younger then and got to see more of them. But the Lord has blessed me with a good daughter. I got nothing to complain about, I don't hold grudges against nobody. The good Lord knows what he is doing."

Footnotes:

[D] Eureka Springs, Ark.

[E] Hot Springs National Park

[F] rustic hotel on mountain near village of Winslow, Ark.

Interviewer: Samuel S. Taylor
Person interviewed: George Johnson
814 W. Ninth Street, Little Rock, Arkansas
Age: 75

GEORGE JOHNSON

"I was born in Richmond, Virginia, September 28, 1862, and came to this country in 1869. My father was named Benjamin Johnson and my mother was named Phoebe Johnson. I don't know the names of my grandmother and grandfather. My father's master was named Johnson; I forget his first name. He was a doctor and lived on Charleston and Morgan Streets. I don't know what my mother's name was before she married my father. And I don't know what her master's name was. She died when I was just three years old.

"The way my father happened to bring me out here was, Burton Tyrus came out here in Richmond stump speaking and telling the people that money grew like apples on a tree in Arkansas. They got five or six boat loads of Negroes to come out here with them. Father went to share cropping on the Red River Bottom on the Chickaninny Farm. He put in his crop, but by the time he got ready to gather it, he taken sick and died. He couldn't stand this climate.

"Then me and my sisters was supposed to be bound out to Henry Moore and his wife. I stayed with them about six years and then I ran off. And I been scouting 'round for myself ever since.

"My occupation has been chiefly public work. My first work was rail roading and steam boating. I was on the Iron Mountain when she was burning wood. That was about fifty some years ago. After that I worked on the steamboats Natchez and Jim Lee. I worked on them as roustabout. After that I would just commence working everywhere I could get it. I came here about forty-five years ago because I liked the city. I was in and out of the city but made this place my headquarters.

"I'm not able to do any work now. I put in for the Old Age Pension two years ago. They told me I would have to prove my age but I couldn't do it any way except to produce my marriage license. I produced them. I got the license right out of this county courthouse here. I was married the last time in 1907 and was forty-five years old then. That will make me seventy-six years old this year—the twenty-eighth day of this coming September. My wife died nine years ago.

"I have heard my father talking a little but old folks then didn't allow the young ones to hear much. My daddy sent me to bed at night. When night came you went to bed; you didn't hang around waiting to hear what the old folks would say.

"My daddy got his leg shot in the Civil War. He said he was in that battle there in Richmond. I don't know which side he was on, but I know he got his leg shot off. He was one-legged. He never did get any pension. I don't know even whether he was really enlisted or not. All I know is that he got his leg shot off in the war.

"When the war ended in 1865, the slaves around Richmond were freed. I never heard my father give the details of how he got his freedom. I was too young to remember them myself.

"I don't know how many slaves Dr. Johnson had but I know it was a good many, for he was a tobacco raiser. I don't remember what kind of houses his slaves lived in. [And I never heard the kind of food we et.] [HW: ?]

"I never heered tell of patrols till I came to Arkansas. I never heered much of the Ku Klux either. I guess that was all the same, wasn't it? Peace wasn't declared here till 1866. I never heered of any of my acquaintances being bothered but I heered the colored people was scared. All I know was that you had to come in early. Didn't, they get you.

"What little schooling I got, I got it by going to night school here. That is been a good many years back—forty years back. I forgot now who was teaching night school. It was some kin of Ishes out here I know.

Opinions

"I think times is tight now. Tighter than I ever knowed 'em to be before. Quite a change in this world now. There is not enough work now for the people and from what I can see, electricity has knocked the laboring man out. It has cut the mules and the men out.

"My opinion of these young people is that they got all the education in the world and no business qualifications. They are too fast for any use."

United States. Work Projects Administration

Interviewer: Miss Irene Robertson
Person interviewed: John Johnson
R.F.D., Clarendon, Arkansas
Age: 73

JOHN JOHNSON

"I was born sixteen miles on the other side of Jackson, Tennessee. The old mistress was Miss Sally, and old master was Mr. Steve Johnson, same name as mine. My papa's name was Louis Johnson but my mama belonged to the Conleys and befo' she married papa her name was Martha Conley. My folks fur as I knowed was field hands. They stayed on at Johnsons and worked a long time after freedom. I was born just befo' freedom. From what I heard all of my folks talkin' the Ku Klux 'fected the colored folks right smart, more than the war. Seemed 'bout like two wars and both of 'em tried their best to draw in the black race. The black race wanted peace all the time. It was Abraham Lincoln whut wanted to free the black race. He was the President. The first war was 'bout freedom and the war right after it was equalization. The Ku Klux muster won it cause they didn't want the colored folks have as much as they have. I heard my folks say they knowed some of the Ku Klux. They would get killed sometimes and then you hear 'bout it. They would be nice as pie in day time and then dress up at night and be mean as they could be. They wanted the colored folks think they was hants and monsters from the bad place. All the Yankees whut wanted to stay after they quit fighting, they run 'em out wid hounds at night. The Ku Klux was awful mean I heard 'em say. Mr. Steve Johnson looked after all his hands. All that stayed on to work for him. He told 'em long as they stayed home at night and behave 'em selves they needn't be scared. They wanter go out at night they had to have him write 'em a pass. Jess like slavery an' they were free.

"The master didn't give 'em nuthin'. He let 'em live in his houses—log houses, and he had 'em fed from the store stead of the smoke house. He give 'em a little money in the fall to pay 'em. 'Bout all the difference they didn't get beat up. If they didn't work he would make 'em leave his place.

"That period—after the Civil War, it sure was hard. It was a de'pression I'll tell you. I never seed a dollar till I was 'bout grown. They called 'em 'wagon wheels.' They was mighty scarce. Great big heavy pieces of silver. I ain't seed one fer years. But they used to be some money.

"Lady, whut you wanter know was fo my days, fo I was born. My folks could answered all dem questions. There was 4 girls and 6 boys in my family.

"Course I did vote. I used to have a heap a fun on election day. They give you a drink. It was plentiful I tell you. I never did drink much. I voted Republican ticket. I know it would sho be too bad if the white folks didn't hunt good canidates. The colored race got too fur behind to be able to run our govmint. Course I mean education. When they git educated they ain't studyin' nuthin' but spendin' all they make and havin' a spreein' time. Lady, that is yo job. The young generation ain't carin' 'bout no govinment.

"The present conditions—that's whut I been tellin' you 'bout. It is hard to get work heap of the time. When the white man got money he sure give the colored man and woman work to do. The white man whut live 'mong us is our best friend. He stand by our color the best. It is a heap my age, I reckon, I can't keep in work. Young folks can pick up work nearly all time.

"I started to pay fer my home when I worked at the mill. I used to work at a shoe and shettle mill. I got holt of a little cash. I still tryin' to pay fer my home. I will make 'bout two bales cotton this year. Yes maam they is my own. I got a hog. I got a garden. I ain't got no cow.

"No maam I don't get no 'sistance from the govmint. No commodities—no nuthin'. I signed up but they ain't give me nuthin'. I think I am due it. I am gettin' so no account I needs it. Lady, I never do waste no money. I went to the show ground and I seed 'em buyin' goobers and popcorn. I seed a whole drove of colored folks pushin' and scrouging in there so feared they wouldn't get the best seat an' miss somepin. Heap of poor white people scrouging in there too all together. They need their money to live on fo cold weather come. Ain't I tellin' you right? I sho never moved outer my tracks. I never been to a show in my life. Them folks come in here wid music and big tent every year. I never been to a show in my life. That what they come here fur, to get the cotton pickin' money. Lady, they get a pile of money fore they leave. Course folks needs it now.

"When I had my mules and rented I made most and next to that when I farmed for a fourth. When I was young I made plenty. I know how cotton an' corn is made now but I ain't able to do much work, much hard work. The

Bible say twice a child and once a man. My manhood is gone fur as work concerned.

"I like mighty well if you govmint folks could give me a little 'sistance. I need it pretty bad at times and can't get a bit."

Interviewer: Mrs. Bernice Bowden
Person interviewed: Letha Johnson
2203 W. Twelfth Street, Pine Bluff, Arkansas
Age: 77

LETHA JOHNSON

"I heered the people say I was born in time of slavery. I was born durin' of the War.

"And when we went back home they said we had been freed four years.

"My father's last owner was named Crawford. He was a awful large man. That was in Monroe County, Mississippi.

"I know they was good to us 'cause we stayed right there after freedom till my father died in 1889. And mama stayed a year or two, then she come to Arkansas.

"After my husband died in 1919, I went to Memphis. Then this girl I raised—her mother willed her to me—I come here to Arkansas to live with her after I got down with the rheumatism so I couldn't wash and iron.

"In my husband's lifetime I didn't do nothin' but farm. And after I went to Memphis I cooked. Then I worked for a Italian lady, but she did her own cookin'. And oh, I thought she could make the best spaghetti.

"I used to spin and make soap. My last husband and I was married fifteen years and eight months and we never did buy a bar of soap. I used to be a good soap maker. And knit all my own socks and stockin's.

"I used to go to a school-teacher named Thomas Jordan. I remember he used to have us sing a song

> 'I am a happy bluebird
> Sober as you see;
> Pure cold water
> Is the drink for me.
> I'll take a drink here
> And take a drink there,
> Make the woods ring
> With my temperance prayer.'

We'd all sing it; that was our school song. I believe that's the onliest one I can remember.

"'Bout this younger generation—well, I tell you, it's hard for me to say. It just puts me to a wonder. They gone a way back there. Seem like they don't have any 'gard for anything.

"I heard 'em 'fore I left Mississippi singin'

> 'Everybody's doin' it, doin' it.'

"'Co'se when I was young they was a few that was wild, but seem like now they is all wild. But I feels sorry for 'em."

Interviewer: Mrs. Bernice Bowden
Person interviewed: Lewis Johnson
713 Missouri Street, Pine Bluff, Arkansas
Age: 87

LEWIS JOHNSON

"I'll be eighty-seven the eighteenth of this month if I live.

"They's a heap of things the human family calls luck. I count myself lucky to be livin' as old as I is.

"Some says it is a good deed I've done but I says it's the power of God.

"I never had but two spells of sickness when I was spectin' to die. Once was in Mississippi. I had a congestis chill. I lay speechless twenty-four hours and when I come to myself they had five doctors in the house with me.

"But my time hadn't come and I'm yet livin' by the help of the good Master.

"I stole off when I was eighteen and got my first marriage license. They was a white fellow was a justice of the peace and he took advantage of my father and he stood for me 'cause he wanted me to work on his place. In them days they'd do most anything to gain labor.

"When they was emigratin' 'em from Georgia to these countries, they told 'em they was hogs runnin' around already barbecued with a knife and fork in their back. Told 'em the cotton growed so tall you had to put little chaps up the stalk to get the top bolls.

"But they tole some things was true. Said in Mississippi the cotton growed so tall and spread so it took two to pick a row, and I found that true.

"Old master always fed his hands good so they could meet the demands when he called on 'em. He worked 'em close but he fed 'em.

"He raised wheat, corn, peas, rye, and oats, and all such like that. Oh, he was a round farmer all right. And he raised feed for his stock too.

"My old boss used to raise sweet potatoes enough to last three years.

"The people of the South was carried through that sweat of freedom. They was compelled to raise cotton and not raise much to eat. They told 'em they could buy it cheaper than raise it, but it was a mistake.

"I used to have a wood yard on the Mississippi and when the steamers come down the river, I used to go aboard and quiz the people from the North. Heap of 'em would get chips of different woods and put it away to carry home to show. And they'd take cotton bolls and some limbs to show the people at home how cotton grows.

"To my idea, the North is wiser than the South. My idea of the North is they is more samissive to higher trades—buildin' wagons and buggies, etc.

"Years ago they wasn't even a factory here to make cloth. Had to send the cotton to the North and then order the cloth from the North, and time they got it the North had all the money.

"In the old days they was only two countries they could depend on to raise tobacco and that was Virginia and South Carolina.

"I can remember a right smart before the War started. Now I can set down and think of every horse's name my old boss had. He had four he kept for Sunday business. Had Prince, Bill, Snap, and Puss. And every Saturday evening he had the boys take 'em in the mill pond and wash 'em off—fix 'em up for Sunday."

United States. Work Projects Administration

Interviewer: Miss Irene Robertson
Person interviewed: Lizzie Johnson,
Biscoe, Arkansas
Age: 65

LIZZIE JOHNSON

"I was born at Holly Springs, Mississippi. My mother was fifteen years old when the surrender come on. Her name was Alice Airs. Mama said she and grandma was sold in the neighborhood and never seen none of her folks after they was sold. The surrender come on. They quit and went on with some other folks that come by. Mama got away from them and married the second year of the surrender. She said she really got married; she didn't jump the broom. Mama was a cook in war times. Grandma churned and worked in the field. Grandma lived in to herself but mama slept on the kitchen floor. They had a big pantry built inside the kitchen and in both doors was a sawed-out place so the cats could come and go.

"My father was sold during of the War too but he never said much about it. He said some of the slaves would go in the woods and the masters would be afraid to go hunt them out without dogs. They made bows and arrows in the woods.

"I heard my parents tell about the Ku Klux come and made them cook them something to eat. They drunk water while she was cooking. I heard them say they would get whooped if they sot around with a book in their hand. When company would come they would turn the pot down and close the shutters and doors. They had preaching and prayed that way. The pot was to drown out the sound.

"They said one man would sell off his scrawny niggers. He wanted fine looking stock on his place. He couldn't sell real old folks. They kept them taking care of the children and raising chickens, turkeys, ducks, geese, and made some of them churn and milk.

"My stepfather said he knowed a man married a woman after freedom and found out she was his mother. He had been sold from her when he was a baby. They quit and he married ag'in. He had a scar on his thigh she recollected. The scar was right there when he was grown. That brought up more talk and they traced him up to be her own boy.

"Hester Swafford died here in Biscoe about seven years ago. Said she run away from her owners and walked to Memphis. They took her up over there. Her master sent one of the overseers for her. She rode astraddle behind him back. They got back about daylight. They whooped her awful and rubbed salt and pepper in the gashes, and another man stood by handed her a hoe. She had to chop cotton all day long. The women on the place would doctor her sores.

"Grandma said she remembered the stars falling. She said it turned dark and seem like two hours sparkles fell. They said stars fell. She said it was bad times. People was scared half to death. Mules and horses just raced. She said it took place up in the day. They didn't have time-pieces to know the time it come on.

"Young folks will be young the way I see it. They ain't much different. Times is sure 'nough hard for old no 'count folks. Young folks makes their money and spends it. We old folks sets back needing. Times is lots different now. It didn't used to be that way."

United States. Work Projects Administration

Interviewer: Mrs. Bernice Bowden
Person interviewed: Louis Johnson
721 Missouri Street, Pine Bluff, Arkansas
Age: 86

LOUIS JOHNSON

"My father said I was fifteen when peace was declared. In slavery days they didn't low colored folks to keep their ages and didn't low em to be educated. I was born in Georgia. I went to a little night school but I never learned to read. I never learned to write my own name.

"I never did see no fightin' a tall but I saw em refugeein' goin' through our country night and day. Said they was goin' to the Blue Ridge Mountains to pitch battle. They was Rebels gettin' out of the way of the Yankees.

"Old master was a pretty tough old fellow. He had work done aplenty. He had a right smart of servants. I wasn't old enough to take a record of things and they didn't low grown folks to ask too many questions.

"I can sit and study how the rich used to do. They had poor white folks planted off in the field to raise hounds to run the colored folks. Colored folks used to run off and stay in the woods. They'd kill old master's hogs and eat em. I've known em to stay six months at a time. I've seen the hounds goin' behind niggers in the woods.

"We had as good a time as we expected. My old master

fed and clothed very well but we had to keep on the go. Some masters was good to em. Yes, madam, I'd ruther be in times like now than slavery. I like it better now—I like my liberty.

"In slavery days they made you pray that old master and mistress would hold their range forever.

"My old master was Bob Johnson. He lived in Muskoge County where I was born. Then he moved to Harris County and that's where the war ketched him. He become to be a widower there.

"I member when the Yankees come and took old master's horses and mules.

"I had a young boss that went to the war and come home with the rheumatism. He was walkin' on crutches and I know they sent him to a refugee camp to see to things and when he come back he didn't have no crutches. I guess the Yankees got em.

"Childern travels now from one seaport to another but in them days they kept the young folks confined. I got along all right 'cept I didn't have no liberty.

"I believe it was in June when they read the freedom papers. They told us we was free but we could stay if we wanted to. My father left Bob Johnson's and went to work for his son-in-law. I was subject to him cause I was a minor, so I went with him. Before freedom, I chopped cotton, hoed corn and drapped peas, but now I was big enough to follow the plows. I was a cowboy too. I tended to the cows. Since I've been grown I been a farmer—always was a farmer. I never would live in town till I got disabled for farming.

"After we was free we was treated better. They didn't lash us then. We was turned loose with the white folks to work on the shares. We always got our share. They was more liberal along that line than they is now.

"After I come to this country of Arkansas I bought several places but I failed to pay for them and lost them. Now my wife and me are livin' on my daughter.

"I been married three times. I married 'fore I left Georgia but me and her couldn't get along. Then I married in Mississippi and I brought her to Arkansas. She died and now I been married to this woman fifty-three years.

"I been belongin' to the church over forty years. I have to belong to the church to give thanks for my chance here now. I think the people is gettin' weaker and wiser."

United States. Work Projects Administration

Interviewer: Miss Irene Robertson
Person interviewed: Mag Johnson,
Clarendon, Arkansas
Age: 65 or 70?

MAG JOHNSON

"Pa was born in North Ca'lina. Ma was born in Virginia. Their names George and Liza Fowler.

"Ma's fust owner what I heard her tell 'bout was Master Ed McGehee in Virginia. He's the one what brung her in a crowd of nigger traders to Somerville, Tennessee. The way it was, a cavalry of Yankees got in back of them. The nigger trader gang drive up. They got separated. My ma and her gang hid in a cave two weeks an' not much to eat. The Yankees overtook 'em hid in the cave and passed on. Ma say one day the nigger traders drive up in front McGehee's yard and they main heads and Master Ed had a chat. They hung around till he got ready and took off a gang of his own slaves wid him. They knowed he was after selling them off when he left wid 'em.

"Ben Trotter in Tennessee bought ma and three more nigger girls. The Yankees took and took from 'em. They freed a long time b'fore she knowed of. She said they would git biscuits on Sunday around. Whoop 'em if one be gone.

"Ole miss went out to the cow pen an' ma jus' a gal like stole outen a piece er pie and a biscuit and et it. The cook out the cow pen too but the three gals was doing about in the house and yard. Ma shut polly up in the shed room. Then she let it out when she et up the pie and biscuit. Ole miss come in. Polly say, 'Liza shut me up, Liza shut me up.' She missed the pie. Called all four the girls and ma said, 'I done et it. I was so hungry.' Ole miss said that what polly talking 'bout, but she didn't understand the bird so very well. Ole miss say, 'I'm goiner tell Ben and have him whoop you.' That scared all four the girls case he did whoop her which he seldom done. She say when Master Ben come they stood by the door in a 'joining room. Ma say 'fore God ole miss tole him. Master Ben sont 'em out to pick up apples. He had a pie a piece cooked next day and a pan of hot biscuits and brown gravy, tole 'em to fill up. He tole 'em he knowed they got tired of corn batter cakes, milk and molasses but it was best he had to give them till the War was done.

"Ma said her job got to be milking, raising and feeding the fowls, chickens, ducks, geese, guineas, and turkeys all. The Yankees discouraged her. They come so many times till they cleaned 'em out she said.

"What they done to shut up polly's mouf was sure funny. He kept on next morning saying, 'Liza shut me up, Liza shut me up.' Liza pulled up her dress and underskirt and walked back'ards, bent down at him. He got scared. He screamed and then he hollered 'Ball-head and no eyes' all that day.

"Ma said they had corn shuckings and corn shellings and brush burnings. Had music and square dancing plenty times.

"When they got free they didn't know what it was nor

what in the world to do with it. What they said 'minds me of folks now what got education. Seems like they don't know what to do nor where to put it.

"Pa said the nigger men run off to get a rest. They'd take to the woods and canebrakes. Once four of the best nigger fellars on their master's place took to the woods for to git a little rest. The master and paddyrolls took after 'em. They'd been down in there long 'nough they'd spotted a hollow cypress with a long snag of a limb up on it. It was in the water. They got them some vines and fixed up on the snag. They heard the dogs and the horn. They started down in the hollow cypress. One went down, the others coming on. He started hollering. But he thought a big snake in there. He brought up a cub on his nearly bare foot. They clem out and went from limb to limb till they got so away the dogs would loose trail. They seen the mama bear come and nap four her cubs to another place. His foot swole up so. They had to tote my pa about. Next day the dogs bayed them up in the trees. Master took them home, doctored his foot. Ast 'em why they runed off and so much to be doing. They tole 'em they taking a little rest. He whooped them every one.

"Pretty soon the Yankees come along and broke the white folks up. Pa went wid the Yankees. He said he got grown in the War. He fed horses for his general three years. He got arm and shoulder wounded, scalped his head. They mustered him out and he got his bounty. He got sixty dollars every three months.

"He died at Holly Grove, Arkansas about fifty years ago. Them was his favorite stories."

Interviewer: Mrs. Bernice Bowden
Person interviewed: Mandy Johnson
607 Cypress Street, Pine Bluff, Arkansas
Age: 92

MANDY JOHNSON

"This is me. I'se old and ain't no 'count. I was done grown when the war started. You know I was grown when I was washin' and ironin'. I stood right there and watched the soldiers goin' to war. I heered the big bell go b-o-n-g, b-o-n-g and everybody sayin' 'There's goin' to be a war, there's goin' to be a war!' They was gettin' up the force to go bless your heart! Said they'd be back by nine tomorrow and some said 'I'm goin' to bring you a Yankee scalp.' And then they come again and want so many. You could hear the old drums go boom—boom. They was drums on this side and drums on that side and them drums was a talkin'! Yes'm, I'se here when it started—milkin' cows, washin' and cookin'. Oh, that was a time. Oh my Lord—them Yankees come in just like blackbirds. They said the war was to free the folks. Lots of 'em got killed on the first battle.

"I was born in Bastrop, Louisiana in February—I was a February colt.

"My old master was John Lovett and he was good to us. If anybody put their hands on any of his folks they'd have him to whip tomorrow. They called us old John's free niggers. Yes ma'm I had a good master. I ain't got a scratch on me. I stayed right in the house and nussed till I'se grown. We had a good time but some of 'em seed sights. I stayed there a year after we was free.

"I married durin' the war and my husband went to war with my uncle. He didn't come back and I waited three years and then I married again.

"You know they used to give the soldiers furloughs. One time one young man come home and he wouldn't go back, just hid out in the cane brake. Then the men come that was lookin' for them that 'exerted' durin' the war and they waited till he come out for somethin' to eat and they caught him and took him out in the bayou and shot him. That was the onliest dead man I ever seen. I seen a heap of live ones.

"The war was gettin' hot then and old master was in debt. Old mistress had a brother named Big Marse Lewis. He wanted to take all us folks and sell us in New Orleans and said he'd get 'em out of debt. But old master wouldn't do it. I know Marse Lewis got us in the jail house in Bastrop and Mars John come to get us out and Marse Lewis shot him down. I went to my master's burial—yes'm, I did! Old mistress didn't let us go to New Orleans either. Oh Lordy, I was young them days and I wasn't afraid of nothin'.

"Oh ho! What you talkin' 'bout? Ku Klux? They come out here just like blackbirds. They tried to scare the people and some of 'em they killed.

"Yes Lord, I seen a heap. I been through a lot and I

seen a heap, but I'm here yet. But I hope I never live to see another war.

"When peace was declared, old mistress say 'You goin' to miss me' and I sho did. They's good to us. I ain't got nothin' to do now but sit here and praise the Lord cause I gwine to go home some day."

United States. Work Projects Administration

Interviewer: Mrs. Carol Graham
Person interviewed: Marion Johnson

MARION JOHNSON

"Howdy, Missy, glad to see you again. As you sees I'm 'bout wound up on my cotton baskets and now I got these chairs to put bottoms in but I can talk while I does this work cause it's not zacting like making baskets.

"'Pears like you got a cold. Now let me tell you what to do for it. Make a tea out of pine straw and mullein leaves an' when you gets ready for bed tonight take a big drink of it an' take some tallow and mix snuff with it an' grease the bottom of your feets and under your arms an' behind your ears and you'll be well in the mornin'.

"Yes'm hits right in the middle of cotton picking time now. Always makes me think of when I was a boy. I picked cotton some but I got lots of whippins 'cause I played too much. They was some chinquapin trees in the fiel' and I jest natchally couldn' help stopping to pick up some 'chanks' now an' then. I likes the fall time. It brings back the old times on the plantation. After frost had done fell we would go possum huntin' on bright moonlight nights and we would mostly find Mr. Possum settin' in the 'simmon tree just helpin' hisself to them good old ripe juicy 'simmons. We'd catch the possum an' then we'd help ourselves to the 'simmons. Mentionin' 'simmons, my mammy sure could make good pies with them. I can most taste them yet and 'simmon bread too.

"He! he! he! jes' look at that boy goin' by with that stockin' on his head. Niggers used to wear stockings on they legs but now they wear them on they heads to make they hair lay down.

"Since this rain we had lately my rheumatism been botherin' me some. I is gone to cutting my fingernails on Wednesday now so's I'll have health; an' I got me a brand new remedy too an' it's a good one. Take live earth worms an' drop them in hot grease an' let them cook till there's no 'semblance of a worm then let the grease cool an' grease the rheumatic parts. You know that rheumatism done come back cause I got out of herbs. I just got to git some High John the Conqueror root an' fix a red flannel sack an' put it in the sack along with five finger grass, van van oil, controllin' powder, magnetic loadstone an' drawin' powder. Now, missy, the way I fixes that sure will ward off evil an' bring heaps of good luck. And I just got to fix myself that. You better let me fix you one too. If you and me had one of them wouldn't neither one of us be ailing. You needs some lucky hand root too to carry round with you all the time. Better let Uncle Marion fix you up.

"Did I ever tell you I used to tell fortunes with cards? But I stopped that cause I got my jack now and it's so much truthfuler than cards. You 'members when I answered that question for you and missy last year and how what I told you come true. Yes'm I never misses now. Uncle Marion can sure help you.

"There goes sister Melissy late with her washin' ergin.

You know, Missy, niggers is always slow and late. They'll be wantin' God to wait on them when they start to heaven. White folks is always on time and they sings 'When The Roll Is Called Up Yonder I'll Be There', and niggers sing 'Don't Call The Roll Till I Get There.' You know I hates for it to get so cool. I'll have to move in off the gallery to work. When I sits on the gallery I sees everybody pass an' changes the time of day with them. 'Howdy, Sister Melissy. Late ergin I see.' Yes, I sees everything that goes on from my gallery. I hates for cool weather to come so's I have to move in.

"Ain't that a cute little feller in long pants? Lawsy me! chillun surely dresses diffunt now from when I was a chap. I didn' know nothin' 'bout no britches; I went in my shirt tail—didn' wear nothin' but a big old long shirt till I was 'bout twelve. You know that little fellow's mama had me treat him for worms. I made him a medicine of jimson weed an' lasses for his mama to give him every morning before breakfast an' that sure will kill 'em. Yes'm, that little fellow is all dressed up. 'Minds me of when I used to dress up to go courtin' my gal. I felt 'bout as dressed up as that little fellow does. I'd take soot out of the chimney and black my shoes then take a biscuit and rub over them to shine 'em. You know biscuits have grease in them and my shoes looked just like they done been shined by the bootblack.

"Law, missy, I don' know nothin' to tell you this time. Maybe if you come back I can think of something 'bout when niggers was in politics after the war but now I just can't 'member nothin'."

United States. Work Projects Administration

Interviewer: Carol Graham (Add.)
Person interviewed: Marion Johnson
El Dorado, Ark.
Age: ?

MARION JOHNSON

"Dar's golden streets and a pearly gate somewhars,
Dar's golden streets and a pearly gate somewhars,
I gwian ter keep on searchin' till I finds hit,
Dar's golden streets and a pearly gate somewhars.

"Dar's perfect peace somewhars,
Dar's perfect peace somewhars,
I gwian ter keep on searchin' till I finds hit,
Dar's perfect peace somewhars.

"Good mornin', Missie! Glad to see you again. I is workin' on chairs again. Got these five to bottom for Mr. Brown and I sho can talk while I does this work.

"Ain't the sunshine pretty this mornin'? I prayed last night that the Lord would let today be sunny. I 'clare, Missie, hits rained so much lately till I bout decided me and all my things was goin' to mildew. Yes'm, me and all-l-l my things. And I done told you I likes to set on my gallery to work. I likes to watch the folks go by. It seems so natchel like to set here and howdy with em.

"I been in this old world a long time, but just can recollect bein' a slave. Since Christmas ain't long past it sets me to thinkin' bout the last time old Sandy Claus come to see us. He brought us each one a stick of candy, a apple and a orange, and he never did come to see us no more after that time cause we peeped. That was the last time he ever filt our stockin'. But you knows how chaps is. We just had to peep.

"You knows I was born and raised in Louisiana. I done told you that many times. And I just wish you could see the vituals on old marster's table at Christmas time. Lawdy, but his table jes groaned with good things. Old Mistress had the cook cookin' for weeks before time it seemed to me. There was hams and turkeys and chickens and cakes of all kinds. They sho was plenty to eat. And they was a present for all the niggers on the place besides the heaps of pretty things that Marster's family got off the tree in the parlor.

"When I first began to work on the farm old master put me to cuttin' sprouts, then when I got big enough to make a field hand, I went to the field then. I done lots of kinds of work—worked in the field, split rails, built fences, cleared new ground and just anything old marster wanted me to do. I members one time I got a long old splinter in my foot and couldn't get it out, so my mammy bound a piece of fat meat round my foot and let it stay bout a couple days, then the splinter come out real easy like. And I was always cutting myself too when I was a chap. You know how careless chaps is. An soot was our main standby for cuts. It would close the gash and heal it. And soot and sugar is extra good to stop bleeding. Sometime, if I would be in the field too far away from the house or anyplace where we could get soot, we would get cobwebbs from the cotton house and different places to stop the bleeding. One time we wasn't close to neither and one the men scraped some felt off from a old black hat and put it on to stop the bleedin'.

"My feets was tough. Didn't wear shoes much till I was grown. Went barefooted. My feets was so tough I could step on stickers and not feel em. Just to show how tough I was I used to take a blackberry limb and take my toes and skin the briers off and it wouldn't hurt my feets.

"Did I ever tell you bout my first pair of breeches? I was bout twelve then and before that I went in my shirt tail. I thought I was goin' to be so proud of my first breeches but I didn't like them. They was too tight and didn't have no pockets. They come just below my knees and I felt so uncomfortable-like that I tore em off me. And did I get a lickin? I got such a lickin' that when my next ones was made I was glad to put em on and wear em.

"I stayed round with marster's boys a lot, and them white boys was as good to me as if I had been their brother. And I stayed up to the big house lots of nights so as to be handy for runnin' for old master and mistress. The big house was fine but the log cabin where my mammy lived had so many cracks in it that when I would sleep down there I could lie in bed and count the stars through the cracks. Mammy's beds was ticks stuffed with dried grass and put on bunks built on the wall, but they did sleep so good. I can most smell that clean dry grass now. Mammy made her brooms from broom sage, and she cooked on a fireplace. They used a oven and a fireplace up at the big house too. I never saw no cookstove till I was grown.

"I members one time when I was a little shaver I et too many green apples. And did I have the bellie ache, whoo-ee! And mammy poured cold water over hot ashes and let it cool and made me drink it and it sure cured me too. I members seein' her make holly bush tea, and parched corn tea too for sickness. Nother time I had the toothache and mammy put some axle grease in the hollow of the tooth and let it stay there. The pain stopped and the tooth rotted out and we didn't have to pull it.

"Whee! Did you see how that car whizzed round the corner? There warn't no cars in my young days. They had mostly two-wheeled carts with shafts for the horse to be hitched in, and lots of us drove oxen to them carts. I plowed oxen many-a-day and rode em to and from the field. Let me tell you, Missy, if you don't know nothin' bout oxen—they surely does sull on you—you beat them and the more you beat the more they sulls. Yes'm, they sure sulls in hot weather, but it never gets too cold for em.

"Howdy, Parson. That sho was good preachin' Sunday. Yes suh, it was fine.

"That's the pastor of our church, an he sho preached two good sermons last Sunday. Sunday mornin' he preached 'Every kind of fish is caught in a net' and that night he preached 'Marvel not you must be born again.' But that mornin' sermon, it capped the climax. Parson sho told em bout it. He say, 'First, they catch the crawfish, and that fish ain't worth much; anybody that gets back from duty or one which says I will and then won't is a crawfish Christian.' Then he say, 'The next is a mudcat; this kind of a fish likes dark trashy places. When you catch em you won't do it in front water; it likes back water and wants to stay in mud. That's the way with some people in church. You can't never get them to the front for nothin'. You has to fish deep for them. The next one is the jellyfish. It ain't got no backbone to face the right thing. That the trouble with our churches today. Too many jellyfishes in em.' Next, he say is the gold fish—good for nothin' but to look at. They is pretty. That the way folks is. Some of them go to church just to sit up and look pretty to everybody. Too pretty to sing; too pretty to say Amen! That what the parson preached Sunday. Well, I'm a full-grown man and a full-grown Christian, praise the Lord. Yes,'m, parson is a real preacher."

United States. Work Projects Administration

VOODOO MAN
UNCLE MARION JOHNSON, EX-SLAVE.
[Date Stamp: OCT 26 1936]

MARION JOHNSON

"Yes young missey ah'll sho tell yo-all whut yo wants ter know. Yes'm ole Uncle Marion sho kin. Mah price is fo' bits fer one question. No'm, not fo' bits fo th' two uv yo but fo' bits each. Yo say yo all ain't got much money and yo all both wants ter know th' same thing. Well ah reckon since yo all is been comin' roun' and tawkin' to ole Uncle Marion ah cud make hit answer th' one question fuh both uv yo fuh fo' bits 'tween yo. No'm ah caint bring hit out heah. Yo all will haft tuh come inside th' house."

"[TR: " should be (]We went inside the house and Uncle Marion unwrapped his voodoo instrument which proved to be a small glass bottle about 2-1/2 inches tall wrapped to the neck in pink washable adhesive tape and suspended from a dirty twine about six inches long. At the top of the twine was a slip knot and in a sly way Uncle Marion would twist the cord before asking the question. If the cord was twisted in one direction the bottle would swing in a certain direction and if the cord was twisted in the other direction the bottle would swing in the opposite direction. Uncle Marion thought that we did not observe this and of course we played dumb. By twisting the cord and slyly working the muscles of his arm Uncle

Marion made his instrument answer his questions in the way that he wished them answered.)

"Now ifn the answer to huh question is yais swing towards huh and ifn taint be still. (The bottle slowly swung toward me.) Now missy see hit have done answered yo question and yo done seed hit say yes. Yes'm hit sho am yes and yo' jes wait and see ifn ole Uncle Marion aint right. Now yo jes answer the same question fuh tother young missy heah. Now ifn the answer is yais yo turn toward huh which am the opposite to which yo jes turnt and ifn the answer is no sta' still. (The bottle then slowly turned around and went in Mrs. Thompson's direction.)

"Yo say whut do ah call dis heah? Ah calls hit a "jack". Yas'm hits a jack an' hit sho will answer any question yo wants ter ask hit. No'm yo cuden ask hit yo-self. Ah would haft ter ask hit fer yo. An' let me tell yo' ole Uncle Marion sho kin help youall chillun. Ah kin help yo all ward off evil and jinx; ah kin help yo all git a job; ah kin help yo all ovah come the ruination uv yo home. Uncle Marion sho cain give yo a helpin good luck hand. Ah cain help yo ovah come yo enemies.

"Now since ah knows yo young misses am in'erested an ah knows yo will sen' othah fokes tuh me what am in trouble ah am gointer tell yo all whut some uv mah magic remidies is so yo all kin tell fokes that ah have them yarbs (herbs) fuh sale. Yes'm ah has them yarbs right hea fuh sale and hit sho will work too.

"Now thar is High John the Conquerer Root. If'n yo totes one o' them roots in yo pocket yo will nevah be widout money. No mam. And you'll always conquer yo troubles an yo enemies. An fokes can sho git them yarbs thru me. Efn Uncle Marion don' have non on han' he sho kin git em for em.

"Den dar is five finger grass, ah kin git dat fuh yo too. Ifn dat is hung up ovah th' bedstid hit brings restful sleep and keeps off evil. Each one uv dem five fingahs stans for sumpin too. One stans fuh good luck, two fuh money, thee fuh wisdom, fo' fuh power an five fuh love.

"Yas'm an ah kin buil' a unseen wall aroun' yo so as ter keep evil, jinx and enemies way fum yo and hit'll bring heaps uv good luck too. The way ah does hit is this way: Ah takes High John the Conqueror Root and fixes apiece of red flannel so as ter make a sack and puts hit in the sack along wid magnetic loadstone, five finger grass, van van oil, controllin' powdah and drawin powdah and the seal uv powah. This heah mus be worn aroun the neck and sprinkle hit ever mornin fuh seven mornins wid three drops uv holy oil. Then theah is lucky han' root. Hit looks jes like a human han'. If yo carries hit on yo person hit will shake yo jinx and make yo a winnah in all kinds o games and hit'll help yo choose winnin numbers."

United States. Work Projects Administration

Interviewer: Miss Irene Robertson
Person interviewed: Martha Johnson, West Memphis
Age: 71

MARTHA JOHNSON

"I was born at Lake Providence, Louisiana second year after the War. Mother's mother was left in Jackson, Tennessee. Mother was sold at Vicksburg, Mississippi. Father's mother was left at Pittsburg, Virginia. Father was brought to Lake Providence and sold to Master Ross and Mr. Coleman was his overseer. He was stripped stark naked and put up on the block. That was Nigger Traders Rule, he said. He was black as men get to be. Mother was three-fourths white. Her master was her father. He had two families. They was raised up in the same house with his white family. Master's white wife raised her and kept her till her death. He was dead I think.

"Then her young white master sold her. He sold his half-sister. She met my father at Vicksburg, Mississippi where he mustered out. She was chambermaid when the surrender came on, on the Gray Eagle boat from Vicksburg to Memphis. Mother died when I was nine years old. Papa had no boys, only three girls. I was his 'Tom Boy.' I did the milking and out-of-door turns. Papa was a small man. He weighed 150 pounds. He carpentered, made and mended shoes, and was a blacksmith. We farmed and farmed. I was chambermaid in Haynes, Arkansas hotel three years. I washed and ironed. I'm not much cook. I never was fond of cooking.

"I never voted. I'm not starting now. I'm too old.

"Times is hard. You can't get ahead no way. It keeps you hustling all the time to live. Times is going pretty fast. In some ways times is better for some people and harder for other people.

"These young folks don't want to be advised and I don't advise them except my own children. I tell them all they listen to. They listen now better than they did when they was younger. They are all grown.

"I don't get no help from nowhere but my children a little. I own my home."

Interviewer: Pernella M. Anderson
Person interviewed: Millie Johnson (Old Bill)
El Dorado, Arkansas
Age: ?

MILLIE JOHNSON

"I was born in Caledonia, Arkansas but I don't know when. I just can't tell you nothing hardly about when I was a child because my mind goes and comes. I was a slave and my white folks were good to me. They let me play and have a good time just like their children did.

"After I got grown I run around terrible. My husband quit me a long time ago. The white folks let me have my way. They said I was mean and if my husband fooled with me, told me to shoot him. I am going back home to Caledonia when I get a chance. My sister's boy brought me up here; Mack Ford is his name.

"A long time ago—I don't know how long it's been—I came out of the back door something hung their teeth in my ankle. I hollered and looked down and it was a big old rattlesnake. I cried to my sister to get him off of me. She was scared, so all I knew to do was run, jump and holler. I ran about—oh, I don't know how far—with the snake hanging to my ankle. The snake would not let me go, and it wasn't but one thing for me to do and that was stop and pull the snake off of me. I stopped and began pulling. I pulled and pulled and pulled and pulled. The snake would not let me go. I began pulling again. After awhile I got it off. When I pulled the snake away the snake brought his mouth full of my meat. You talk about hurting, that like to have killed me. That place stayed sore for twenty years before it healed up. After it had been healed a couple years I then scratched the place on a bob wire that inflamed it. That has been about 25 or 30 years ago and it's been sore ever since. Lord, I sure have been suffering too. As soon as it gets well I am going back to Caledonia. I am praying for God to let me live to get back home. Mack Ford is the cause of me being up here.

"I was born in slavery time way before the War. My name is Millie Johnson but they call me Bill."

Interviewer: Miss Irene Robertson
Person interviewed: Rosie Johnson,
Holly Grove, Arkansas
Age: 76

ROSIE JOHNSON

"I was born and raised on Mr. Dial's place. Mama belong to them. My papa belong to Frank Kerr. His old mistress' name Jane Roberts in Alabama. His folks come from Alabama. He say Jane Roberts wouldn't sell her slaves. They was aired (heired) down mong the children. David Dial had sebral children and mama was his house girl and nurse. They was married in Dial's yard. My papa name Jacob Kerr. They took me to Texas when I warn't but two years old. We rode in the covered wagon where they hauled the provisions. They muster stayed a pretty good time. I heard em talkin' what all they raised out there and what a difference they found in the country. They wanted to go. They didn't wanter be in the war they said. It was too close to suit them.

"I recken I was too small to recollect the Ku Klux. I heard em talk bout how mean the Jayhaws was.

"I never voted. What business I got votin' I would jes' lak you tell me? I don't believe in it no more'n nuthin'.

"I been farmin' all my life. I had fourteen children. Eight livin' now. They scattered bout up North. It took meat and bread to put in their mouths and somebody workin' to get it there I tell you. There ain't a lazy bone in me. I jes' give out purty nigh. I wash and iron some when I ken get it.

"I got a hog and a garden. I ain't got nuthin' else. I don't own no house, no place. I got a few chickens bout the place what eat up the scraps what the pig don't get.

"I signed up three years ago. I don't get nuthin' now. What I scrape round and make is all I has.

"I was born in June 1861. I don't recollect what day they said. Pear lack it been so long. When it come to work I recken I is had a hard time all my life. I never minded nuthin' till I got so slow and no count."

Interviewer: Samuel S. Taylor
Person interviewed: Saint Johnson
Izard Street, Little Rock, Arkansas
Age: —
Occupation: Drayman

SAINT JOHNSON

"As far as slavery is concerned I know nothing about it except as the white people told me. My mother would ask me what they told me and I would tell her that Miss Annie said I didn't have to call her father 'Master' any more. And she would say, 'No, you don't.'

"My father's name was Wiley Johnson. He was ninety years old when he died. He was born in Cave Spring, Georgia, in Floyd County. My mother was born in the same place. Both of them were Johnsons. They were married during slavery times. I don't know what her name was before she married.

"Anyway, I've told you enough. I've told you too much. How come they want all this stuff from the colored people anyway? Do you take any stories from the white people? They know all about it. They know more about it than I do. They don't need me to tell it to them.

"I don't tell my age. I just say I was born after slavery. Then I can't be bothered about all this stuff about records. Colored people didn't keep any records. How they goin' to know when they were born or anything? I don't believe in all that stuff.

"You know these young people as well as I do. They ain't nothin'.

"I ain't got nothin' to say about politics. You know what the truth is. Why don't you say it? You don't need to hide behind my words. You're educated and I'm not; you don't need to get anything from me.

"Yes, I had some schoolin'. But you know more about these things than I do."

Interviewer's Comment

At first, I thought I wouldn't write this interview up; but afterwards I thought: Maybe this interview will be of interest to those who want the work done. It represents the attitude of a very small, but definite, minority. About five persons out of a hundred and fifty contacted and more than eighty written up have taken this attitude.

Johnson is reputed to have been born in slavery, but he says not. He had a high school education. He is a good man, wholesome in all his contacts, despite the apparent intolerance of his private remarks to the interviewer.

Interviewer: Samuel S. Taylor
Person interviewed: Willie Johnson (female)
1007 Izard, Little Rock, Arkansas
Age: 71

WILLIE JOHNSON

"My father said he had a real good master. When he got up large enough to work, his master learned him a trade. He learned the mechanic's trade, such as blacksmithing and working in shops. He learned him all of that. And then he learned him to be a shoemaker. You see, he learned him iron work and woodworking too. And he never whipped him during slavery time. Positively didn't allow that.

"My father's name was Jordan Kirkpatrick. His master was named Kirkpatrick also. My father was born in Tennessee in Sumner County.

"My father married in slave time. You know, they married in slave time. I have heard people talking about it. I have heard some people say they married over 'gain when freedom came. My father had a marriage certificate, and I didn't hear him say anything about being married after freedom. I have seen the certificate lots of times. I don't know the date of it. The certificate was issued in Sumner County, Tennessee.

"My father and mother belonged to different masters. My mother's master was a Murray. She had a good many people. Her name before she married was Mary Murray. I don't know just how my mother and father met. The two places weren't far apart. They lived a good distance from each other though, and I remember hearing him tell how he had to go across the fields to get to her house after he was through with the day's work. The pateroles got after him once. They didn't catch him, so they didn't do anything to him. He skipped them some way or another.

"I have heard them say that before the slaves were set free the soldiers were going 'round doing away with everything that they could get their hands on. Just a while before they were set free, my father took my mother and the children one night and slipped off. He went to Nashville. That was during the War. It wasn't long after that till everybody was set free. They never did capture him and get him back.

"During the War they went around pressing men into service. Finally once, they caught him but they let him go. I don't know how he got away.

"I can remember he said once they got after him and there was a white man and his family living in the house. He rented a room from the white man. That was in Nashville. These pateroles or whatever they was got after him and claimed they were coming to get him, and the old man and the old woman he stayed with took him upstairs and said they would protect him if the pateroles came back. I don't know whether they came back or not, but they never got him.

"My father supported himself and his family in Nashville by following his trade. He seems to have gotten along all right. He never seemed to have any trouble that I heard him speak of.

"I was born in 1867 in Nashville, Tennessee, about half a block from the old Central Tennessee College[G]. I think it became Walden University later on, and I think that it's out now. That's an old school. My oldest sister was graduated from it. I could have been if I hadn't taken up the married notion.

"I got part of my schooling in Nashville and part here. When I left Nashville, I was only a child nine years old. I only went to school four sessions after we came out here. I didn't like out here. I wanted to stay back home. My father came out here because he had heard that he could make more money with his trade here than he could in Nashville, which he did. He was shoeing horses and building wagons and so on. Just in this blacksmithing and carpenter work.

"I wanted to learn that. I would stay 'round the shop and help him shoe horses. But they wouldn't let me take it up. I got so I could do carpenter work pretty good. First I learned how to make a box square—that is a hard job when a person doesn't know much.

"I never heard my father say anything about the food the slaves ate. I have heard him talk about the good times they had around hog killing. His master raised sweet potatoes and corn and wheat and things like that. I guess they ate just about what they raised.

"My father never was a sharecropper. He knew nothing of rural work except the mechanical side of it. He could make or do anything that was needed in fixing up something to do farm work with. I have seen him make and sharpen plows. The first cotton stalk cutter that was made within ten miles of here was made by my father.

The people 'round here were knocking off cotton stalks with sticks until my father began making the cutter. Then everybody began using his cutter. That is, the different farmers and sharecroppers around here began using them. I was scared of the first one he made. He made six saws or knives and sharpened them and put them on a section of a log so that it could be hitched to a mule and pulled through the fields and cut the cotton stalks down.

"My mother's old master was her father. I think my father's father was a Negro and his mother was an Indian. My mother's mother was an American woman, that is, a slavery woman. My mother and father were lucky in having good people. My mother was treated just like one of her master's other children. My father's master had an overseer but he never was allowed to touch my father. Of course my mother never was under an overseer."

Footnotes:

[G] [HW: Central Tennessee College estab. about 1866-7.]

Interviewer: Miss Irene Robertson
Person interviewed: Angeline Jones
Near Biscoe and Brinkley, Arkansas
Age: 79
[Date Stamp: May 31 1938]

ANGELINE JONES

"I was born in Memphis, Tennessee. Mother was cooking. Her name was Marilla Harris and she took my pa's name, Brown. He was Francis Brown. I was three years old when the surrender come on. Then grandma, my mama and pa and me and my brother come with a family to Biscoe. There wasn't no Biscoe but that's where we come to anyhow. Mama and grandma cooked for a woman. They bought a big farm and started clearing. Some of it was cleared. Mama's been dead forty years. I farmed all my whole life. I don't know nothing else.

"Grandma had a right smart to say during slavery times. She was cooking for her mistress and had a family. She'd hide good things to take to her children. The mistress kept a polly parrot about in the kitchen. Polly would tell on grandma. Caused grandma to get whoopings. She talked like a good many of 'em. She got sick. The woman what married grandma's brother was to take her place. She wasn't going to be getting no whoopings. She sewed the parrot up. He got to dwindling. They doctored him. She clipped his tongue at the same time so he never could do no good talking. He died. They never found out his trouble. Grandma said they worried about the parrot but she never did; she knowed what been done. Grandma come from Paris, Tennessee but I think the same folks fetched 'er. I don't think she said she was sold. She said slavery times was hard. Mama didn't see as hard times as grandma had. Grandma shielded her in the work part a whole heap to get to live where she did. They loved to be together. She's been dead and left me forty odd years. I works and support myself, and my kin folks help all they can."

Interviewer: Mrs. Bernice Bowden
Person interviewed: Charlie Jones
1303 Ohio Street, Pine Bluff, Arkansas
Age: 76

CHARLIE JONES

"I was borned in '61 in the State of Mississippi August the 15th.

"I member just a little bout the War. Yes'm, I member seein' the soldiers. They was walkin'—just a long row of em. Had guns across their shoulders and had them canteens. I member we chilluns run out to the road and got upon the bars and watched em go by. I think it was after they had fought in Vicksburg and was comin' back towards Memphis.

"My mother belonged to the Harrises and we stayed with her and my father belonged to the Joneses.

"I member how they used to feed us chillun. They had a big cook kitchen at the big house and we chillun would be out in the yard playin'. Cook had a big wooden tray and she'd come out and say 'Whoopee!' and set the tray on the ground. Sometimes it was milk and sometimes it would be potlicker. We'd fall down and start eatin'. Get out [TR: our?] heads in and crowd just like a lot of pigs.

"After freedom we went to old Colonel Jones and worked on the shares. I wasn't big enough to work but I member when we left the Harris place. I know they wasn't so cruel to em. Didn't have no overseer. Some of the people had cruel overseers.

"I went to school after the War a right smart. I got as far as the third grade. Studied McGuffy's Reader and the old Blue Back Speller. Yes'm, sure did.

"I come here to Arkansas wid my parents in '78. Come right here to Jefferson County, down at Fairfield on the Lambert place.

"All my life I've farmed. I worked on the shares and rented too. Could make the most money rentin'. I got everywhere from 4¢ to 50¢ a pound for cotton. I had cows and hogs and chickens and raised some corn.

"I made a garden and made a little cotton and corn last year on government land on the old river bank.

"I heered of the Klu Klux but they never did bother me.

"I voted the Publican ticket and never had no trouble.

"I been right around this town fifteen years and I own this home. I worked about six months at the shops but the rest of the time I farmed.

"Heap of things I'd do when I was young the young folks won't do now."

Interviewer: Mrs. Bernice Bowden
Person interviewed: Cyntha Jones
3006 W. Tenth Avenue, Pine Bluff, Arkansas
Age: 88

CYNTHA JONES

"Well, here's one of em. Born down in Drew County.

"Simpson Dabney was old master and his wife named Miss Adeline.

"I reckon I do remember bout the War. Yes ma'am, the Yankees come and they had me scared. I wouldn't know when they got in the yard till they was all around me. Had me holdin' the bridles.

"My young missis' husband was in the War and when they fought the last battle at Princeton, she had me drive the carriage. When I heard them guns I said we better go back, so I turned round and made them horses step so fast my dress tail stood out straight. I thought they was goin' to kill us all. And when we got home all the windows was broke. Miss Nancy say, 'Cyntha, somebody come and broke all my windows,' but it was them guns broke em.

"Old master was a doctor but my young missis' husband wasn't nothin' but a hunter till they carried him to war. He was so skeered they had to most drag him.

"I seen two wars and heered tell of another.

"I member when the Yankees come and took things I just fussed at em. I thought what was my white folks' things was mine too. But when they got my old master's horse my daddy went amongst em and got it back cause he had charge of the stock. I don't know whether he got em at night or not but I know he went in the daytime and come back in the daytime.

"Old master's children and my father's children worked in the field just alike. He wouldn't low a overseer on the place, or a patroller either.

"Dr. Dabney and his sister raised my mother. They brought her from some furrin' country to Arkansas. And when he married, my mother suckled every one of his children.

"I just worked in the house and nussed. Never worked in the field till I was grown and married. I was nineteen when I married the fust time. I stayed right there in that settlement till the second year of surrender.

"When I was twenty-one they had me fixed up for a midwife. Old Dr. Clark was the one started me. I never went to school a minute in my life but the doctors would read to me out of their doctor books till I could get a license. I got so I could read print till my eyes got so bad. Old Dr. Clark was the one learned me most and since he died I ain't never had a doctor mess with me.

"In fifteen years I had 299 babies on record right there in Rison. That's where I was fixed up at—under five doctors. And anybody don't believe it, they can go down there and look up the record.

"We had plenty to eat in slave times. Didn't have to go

to the store and buy it by the dribble like they does now. Just go to the smokehouse and get it.

"I got such a big mind and will I wants to get about and raise something to eat now so we wouldn't have to buy everything, but I ain't able now. I've had twenty-one children but if I had em now they'd starve to death.

"I been married four times but they all dead—every one of em.

"When freedom come my old master give my mother $500 cause she saved his money for him when the Yankees come. She put it in the bed and slept on it. He had four farms and he told her she could have ary one of em and any of the stock, but my father had done spoke for a place in Cleveland County—he had done bought him a place.

"And old master on his dying bed, he asked my mother to take his two youngest children and raise em cause their mother was sickly, but she didn't do it.

"I don't know hardly what to think of this younger generation. Used to be they'd go to Sunday school barefooted but now'days, time they is born they got shoes and stockin's on em.

"I used to spin, knit and weave. I even spun thread to make these ropes they use to plow. I could spin a thread you could sew with, and weave cloth with stripes and flowers. Have to know how to dye the thread. That's all done in the warp. Call the other the filler.

"Now let me tell you, when that was goin' on and you raised your meat and corn and potatoes, that was livin'!"

United States. Work Projects Administration

Interviewer: Mrs. Bernice Bowden
Person interviewed: Edmond Jones
1824 W. Second, Pine Bluff, Arkansas
Age: 75

EDMOND JONES

"I growed up in the war. I remember seein' the soldiers—hundreds and thousands of em. Oh, yes'm, I growed up in the war. I was born under Abraham Lincoln's administration and then Grant.

"I remember when that old drum beat everbody had to be in bed at nine o'clock. That was when they had martial law. Hays knocked that out you know. That was when they had the Civil Rights Bill. I growed up in that.

"Abraham Lincoln issued the Proclamation of Freedom in January and I was born in May so you might say I was born right into freedom.

"I always say I was born so close to slavery I could smell it, just like you cookin' somethin' for dinner and I smelled it.

"I tell these young people I can look back to my boy days quick as they can.

"Yes'm, I don't know anything bout slavery. My people say they come from North Carolina, but I been right here on this spot of ground for forty-four years. I come here when they was movin' the cemetery.

"My mother was a cook here for Mrs. Reynolds. After I growed up here I went out to my father where he was workin' on the shares and stayed there a year. I married quite young and bought a place out there. I said I was twenty-one when I got the license but I wasn't but twenty.

"In old times everbody thought of the future and had all kinds of things to eat. First prayer I was taught was the Lord's Prayer—'Give us this day our daily bread.' I said sure was a long time bein' answered cause now we're gettin' it—just our daily bread.

"I never had no luck farmin'—ever' time I farmed river overflowed. I raised everthing I needed or I didn't have it. Had as high as thirty head of cows at one time.

"I went to work as janitor at Merril School to take the regular janitor's place for just two months and how long you reckon I stayed there? Twenty years. Then I come here and sit down and haven't done anything since.

"The first school I went to was in the First Baptist Church on Pullen Street. They had it there till they could put up a building.

"I went to nine different teachers and all of em was white. They was sent here from the North. We studied McGuffy's reader and you stayed with it till you learned it. I got it till today—in my head you understand.

"Sure, Lord, I used to vote and hold ever' kind of office. Used to be justice of the peace six years. I said I been in everthing but a bull fight.

"I've traveled ever' place—Niagara Falls, Toronto,

Canada. I been in two World's Fairs and in several inaugurations. Professor Cheney says I know more history than any the teachers at the college."

United States. Work Projects Administration

Interviewer: Mrs. Bernice Bowden
Person interviewed: Eliza Jones
610 E. Eighteenth, Pine Bluff, Arkansas
Age: 89

ELIZA JONES

"Yes ma'am, this is Eliza. I was born in slave times and I knowed how to work good.

"You know I was grown in time of the War 'cause I married the first year of freedom.

"Belonged to a widow named Edna Mitchell. That was in Tennessee near Jackson. Oh Lawd, my missis was good to all her niggers—if you should call 'em that.

"She had two men and three women. My mother was the cook. Let's see—Sarah was one, Jane was two, and Eliza was three. (I was Eliza.) Then there was Doc and Uncle Alf. I reckon he was our uncle. Anyway we all called him Uncle Alf. He managed the business—he was the head man and Doc was next. And Miss Edna raised us all to grown.

"Now I'm tellin' you right straight along. I try to tell the truth. I forgits and I can't remember ever'thing like it ought to be but I hit at it.

"Things is hard this year and I don't know how come. I guess it's 'cause folks is so wicked. They is livin' fast—black and white.

"How many chillun? Now, you'd be s'prised. I hardly ever tell folks how many. I had fifteen; I was a good breeder. But they is all dead but one, and they ain't doin' me no good. Never raised but two. Most of 'em just died when they was born.

"I'd a been better off if I had stayed single a while longer and went to school and learned how to read and write and figger. But I went to another kind of a school.

"But I sure has been blest. I been here a long time, got a chile to cook me a little bread—don't have to worry 'bout dat.

"I had to send clean back to where I j'ined the Metropolitan to get my age. That was in Cairo, Illinois 'cause I'd lived there fifteen years. But when my daughter and her husband come here and got settled, why I come to finish it out.

"Yes ma'am, I sure have worked hard. I've plowed, split wood, and done a little bit of ever'thing. But it was all done since freedom. In slavery times I was a house girl. I tell you I was a heap better off a slave than I was free.

"After freedom we had to go and get what we could get to do and work hard.

"They used to talk 'bout ha'nts and squinch owls. Say it was a sign of somebody dead. But I don't believe in that. 'Course what I don't believe in somebody else does."

Interviewer: Samuel S. Taylor
Person interviewed: Evelyn Jones
815 Arch Street, Little Rock, Arkansas
Age: Between 68 and 78?

EVELYN JONES

"I was born in Lonoke County right here in Arkansas. My father's name—I don't know it. I don't know nothin' 'bout my father. My mother's name was Mary Davis.

"My daddy died when I was five weeks old. I don't know nothin' 'bout 'im. Just did manage to git here before he left. I don't know the date of my birth. I don't know nothin' 'bout it and I ain't goin' to tell no lie.

"I have nineteen children. My youngest living child is twenty-eight years old. My oldest living is fifty-three. I have four dead. I don't know how old the oldest one is. That one's dead.

"I have a cousin named Harry Jordan. He lives 'round here somewheres. You'll find him. I don't know where he lives. He says he knows just how old I am, and he says that I'm sixty-eight. My daughter here says I'm seventy. And my son thinks I'm older. Don't nobody know. My daddy never told me. My mama was near dead when I was born; what could she tell me? So how am I to know?

"My mother was born in slavery. She was a slave. I don't know nothin' 'bout it. My mother came from Tennessee. That's what she told me. I was born in a log cabin right here in Arkansas. I was born in a log cabin right in front of the white folks' big house. It was not far from the white folks' graveyard. You know they had a graveyard of their own. Old Bill Pemberton, that was the name of the man owned the place I was born on. But he wasn't my mother's owner.

"I don't know where my father come from. My mother said she had a good time in slavery. She spoke of lots of things but I don't remember them.

"My grandma told me about when she went to church she used to carry her good clothes in a bundle. When she got near there, she would put them on, and hide her old clothes under a rock. When she come out from the meeting, she would have to put on her old clothes again to go home in. She didn't dare let the white folks see her in good clothes.

"I think my mother's white people were named Jordans. My mother and them all belonged to the young mistress. I think her name was Jordan. Yes, that's what it was—Jordan.

"Grandmammy had so many children. She had nineteen children—just like me. My grandmammy was a great big old red woman. She had red hair too. I never heard her say nothin' 'bout nobody whippin' her and my granddaddy. They whipped all them children though. My mama just had six children.

"Mama said her master tried to keep her in slavery after freedom. My mama worked at the spinning-wheel. When she heard the folks say they was through with the

War, she was at the spinning-wheel. The white folks ought a tol' them they was free but they didn't. Old Jordan carried them down in De Valla Bluff. He carried them down there—called hisself gittin' away from the Yankees. But the Yankees told mama to quit workin'. They tol' her that she was free. My mama said she was in there at the wheel spinning and the house was full of white men settin' there lookin' at her. You don't see that sort of thing now.

"They had a man—I don't know what his name was. He stalled them steers, stalled 'em twice a day. They used to pick cotton. I dreamed about cotton the other night.

"My father farmed after slavery. I never heard them say they were cheated out of nothin'. I don't know whether they was or not. I'll tell you the truth. I didn't pay them no 'tention. Mighty little I can remember."

United States. Work Projects Administration

Interviewer: Miss Irene Robertson
Person interviewed: John Jones,
Brinkley, Arkansas
Age: 71

JOHN JONES

"I was raised an orph'ant but I was born in Tennessee. I lived over there and farmed till 'bout fifty year ago. I come out here wid Mr. Woodson to pick cotton. He dead now and I still tryin' to work all I can.

"I haben voted in thirty-five year. Because I couldn't vote in the Primary, then I say I wouldn't vote 'tall. I don't care if the women want to vote. Don't do no good nohow.

"I farmed all my life 'ceptin' 'bout ten years I worked on the section. I got so I couldn't stand up to it every day and had to farm again.

"I never considered times hard till I got disabled to work. It mighty bad when you can't get no jobs to do. My hardest time is in the winter. I has a garden and chickens but I ain't able to buy a cow. Man give me a little pig the other day. He won't be big enough to eat till late next spring. Every winter times is hard for me. It's been thater wa's ever since I begin not to be able to get about. Helped by the PWA."

United States. Work Projects Administration

Interviewer: Mrs. Bernice Bowden
Person interviewed: John Jones
3109 W. 10th Avenue, Pine Bluff, Arkansas
Age: 82

JOHN JONES

"I come here in 1856—you can figure it out for yourself. I was born in Arkansas, fifty miles below here.

"I remember the soldiers. I know I was a little boy drivin' the gin. Had to put me upon the lever. You see, all us little fellows had to work.

"I remember seein' the Indians goin' by to fight at Arkansas Post. They fought on the southern side. When I heard the cannons, I asked my mama what it was and she said 'twas war.

"John Dye—that was my young master—went to the War but Ruben had a kind of afflicted hand and he didn't go.

"Our plantation was on the river and I used to see the Yankee boats go down the river.

"My papa belonged to the Douglases and mama belonged to the Dyes. I was born on the Douglas place and I ain't been down there in over fifty years. They said I was born in March but I don't know any more bout it than a rabbit.

"Papa said he was raised up in the house. Said he didn't do much work—just tended to the gin.

"I remember one night the Ku Klux come to our house. I was so scared I run under the house and stayed till ma called me out. I was so scared I didn't know what they had on.

"I remember when some of the folks come back from Texas and they said peace was declared.

"I think my brother run off and jined the Yankees and come here when they took Pine Bluff. War is a bad thing. I think they goin' keep on till they hatch up another one.

"I didn't go to school much. I was the oldest boy at home and I had to plow. I went seven days all told and since then I learned ketch as ketch can. I can read and write pretty well. It's a consolation to be able to read. If you can't get all of it, you can get some of it.

"Been here in Jefferson County ever since 1867. I come here from Lincoln County.

"After freedom my papa moved my mama down on the Douglas place where he was and stayed one year, then moved on the Simpson place in Lincoln County, and then come up here in Jefferson County. I remember all the moves.

"I remember down here where Kientz Bros, place is was the gallows where they hung folks in slavery times. You know—when they had committed some crime.

"Yes'm, I voted but I never held any office.

"I know I don't look my age but I can tell you a heap of things happened before emancipation.

"I think the people are better off free—they got liberty."

United States. Work Projects Administration

Interviewer: Mrs. Bernice Bowden
Person interviewed: Lidia Jones
228 N. Oak Street, Pine Bluff, Arkansas
Age: 94
Occupation: None—blind

LIDIA JONES

"I was born in Mississippi and emigrated to Arkansas. Born on the Peacock place. Old John Patterson was my old master.

"My first goin' out was to the cow pen, then to the kitchen, and then they moved me to Mrs. Patterson's dining-room.

"I helped weave cloth. Dyed it? I wish you'd hush! My missis went to the woods and got it. All I know is, she said it was indigo. She had a great big kittle and she put her thread in that. No Lord, she never bought her indigo—she raised it.

"Oh, Miss Fannie could do most anything. Made the prettiest counter-panes I ever saw. Yes ma'am, she could do it and did do it.

"She had a loom half as big as this house. Lord a mercy, a many a time I went dancin' from that old spinnin'-wheel.

"They made all the clothes for the colored folks. They'd be sewin' for weeks and months.

"Miss Fannie and Miss Frances—that was her daughter—they wove such pretty cloth for the colored. You know, they went and made themselves dresses and the white and colored had the same kind of dresses.

"Yes Lord, they had some folks.

"Miss Frances wore hoops but Miss Fannie didn't.

"During of the War them Yankees come down the river; but to tell the truth, we run and hid and never seen 'em no more.

"They took Mars John's fine saddle horse named Silver Heels. Yes ma'am, took saddle and bridle and the horse on top of 'em. And he had a mare named Buchanan and they took her too. He had done moved out of the big house down into the woods. Called hisself hidin' I reckon. And he had his horses tied down by the river and the Yankees slipped up on him and took the horses.

"Yankees burned his house and gin house too and set fire to the cotton. Oh Lord, I don't like to talk about it. Them Yankees was rough.

"Right after freedom our white folks left this country and went to Missouri and the last account I heard of 'em they was all dead.

"After freedom, folks scattered out just like sheep.

"I'm tryin' to study 'bout some songs but I can't think of nothin' but Dixie."

Interviewer: Mrs. Bernice Bowden
Person interviewed: Lydia Jones
228 North Oak Street, Pine Bluff, Arkansas
Age: 93

LYDIA JONES

"My name's Lydia—Lydia Jones. Oh my God I'se born in Mississippi. I wish you'd hush—I know all about slavery.

"I never had but one master. That was old John Patterson. No he want good to me. I wish you'd hush! I had two young masters—Marse John and Marse Edward. Marse John go off to war and say he gwine whip them Yankees with his pocket knife, but he didn't do it. They said the war was to keep the colored folks slaves. I tell you I've heard them bull whips a ringin' from sun to sun.

"After the war when they told us we is free, they said to hire ourselves out. They didn't give us a nickel when we left.

"I heered talk of the Ku Klux and they come close enough for us to be skeered but I never seen none of 'em. We never had no slave uprisin's on our plantation—old John Patterson would a shot 'em down. I tell you he was a rabid man.

"I used to pick cotton and chop cotton and help weave the cloth. My old mistress—Miss Fannie—used to go to the woods and get things to dye the cloth. She would dye some blue and some red.

"Only song I 'member is Dixie. I heered talk of some others but God knows I never fooled with 'em.

"Yes'm I believes in hants. Let me tell you something. My mama seen my daddy after he been dead a long time. He come right up through the crack by the fireplace and he said 'Don't you be afraid Emmaline' but she was agoin'. They had to sing and pray in the house 'fore my mama would go back but she never seen him again.

"I'se been blind now for three years and I lives with my granddaughter but lady, I'll tell you the truth—I been around. Yes, madam, I is."

Interviewer: Mrs. Bernice Bowden
Person interviewed: Liza Jones (Cookie)
610 S. Eighteenth Street, Pine Bluff, Ark.
Age: 88

LIZA JONES

"Come in, this is Cookie. Well, I do know a heap about slavery, cause I worked. I stayed in the house; I was house girl. They called me Cookie cause I used to cook so much.

"That was in Madison County, near Jackson, Tennessee. My mistress was good to me. Yes'm, I got along all right but a heap of others got along all wrong.

"Mistress took care of us in the cold and all kinds of weather. She sho did.

"She had four women and four men. We had plenty to eat. She had hogs and sheep and geese and always cooked enough for all of us. Whatever she had to eat we had.

"We clothed our darkies in slavery times. I was a weaver for four years and never done nothin' else. Yes ma'm, I was a house woman and I am now.

"Yes ma'm, I member seein' different kinds of soldiers. I member once some Rebels come to old mistress to get somethin' to eat but before it was ready the Yankees come and run em off. They didn't have time to eat it all so us colored folks got the rest of it.

"Old mistress had a son Mac and he was in the war. The Yankees captured him and carried him to Chicago and put him in a warehouse over the water.

"Old mistress was a good old Christian woman. All the darkies had to come to her room to prayermeetin' every night. She didn't skip no nights. And her help didn't mind workin'. They'd go the length for her, Miss.

"After I was grown I went most anywhere, but when I was little I sho set on old mistress' dress tail. I used to go to church with her. She'd say, "Open your mouf and sing" and I'd just holler and sing. I can member now how loud I used to holler.

"Aint no use in talkin', I had a good mistress. I never was sold. Old mistress wouldn't sell. There was a speculator come there and wanted to buy us. When we was free, old mistress say, "Now I could a sold you and had the money, and now you is goin' to leave." But they didn't, they stayed. Some stayed with old mistress till she died, but I didn't. I married the first year of freedom.

"My mistress and me spin a many a cut of cotton together. She couldn't beat me neither. If that old soul was livin' today, I'd be right with her. I was gettin' along. I didn't know nothin' but freedom.

"I had freedom then and I ain't been free since, didn't have no sponsibility. But when they turned you loose, you had your doctor bill and your grub bill—now wasn't you a slave then?

"My mammy was a cook and her name was Katy.

"After I was married we went to live at Black Ankle.

I learned to cook and I sho did cook for the white folks twenty-one years. I used to go back and see old mistress. If I stay away too long, she send for me.

"How many childen I had? You want the truth? Well, fifteen, but never had but three to live any length of time.

"Well, I told you the best I know and the straightest I know. If I can't tell you the truth, I'm not goin' to tell you nothin'.

"Yes, honey, I saw the Ku Klux."

United States. Work Projects Administration

Interviewer: Miss Irene Robertson
Person interviewed: Lucy Jones,
Marianna, Arkansas
Age: Born 1866
[Date Stamp: MAY 11 1938]

LUCY JONES

"I was raised second year after the surrender. I don't know a father or mother. They was dead when I was five years old. I had no sisters nor brothers. Mrs. Cynthia Hall raised me. She raised my mother. Master Hall was her husband. They was old people and they was so good to me. They had no children and I lived in the house with them. I never went to school a day in my life. I can't read. I can count money.

"My mother was dark. I married when I was fifteen years old. I have four children living. They are all dark. They are about the same color but darker than I am.

"No ma'am, I don't believe one could be voodooed. I lived nearly all my life with white folks and they don't heed no foolishness like that, do they? I cooked, worked in the field, washed and ironed.

"I married three times. The first time at Raymond, Mississippi. I never had no big weddings.

"Seems like some folks have lost their grip and ain't willing to start over. I don't know much to say for the young people. They are not smart. They got more schooling. They try to shirk all the work they can. I never seen no Ku Klux in my life. People used to raise nearly all their living at home and now they depend on buying nearly everything. Well, I think it is bad."

Interviewer: Samuel S. Taylor
Person interviewed: Mary Jones
1017 Dennison, Little Rock, Arkansas
Age: 72

MARY JONES

"I was born on the twenty-second of March, 1866, in Van Buren, Arkansas. I had six children. All of them were bred and born at the same place.

"I was born in a frame house. My father used to live in the country, but I was born in the town. He bought it just as soon as he come out of the army and married right away and bought this home. I don't know where he got his money from. I guess he saved it. He served in the Union army; he wasn't a servant. He was a soldier, and drawed his pay. He never run through his money like most people do. I don't know whether he made any money in slavery or not but he was a carpenter during slave times and they say he always had plenty of money. I guess he had saved some of that too.

"My mother was married twice. Her name was Louisa Buchanan. My father was named Abraham Riley. My stepfather was named Moses Buchanan. My father was a soldier in the old original war (the Civil War)—the war they ended in 1865.

"I disremember who my mother's master was but I think it was a man named Johnson. I didn't know my father's people. She married him from White County up here. Her and him, they corresponded mostly in letters because he traveled lots. He looked like an Indian. He had straight hair and was tall and rawboned and wore a Texas hat. I had his picture but the pictures fade away. My father was a sergeant. He died sometime after the war. I don't remember when because I wasn't old enough. I can just remember looking at the corpse. I was too small to do any grieving.

"My mother was a nurse in slavery times. She nursed the white folks and their children. She did the housework and such like. She was a good cook too. After freedom, when the old folks died out, she cooked for Zeb Ward—you know him, head of the penitentiary. She used to cook for the Jews and gentiles. That her kind of work. That was her occupation—good cook. She could make all kinds of provisions. She could make preserves and they had a big orchard everywhere she worked.

"I have heard my mother talk about pateroles, jayhawkers, and Ku Klux, but I never knew of them myself. I have heard say they were awful bad—the Ku Klux or somethin'.

"My mother's white folks sold her. I don't know who they sold her to or from. They sold her from her mother. I don't know how she got free. I think she got free after the war ceased. But she had a good time all her life. She had a good time because she was a good cook, and a good nurse, and she had good white folks. My grandma, she had good folks too. They was free before they were free, my ma and grandma. They was just as free before freedom as they were afterwards. My mother had seven children and two sets of twins among them. But I am the only one living.

Occupation

"They say that I'm too old to work now; so I can't make nothin' to keep my home goin'. I have five children living. Two are away from here—one in Michigan, and another in Illinois. I have three others but they don't make enough to help me much. I used to work 'round the laundries. Then I used to work 'round with these colored restaurants. I worked with a colored woman down by the station for twelve or fifteen years. I first helped her wash and iron. She ironed and hired other girls to wait table and wash dishes and so on. Them times wasn't like they are now. They'd hire you and keep you. Then I worked at a white boarding house on Second and Cross. I quit working at the laundries because of the steady work in the restaurants. After the restaurants I went to work in private families and worked with them till I got so I couldn't work no more. Maybe I could do plenty of things, but they won't give me a chance.

"I have been married twice. My second husband was John Jones. He always went by the name of his white folks. They were named Ivory. He came from up in Searcy. I got acquainted with him and we started going together. He'd been married before and had children up in Searcy. He got his leg cut off in a accident. He was working over to the shop lifting ties with another helper and this man helping him gave way on his side and let his end fall. It fell across my husband's foot and blood poison set in and caused him to lose his foot and leg. He had his foot cut off at the county hospital and made himself a peg-leg. He cut it out hisself while he was at the hospital. He lived a long while after that. He died on Tenth and Victory. My first husband was Henry White. He was a shop worker too—the Iron Mountain.

"We went to school together. I lost my health before I married, and I had to stop going to school. The doctor was a German and lived on Cross between Fifth and Sixth. He said that he ought to have written the history of my life to show what I was cured of because I was paralyzed two years. My head was drawed 'way back between my shoulders. I lived with my first husband about six years. He died with T.B. in Memphis, Tennessee. He had married again when he died. We got so we couldn't agree, so I thought it was best for him to live with his mother and me to live with mine. We quit under good conditions. I had a boy after he was separated from me.

"I don't know what to say about the people now. I don't get 'round much. They aren't like they used to be. The young people don't like to have you 'round them. I never did object to any of my children gettin' married because my mother didn't object to me.

"I know Mr. Gillespie. (He passed at the time—ed.) He comes to see me now and then. All my people are dead now 'cept my children."

Interviewer's Comment

Brother Gillespie has a story turned in previously. Evidently he is making eyes at the old lady; but the romance is not likely to bud. She has lost the sight of one eye apparently through a cataract which has spread over the larger part of the iris. Nevertheless, she is more active than he is, and apparently more competent, and she isn't figuring on making her lot any harder than it is.

United States. Work Projects Administration

Interviewer: Mrs. Bernice Bowden
Person interviewed: Mary Jones
509 E. 23rd Avenue, Pine Bluff, Arkansas
Age: 78
[Date Stamp: MAY 31 1938]

MARY JONES

"I was born three weeks 'fore Christmas in South Carolina.

"I 'member one time the Yankees come along and I run to the door. I know ma made me go back but I peeped out the window. You know how children is. They wore great big old hats and blue coats.

"'Nother time we saw them a comin' and said, 'Yonder come the Yankees' and we run. Ma said, 'Don't run, them's the Yankees what freed you.'

"Old mis' was named Joanna Long and old master was Joe Long. I can't remember much, I just went by what ma said.

"I went to school now and then on account we had to work.

"We had done sold out in South Carolina and was down at the station when some of the old folks said if we was goin' to the Mississippi bottoms where the panthers and wolves was we would never come back. We thought we was comin' to Arkansas but when we found out we was in the Mississippi bottoms. We stayed there and made two crops, then we come to Arkansas.

"The way the younger generation is livin' now, the Lord can't bless 'em. They know how to do right but they won't do it. Yes ma'am."

Interviewer: Mrs. Bernice Bowden
Person interviewed: Nannie Jones
1601 Saracen Street, Pine Bluff, Arkansas
Age: 81

NANNIE JONES

"Good morning. Come in. I sure is proud to see you. Yes ma'am, I sure is.

"I was born in Chicot County. I heerd Dr. Gaines say I was four years old in slavery times. I know I ain't no baby. I feels my age, too—in my limbs.

"I heerd 'em talk about a war but I wasn't big enough to know about it. My father went to war on one side but he didn't stay very long. I don't know which side he was on. Them folks all dead now—I just can remember 'em.

"Dr. Gaines had a pretty big crew on the place. I'm gwine tell you what I know. I can't tell you nothin' else.

"Now I want to tell it like mama said. She said she was sold from Kentucky. She died when I was small.

"I remember when they said the people was free. I know they jumped up and down and carried on.

"Dr. Gaines was so nice to his people. I stayed in the house most of the time. I was the little pet around the house. They said I was so cute.

"Dr. Gaines give me my age but I lost it movin'. But

I know I ain't no baby. I never had but two children and they both livin'—two girls.

"Honey, I worked in the field and anywhere. I worked like a man. I think that's what got me bowed down now. I keeps with a misery right across my back. Sometimes I can hardly get along.

"Honey, I just don't know 'bout this younger generation. I just don't have no thoughts for 'em, they so wild. I never was a rattlin' kind of a girl. I always was civilized. Old people in them days didn't 'low their children to do things. I know when mama called us, we'd better go. They is a heap wusser now. So many of 'em gettin' into trouble."

Interviewer: Mrs. Bernice Bowden
Person interviewed: Reuben Jones
Ezell Quarters, Pine Bluff, Arkansas
Age: 85

REUBEN JONES

"Well, I'm one of em. I can tell you bout it from now till sundown.

"I was born at Senatobia, Mississippi, this side of Jackson. Born in '52 on April the 16th. That's when I was born.

"Old man Stephen Williams was my master in time of the war and before the war, too. He was pretty good to me. Give me plenty of something to eat, but he whipped me. Oh, I specked I needed it. Put me in the field when I was five years old. Put a tar cap on my head. I was so young the sun made my hair come out so they put that tar cap on my head.

"I member when they put the folks on blocks as high as that house and sell em to the highest bidder. No ma'm, I wasn't sold cause my mother had three or four chillun and boss man wouldn't sell dem what had chillun cause dem chillun was hands for him.

"They made me hide ever'thing they had from the Yankees. Yes'm, I seen em come out after the fodder and the corn. We hid the meat and the mules and the money. Drove the mules in the cave. Kept em der till the Yankees left. We dug the hole for the meat but old marse dug the hole for the money.

"I used to help put timbers on the bridge to keep the Yankees out but dey come right on through just the same. Took the ox wagon but dey sent it back.

"Couldn't go nowhere without a pass. Had a whippin' block right at the horse trough. Yes ma'm, they'd eat you up. I mean they'd whip you, but they give you plenty of somethin' to eat.

"My mother was the weaver and they had a tanyard on the place.

"In slavery days couldn't go see none of your neighbors without a pass. People had meetin' right at the house. Dey'd have prayer and singin'. I went to em. I could sing—Lord yes. I used to know a lot of old songs—'Am I A Soldier of the Cross?'.

"Lord yes, ma'm, don't talk! When the soldiers come out where we was I could hear the guns. Had a battle right in town. Rebels just as scared of the Yankees as if twas a bear. I seed one or two of em come to town and scare the whole business.

"I never knowed but one man run off and jined the Yankees. Carried his master's finest ridin' hoss and a mule. He always had a fine hoss and Yankees come and took it. When the Yankees come out the last time, my owners cleaned out the smoke house and buried the meat.

"I helped gin cotton when I wasn't big enough to stand up to the breast. Stood upon a bench and had a lantern hung up so I could see fore daylight. Yes ma'm, great big gin house. Yes ma'm, I sho has worked—all kinds and plowin'.

"Now my old boss called me Tony—that's what he called me.

"When peace come, we had done gathered our crop and we left there a week later. You know people usually hunts their kinfolks and we went to Hernando. Come to Arkansas in '77. Got offin de boat right der at de cotehouse. Pine Bluff wasn't nothin' when I come here.

"I used to vote. I aimed to vote the Republican ticket—I don't know.

"Oh yes ma'm, I seed the Ku Klux, yes ma'm. They're bad, too. Lord I seed a many of them. They come to my house. I went to the door and that's as far as I went. That was in Hernando. I went back to my old home in Hernando bout three months ago. Went where I was bred and born but I didn't know the place it was tore up so.

"This younger generation whole lot different from when I was comin' up. Yes'm, it's a whole lot different. They ain't doin' so well. I have always tended to my own business. Cose I been arrested for drivin' mules with sore shoulders. Didn't put me in jail, but the officers come up. That was when I was workin' on the Lambert place. I told em they wasn't my mules so they let me go.

"I can't tell you bout the times now. I hope it'll get better—can't get no wusser."

United States. Work Projects Administration

Interviewer: Miss Irene Robertson
Person interviewed: Vergil Jones,
Brinkley, Arkansas
Age: 70

VERGIL JONES

"My parents was Jane Jones and Vergil Jones. Their owner was Colonel Jones in Alabama. Papa went to the war and served four years. He got a $30 a month Union pension long as he lived. He was in a number of places. He fought as a field man. He had a long musket he brought home from the war. He told us a heap of things long time ago. Seem lack folks set down and talked wid their children more'n they do nowdays.

"Papa come to this State after the surrender. He married here. I am the oldest of seven children. Mama was in this State before the war. She was bought when she was a girl and brought here. I don't know if Colonel Jones owned her or if papa had seen her somewhere else. He come to her and they married. My mama was a house girl some and she washed and ironed for Miss Fannie Lambert. They had a big family and a big farm. Their farm was seven miles this side of Indian Bay, eight miles to Clarendon. They had thirteen in family and mama had seven children made nine in her family. She had a bed piled full of starched clothes white as snow. Lamberts had three sets of twins. Our family lived with the Lamberts 23 or 24 years. We started working for Mr. B. J. Lambert and

Miss Fannie (his wife). Mama nursed me and R. T. from the same breast. We was raised up grown together and I worked for R. T. till he died. We played with J. L. Black too till he was grown. He was county judge and sheriff of this county (Monroe).

"Folks that helped me out is about all dead. I pick cotton but I can't pick very much. Now I don't have no work till chopping cotton times comes on. It is hard now. I would do jobs but I don't hear of no jobs to be done. I asked around but didn't find a thing to do.

"I heard about the Ku Kluxes. My papa used to dodge the Ku Kluxes. He lay out in the bushes from them. It was bad times. Some folks would advise the black folks to do one way and then the Ku Kluxes come and make it hot for them. One thing the Ku Kluxes didn't want much big gatherings among the black folks. They break up big gatherings. Some white folks tell them to do one thing and then some others tell them to do some other way. That is the way it was. The Ku Kluxes was hot headed. Papa wasn't a bad man but he was afraid they did do so much. He was on the lookout and dodged them all the time.

"I haven't voted for a long time. I couldn't keep my taxes up.

"I don't own a home. I pay $4 rent for it. It is a cold house—not so good. I have farmed all my life. I still farm. Times got so that nobody would run you (credit you) and I come here to get jobs between farming. I still farm. They hire mostly by the day—day labor. Them two things and my dis'bility is making it mighty hard for me to live. I work at any jobs I can get.

"I signed up for the Old Age Pension. They said I couldn't work, I was too old. I wanted to work on the government work. I never got nothing. I don't get no kind of help. I thought I didn't know how to get into the Old Age Pension reason I didn't get it. It would help keep in wood this wet weather when work is scarce."

United States. Work Projects Administration

Interviewer: Miss Irene Robertson
Person interviewed: Walter Jones,
Brinkley, Arkansas
Age: 72

WALTER JONES

"My father run away scared of the Yankees. He got excited and left. My mother didn't want him to leave her. She was crying when he left. My father belong to the Wilsons. Mother was sold on the block in Richmond, Virginia when she was twelve years old and never seen her mother again. Mother belong to Charles Hunt. Her name was Lucy Hunt. She married three times. Charles Hunt went to market to buy slaves. We lived in Hardeman County, Tennessee when I was born but he sent us to Mississippi. She worked in the field then but before then she was a house girl. No, she was black. We are all African.

"I got eight children. When my wife died they finished scattering out. I come here from Grand Junction, Mississippi. I eat breakfast on Christmas day 1883 at Forrest City and spent the day at Hazen. I come with friends. We paid our own ways. We come on the train and boat and walked some.

"No, I don't take stock in voting. I never did. I have voted so long ago I forgot it all.

"The biggest thing I can tell you ever happened to us more than I told you was in 1878 I had yellow fever. Dr.

Milton Pruitt come to see me. The next day his brother come to see me. Dr. Milton died the next day. I got well. At Grand Junction both black and white died. Some of both color got well. A lot of people died.

"How am I making a living? I don't make one. Mr. Ashly lets me live in a house and gives me scrap meat. I bottom chairs or do what I can. I past heavy work. The Welfare don't help me. I farmed, railroaded nearly all my life. Public work this last few years."

Interviewer: Samuel S. Taylor
Person interviewed: Oscar Felix Junell
1720 Brown Street, Little Rock, Arkansas
Age: 60

OSCAR FELIX JUNELL

"My father's name was Peter Junell, Peter W. Junell. I don't know what the W. was for. He was born in Ouachita County near Bearden, Arkansas. Bearden is an old town. It is fourteen miles from Camden. My dad was seventy-five years old when he died. He died in 1924. He was very young in the time of slavery. He never did do very much work.

"His master was named John Junell. That was his old master. He had a young master too, Warren Junell. His old master given him to his young master, Warren. My father's mother and father both belonged to the Junells. His mother's name was Dinah, and his father's name was Anthony. All the slaves took their last names after their owners. They never was sold, not in any time that my father could remember.

"As soon as my father was large enough to go to walkin' about, his old master given him to his son, Master Warren Junell. Warren would carry him about and make him rassle (wrestle). He was a good rassler. As far as work was concerned, he didn't do nothing much of that. He just followed his young master all around rasslin.

"His masters was good to him. They whipped slaves

sometimes, but they were considered good. My father always said they was good folks. He never told me how he learnt that he was free.

"Pretty well all the slaves lived in log cabins. Even in my time, there was hardly a board house in that county. The food the slaves ate was mostly bread and milk—corn bread. Old man Junell was rich and had lots of slaves. When he went to feed his slaves, he would feed them jus like hogs. He had a great long trough and he would have bread crumbled up in it and gallons of milk poured over the bread, and the slaves would get round it and eat. Sometimes they would get to fighting over it. You know, jus like hogs! They would be eatin and sometimes one person would find somethin and get holt of it and another one would want to take it, and they would get to fightin over it. Sometimes blood would get in the trough, but they would eat right on and pay no 'tention to it.

"I don't know whether they fed the old ones that way or not. I jus heered my father tell how he et out of the trough hisself.

"I have heered my father talk about the pateroles too. He talked about how they used to chase him. But he didn't have much experience with them, because they never did catch him. That was after the war when the slaves had been freed, but the pateroles still got after them. My father remember how they would catch other slaves. One night they went to an old man's house. It was dark and the old man told them to come on in. He didn't have no gun, but he took his ax and stood behind the door on the hinge side. It was after slavery. When he said for them to come in, they rushed right on in and the old man killed three or four of them with his ax. He was a old African, and they never had been able to do nothin' with him, not even in slavery time. I never heard that they did nothin' to the old man about it. The pateroles was outlaws anyway.

"I heard my father say that in slavery time, they took the finest and portlies' looking Negroes—the males—for breeding purposes. They wouldn't let them strain themselves up nor nothin like that. They wouldn't make them do much hard work."

United States. Work Projects Administration

Interviewer: Miss Irene Robertson
Person interviewed: Sam Keaton,
Brinkley, Ark.
Age: 78

SAM KEATON

"I was born close to Golden Hill down in Arkansas County. My parents names was Louana and Dennis Keaton. They had ten children. Their master was Mr. Jack Keaton and Miss Martha. They had four boys. They all come from Virginia in wagons the second year of the war—the Civil War. I heard 'em tell about walking. Some of em walked, some rode horse back and some in wagons. I don't know if they knowed bout slave uprisings or not. I know they wasn't in em because they come here wid Mr. Jack Keaton. It was worse in Virginia than it was down here wid them. Mr. Keaton didn't give em nothing at freedom. They stayed on long as they wanted to stay and then they went to work for Mr. Jack Keaton's brother, Mr. Ben Keaton. They worked on shares and picked cotton by the hundred. My parents staid on down there till they died. I been working for Mr. Floria for thirty years.

"My father did vote. He voted a Republican ticket. I haven't voted for fifty years. They that do vote in the General election know very little bout what they doing. If they could vote in the Primary they would know but a mighty little about it. The women ain't got no business voting. Their place is at home. They cain't keep their houses tidied up and like they oughter be and go out and work regularly. That's the reason I think they oughter stay at home and train the children better than it being done.

"I think that the young generation is going to be lost. They killing and fighting. They do everything. No, they don't work much as I do. They don't save nothing! They don't save nothing! Times is harder than they used to be some. Nearly everybody wants to live in town. My age is making times heap harder for me. I live with my daughter. I am a widower. I owns 40 acres land, a house, a cow. I made three bales cotton, but I owe it bout all. I tried to get a little help so I could get out of debt but I never could get no 'sistance from the Welfare."

Interviewer: Watt McKinney
Person interviewed: Tines Kendricks,
Trenton, Arkansas
Age: 104

TINES KENDRICKS

"My name is Tines Kendricks. I was borned in Crawford County, Georgia. You see, Boss, I is a little nigger and I really is more smaller now dan I used to be when I was young 'cause I so old and stooped over. I mighty nigh wore out from all these hard years of work and servin' de Lord. My actual name what was give to me by my white folks, de Kendricks, was 'Tiny'. Dey called me dat 'cause I never was no size much. Atter us all sot free I just changed my name to 'Tines' an' dats what I been goin' by for nigh on to ninety years.

"'Cordin' to what I 'member 'bout it, Boss, I is now past a hundred and four year old dis past July de fourth two hours before day. What I means is what I 'member 'bout what de old mars told me dat time I comed back to de home place atter de War quit an' he say dat I past thirty then. My mammy, she said I born two hours before day on de fourth of July. Dat what dey tole me, Boss. I is been in good health all my days. I ain't never been sick any in my life 'scusin' dese last years when I git so old and feeble and stiff in de joints, and my teef 'gin to cave, and my old bones, dey 'gin to ache. But I just keep on livin' and trustin' in de Lord 'cause de Good Book say, 'Wherefore de evil days come an' de darkness of de night draw nigh, your strength, it shall not perish. I will lift you up 'mongst dem what 'bides wid me.' Dat is de Gospel, Boss.

"My old mars, he was named Arch Kendricks and us lived on de plantation what de Kendricks had not far from Macon in Crawford County, Georgia. You can see, Boss, dat I is a little bright an' got some white blood in me. Dat is 'counted for on my mammy's side of de family. Her pappy, he was a white man. He wasn't no Kendrick though. He was a overseer. Dat what my mammy she say an' then I know dat wasn't no Kendrick mixed up in nothin' like dat. Dey didn't believe in dat kind of bizness. My old mars, Arch Kendricks, I will say dis, he certainly was a good fair man. Old mis' an' de young mars, Sam, dey was strickly tough an', Boss, I is tellin' you de truth dey was cruel. De young mars, Sam, he never taken at all atter he pa. He got all he meanness from old mis' an' he sure got plenty of it too. Old mis', she cuss an' rare worse 'an a man. Way 'fore day she be up hollerin' loud enough for to be heered two miles, 'rousin' de niggers out for to git in de fields even 'fore light. Mars Sam, he stand by de pots handin' out de grub an' givin' out de bread an' he cuss loud an' say: 'Take a sop of dat grease on your hoecake an' move erlong fast 'fore I lashes you.' Mars Sam, he was a big man too, dat he was. He was nigh on to six an' a half feet tall. Boss, he certainly was a chile of de debbil. All de cookin' in dem days was done in pots hangin' on de pot racks. Dey never had no stoves endurin' de times what I is tellin' you 'bout. At times dey would give us enough to eat. At times dey wouldn't—just 'cordin' to how dey feelin' when dey dishin' out de grub. De biggest what dey would give de field hands to eat would be de truck what us had on de place like greens, turnips, peas, side meat, an' dey sure would cut de side meat awful thin too, Boss. Us allus had a heap of corn-meal dumplin's an' hoecakes. Old mis', her an' Mars Sam, dey real stingy. You better not leave no grub on your plate for to throw away. You sure better eat it all iffen you like it or no. Old mis' and Mars Sam, dey de real bosses an' dey was wicked. I'se tellin' you de truth, dey was. Old mars, he didn't have much to say 'bout de runnin' of de place or de handlin' of de niggers. You know all de property and all the niggers belonged to old mis'. She got all dat from her peoples. Dat what dey left to her on their death. She de real owner of everything.

"Just to show you, Boss, how 'twas with Mars Sam, on' how contrary an' fractious an' wicked dat young white man was, I wants to tell you 'bout de time dat Aunt Hannah's little boy Mose died. Mose, he sick 'bout er week. Aunt Hannah, she try to doctor on him an' git him well an' she tell old mis' dat she think Mose bad off an' orter have de doctor. Old mis', she wouldn't git de doctor. She say Mose ain't sick much, an' bless my Soul, Aunt Hannah she right. In a few days from then Mose is dead. Mars Sam, he come cussin' an' tole Gabe to get some planks an' make de coffin an' sont some of dem to dig de grave over dere on de far side of de place where dey had er buryin'-groun' for de niggers. Us toted de coffin over to where de grave was dug an' gwine bury little Mose dar an' Uncle Billy Jordan, he was dar and begun to sing an' pray an' have a kind of funeral at de buryin'. Every one was moanin' an' singin' an' prayin' and Mars Sam heard 'em an' come sailin' over dar on he hoss an' lit right in to cussin' an' rarein' an' say dat if dey don't hurry an' bury dat nigger an' shut up dat singin' an' carryin' on, he gwine lash every one of dem, an' then he went to cussin' worser an' 'busin' Uncle Billy Jordan. He say iffen he ever hear of him doin' any more preachin' or prayin' 'round 'mongst de niggers at de grave-yard or anywheres else, he gwine lash him to death. No suh, Boss, Mars Sam wouldn't even 'low no preachin' or singin' or nothin' like dat. He was wicked. I tell you he was.

"Old mis', she ginrally looked after de niggers when dey sick an' give dem de medicine. An' too, she would get de doctor iffen she think dey real bad off 'cause like I said, old mis', she mighty stingy an' she never want to lose no nigger by dem dyin'. How-some-ever it was hard some time to get her to believe you sick when you tell her dat you was, an' she would think you just playin' off from work. I have seen niggers what would be mighty near dead before old mis' would believe them sick at all.

"Before de War broke out, I can 'member there was some few of de white folks what said dat niggers ought to be sot free, but there was just one now an' then that took that stand. One of dem dat I 'member was de Rev. Dickey what was de parson for a big crowd of de white peoples in dat part of de county. Rev. Dickey, he preached freedom for de niggers and say dat dey all should be sot free an' gived a home and a mule. Dat preachin' de Rev. Dickey done sure did rile up de folks—dat is de most of them like de Kendricks and Mr. Eldredge and Dr. Murcheson and Nat Walker and such as dem what was de biggest of the slaveowners. Right away atter Rev. Dickey done such preachin' dey fired him from de church, an' 'bused him, an' some of dem say dey gwine hang him to a limb, or either gwine ride him on a rail out of de country. Sure enough dey made it so hot on dat man he have to leave clean out of de state so I heered. No suh, Boss, they say they ain't gwine divide up no land with de niggers or give them no home or mule or their freedom or nothin'. They say dey will wade knee deep in blood an' die first.

"When de War start to break out, Mars Sam listed in de troops and was sent to Virginny. There he stay for de longest. I hear old mis' tellin' 'bout de letters she got from him, an' how he wishin' they hurry and start de battle so's he can get through killin' de Yankees an' get de War over an' come home. Bless my soul, it wasn't long before dey had de battle what Mars Sam was shot in. He writ de letter from de hospital where they had took him. He say dey had a hard fight, dat a ball busted his gun, and another ball shoot his cooterments (accouterments) off him; the third shot tear a big hole right through the side of his neck. The doctor done sew de wound up; he not hurt so bad. He soon be back with his company.

"But it wasn't long 'fore dey writ some more letters to old mis' an' say dat Mars Sam's wound not gettin' no better; it wasn't healin' to do no good; every time dat they sew de gash up in his neck it broke loose again. De Yankees had been puttin' poison grease on the bullets. Dat was de reason de wound wouldn't get well. Dey feared Mars Sam goin' to die an' a short time atter dat letter come I sure knowed it was so. One night just erbout dusk dark, de screech owls, dey come in er swarm an' lit in de big trees in de front of de house. A mist of dust come up an' de owls, dey holler an' carry on so dat old mars get he gun an' shot it off to scare dem erway. Dat was a sign, Boss, dat somebody gwine to die. I just knowed it was Mars Sam.

"Sure enough de next day dey got de message dat Mars Sam dead. Dey brung him home all de way from Virginny an' buried him in de grave-yard on de other side of de garden wid his gray clothes on him an' de flag on de coffin. That's what I'se telling you, Boss, 'cause dey called all de niggers in an' 'lowed dem to look at Mars Sam. I seen him an' he sure looked like he peaceful in he coffin with his soldier clothes on. I heered atterwards dat Mars Sam bucked an' rared just 'fore he died an' tried to get outen de bed, an' dat he cussed to de last.

"It was this way, Boss, how come me to be in de War. You see, they 'quired all of de slaveowners to send so many niggers to de army to work diggin' de trenches an' throwin' up de breastworks an' repairin' de railroads what de Yankees done 'stroyed. Every mars was 'quired to send one nigger for every ten dat he had. Iffen you had er hundred niggers, you had to send ten of dem to de army. I was one of dem dat my mars 'quired to send. Dat was de worst times dat dis here nigger ever seen an' de way dem white men drive us niggers, it was something awful. De strap, it was goin' from 'fore day till 'way after night. De niggers, heaps of 'em just fall in dey tracks give out an' them white men layin' de strap on dey backs without ceastin'. Dat was zackly way it was wid dem niggers like me what was in de army work. I had to stand it, Boss, till de War was over.

"Dat sure was a bad war dat went on in Georgia. Dat it was. Did you ever hear 'bout de Andersonville prison in Georgia? I tell you, Boss, dat was 'bout de worstest place dat ever I seen. Dat was where dey keep all de Yankees dat dey capture an' dey had so many there they couldn't nigh take care of them. Dey had them fenced up with a tall wire fence an' never had enough house room for all dem Yankees. They would just throw de grub to 'em. De mostest dat dey had for 'em to eat was peas an' the filth, it was terrible. De sickness, it broke out 'mongst 'em all de while, an' dey just die like rats what been pizened. De first thing dat de Yankees do when dey take de state 'way from de Confedrits was to free all dem what in de prison at Andersonville.

"Slavery time was tough, Boss. You Just don't know how tough it was. I can't 'splain to you just how bad all de niggers want to get dey freedom. With de 'free niggers' it was just de same as it was wid dem dat was in bondage. You know there was some few 'free niggers' in dat time even 'fore de slaves taken outen bondage. It was really worse on dem dan it was with dem what wasn't free. De slaveowners, dey just despised dem 'free niggers' an' make it just as hard on dem as dey can. Dey couldn't get no work from nobody. Wouldn't airy man hire 'em or give 'em any work at all. So because dey was up against it an' never had any money or nothin', de white folks make dese 'free niggers' sess (assess) de taxes. An' 'cause dey never had no money for to pay de tax wid, dey was put up on de block by de court man or de sheriff an' sold out to somebody for enough to pay de tax what dey say dey owe. So dey keep these 'free niggers' hired out all de time most workin' for to pay de taxes. I 'member one of dem 'free niggers' mighty well. He was called 'free Sol'. He had him a little home an' a old woman an' some boys. Dey was kept bounded out nigh 'bout all de time workin' for to pay dey tax. Yas suh, Boss, it was heap more better to be a slave nigger dan er free un. An' it was really er heavenly day when de freedom come for de race.

"In de time of slavery annudder thing what make it tough on de niggers was dem times when er man an' he wife an' their chillun had to be taken 'way from one anudder. Dis sep'ration might be brung 'bout most any time for one thing or anudder sich as one or tudder de man or de wife be sold off or taken 'way to some other state like Louisiana or Mississippi. Den when a mars die what had a heap of slaves, these slave niggers be divided up 'mongst de mars' chillun or sold off for to pay de mars' debts. Then at times when er man married to er woman dat don't belong to de same mars what he do, then dey is li'ble to git divided up an' sep'rated most any day. Dey was heaps of nigger families dat I know what was sep'rated in de time of bondage dat tried to find dey folkses what was gone. But de mostest of 'em never git togedder ag'in even after dey sot free 'cause dey don't know where one or de other is.

"Atter de War over an' de slaves taken out of dey bondage, some of de very few white folks give dem niggers what dey liked de best a small piece of land for to work. But de mostest of dem never give 'em nothin' and dey sure despise dem niggers what left 'em. Us old mars say he want to 'range wid all his niggers to stay on wid him, dat he gwine give 'em er mule an' er piece er ground. But us know dat old mis' ain't gwine agree to dat. And sure enough she wouldn't. I'se tellin' you de truth, every nigger on dat place left. Dey sure done dat; an' old mars an' old mis', dey never had a hand left there on that great big place, an' all that ground layin' out.

"De gov'ment seen to it dat all of de white folks had to make contracts wid de niggers dat stuck wid 'em, an' dey was sure strict 'bout dat too. De white folks at first didn't want to make the contracts an' say dey wasn't gwine to.

So de gov'ment filled de jail with 'em, an' after that every one make the contract.

"When my race first got dey freedom an' begin to leave dey mars', a heap of de mars got ragin' mad an' just tore up truck. Dey say dey gwine kill every nigger dey find. Some of them did do dat very thing, Boss, sure enough. I'se tellin' you de truth. Dey shot niggers down by de hundreds. Dey jus' wasn't gwine let 'em enjoy dey freedom. Dat is de truth, Boss.

"Atter I come back to de old home place from workin' for de army, it wasn't long 'fore I left dar an' git me er job with er sawmill an' worked for de sawmill peoples for about five years. One day I heered some niggers tellin' about er white man what done come in dar gittin' up er big lot of niggers to take to Arkansas. Dey was tellin' 'bout what a fine place it was in Arkansas, an' how rich de land is, an' dat de crops grow without working, an' dat de taters grow big as er watermelon an' you never have to plant 'em but de one time, an' all sich as dat. Well, I 'cided to come. I j'ined up with de man an' come to Phillips County in 1875. Er heap er niggers come from Georgia at de same time dat me an' Callie come. You know Callie, dats my old woman whats in de shack dar right now. Us first lived on Mr. Jim Bush's place over close to Barton. Us ain't been far off from dere ever since us first landed in dis county. Fact is, Boss, us ain't been outen de county since us first come here, an' us gwine be here now I know till de Lord call for us to come on home."

United States. Work Projects Administration

FOLKLORE SUBJECTS

Name of interviewer: Watt McKinney
Subject: Superstitious beliefs
Story—Information (If not enough space on this page, add page)

This information given by: Tines Kendricks (C)
Place of residence: Trenton, Arkansas
Occupation: None
Age: 104

TINES KENDRICKS

[TR: Personal information moved from bottom of form.]

There is an ancient and traditional belief among the Southern Negroes, especially the older ones, that the repeated and intermitted cries of a whippoorwill near a home in the early evenings of summer and occurring on successive days at or about the same time and location; or the appearance of a highly excited redbird, disturbed for no apparent reason, is indicative of some imminent disaster, usually thought to be the approaching death of some member of the family.

Tines Kendricks, who says that he was born the slave of Arch Kendricks in Crawford County, Georgia, two hours before day on a certain Fourth of July, one hundred and four years ago, recalls several instances in his long and eventful life in which he contends the accuracy of these forecasts was borne out by subsequent occurrences. The most striking of these he says was the time his young master succumbed from the effect of a wound received at the first battle of Manassas after hovering between life and death for several days. The young master, Sam Kendricks, who was the only son of his parents, volunteered at the beginning of the War and was attached to the army in Virginia. He was a very impetuous, high-spirited young man and chafed much under the delay occasioned between the time of his enlistment and first battle, wanting to have the trouble over with and the difficulties settled which he honestly thought could be accomplished in the first engagement with that enemy for whom he held such profound contempt. Sam Kendricks, coming as he did from a long line of slave-owning forebears, was one of those Southerners who felt that it was theirs to command and the duty of others to obey. They would brook no interference with the established order and keenly resented the attitude and utterances of Northern press and spokesmen on the slavery question. Tines Kendricks recalls the time his young master took leave of his home and parents for the war and his remarks on departing that his neck was made to fit no halter and that he possessed no mite of fear for Yankee soldier or Yankee steel. Soon after the battle of Manassas, Arch Kendricks was advised that Sam had suffered a severe wound in the engagement. It was stated, however, that the wound was not expected to prove fatal. This sad news of what had befallen the young master was soon communicated throughout the entire length and breadth of the great plantation and in the early evening of that day Tines sitting in the door of his cabin in the slave quarters a short distance from the master's great house heard the cry of a whippoorwill and observed that the voice of this night bird seemed to arise from the dense hedge enclosing the spacious lawn in front of the home. Disturbed and filled with a sense of foreboding at this sound of the bird, he earnestly hoped and prayed that the cry would not be repeated the following evening, but to his great disappointment it was heard again and nearer the house than before. On each succeeding evening according to Tines Kendricks the call of the bird came clearly through the evening's stillness and each time he noticed that the cry came from a spot nearer the home until at last the bird seemed perched beneath the wide veranda and early on the morning following, a very highly excited redbird darted from tree to tree on the front lawn. The redbird continued these peculiar actions for several minutes after which it flew and came to rest on the roof of the old colonial mansion directly above the room formerly occupied by the young master. Tines was convinced now that the end had come for Sam Kendricks and that his approaching death had been foretold by the whippoorwill and that each evening as the bird approached nearer the house and uttered his night cry just so was the life of young Sam Kendricks slowly nearing its close and the actions of the redbird the following day was revealing evidence to Tines that the end had come to his young master which indeed it had as proven by a message the family received late in the morning of this same day.

United States. Work Projects Administration

Interviewer: Miss Irene Robertson
Person interviewed: Frank Kennedy,
Holly Grove, Arkansas
Age: 65 or 70?

FRANK KENNEDY

"My parents' name was Hannah and Charles Kennedy. They b'long to Master John Kennedy. I was raised round Aberdeen, Mississippi but they come in there after freedom. I heard em talk but I couldn't tell you much as where they come from. They said a young girl bout got her growth would auction off for more than any man. They used em for cooks and house women. I judge way they talked she be fifteen or sixteen years old. They brought $1,600 and $2,000. If they was scared up, where they been beat, they didn't sell off good. I knowed Master John Kennedy.

"The Ku Klux come round but they didn't bother much. They would bother if you stole something. Another thing they made em stay close bout their own places and work. I don't know bout freedom.

"I been farmin' and sawmillin' at Clarendon. I gets jobs I can do on the farms now. I got rheumatism so I can't get round. I had this trouble five years or longer now.

"The times is worse, so many folks stealin' and killin'. The young folks don't work steady as they used to. Used to get figured out all you raised till now they refuse to work less en the money in sight. They don't work hard as I allers been workin'.

"I got one girl married. I don't have no land nor home. I works for all I have yet.

"I have voted—not lately. I think my color outer vote like the white folks do long as they do right. The women takin' the mens' places too much it pears like. But they may be honester. I don't know how it will be."

Interviewer: Samuel S. Taylor
Person interviewed: Mrs. A. (Adrianna) W. Kerns
800 Victory Street, Little Rock, Arkansas
Age: 85

KERNS ADRIANNA

"When they first put me in the field, they put me and Viney to pick up brush and pile it, to pick up stumps, and when we got through with that, she worked on her mother's row and I worked on my aunt's row until we got large enough to have a row to ourselves. Me and Viney were the smallest children in the field and we had one row each. Some of the older people had two rows and picked on each row.

"My birthday is on the fourth of November, and I am eighty-five years old. You can count back and see what year I was born in.

Relatives

"My mother's first child was her master's child. I was the second child but my father was Reuben Dortch. He belonged to Colonel Dortch. Colonel Dortch died in Princeton, Arkansas, Dallas County, about eighty-six miles from here. He died before the War. I never saw him. But he was my father's first master. He used to go and get goods, and he caught this fever they had then—I think it was cholera—and died. After Colonel Dortch died, his son-in-law, Archie Hays, became my father's second master. Were all with Hays when we were freed.

"My father's father was a white man. He was named Wilson Rainey. I never did see him. My mother has said to me many a time that he was the meanest man in Dallas County. My father's mother was named Viney. That was her first name. I forget the last name. My mother's name was Martha Hays, and my grandmother's name on my mother's side was Sallie Hays. My maiden name was Adrianna Dortch.

A Devoted Slave Husband

"I have heard my mother tell many a time that there was a slave man who used to take his own dinner and carry it three or four miles to his wife. His wife belonged to a mean white man who wouldn't give them what they needed to eat. He done without his dinner in order that she might have enough. Where would you find a man to do that now? Nowadays they are taking the bread away from their wives and children and carrying it to some other woman.

Patrollers

"A Negro couldn't leave his master's place unless he had a pass from his master. If he didn't have a pass, they would whip him. My father was out once and was stopped by them. They struck him. When my father got back home, he told Colonel Dortch and Colonel Dortch went after them pateroles and laid the law down to them—told them that he was ready to kill 'em.

"The pateroles got after a slave named Ben Holmes once and run him clean to our place. He got under the bed and hid. But they found him and dragged him out and beat him.

Work

"I had three aunts in the field. They could handle a plow and roll logs as well as any man. Trees would blow down and trees would have to be carried to a heap and burned.

"I been whipped many a time by my mistress and overseer. I'd get behind with my work and he would come by and give me a lick with the bull whip he carried with him.

"At first when the old folks cut wood, me and Viney would pick up chips and burn up brush. We had to pick dry peas in the fall after the crops had been gathered. We picked two large basketsful a day.

"When we got larger we worked in the field picking cotton and pulling corn as high as we could reach. You had to pull the fodder first before you could pull the corn. When we had to come out of the field on account of rain, we would go to the corn crib and shuck corn if we didn't have some weaving to do. We got so we could weave and spin. When master caught us playing, he would set us to cutting jackets. He would give us each two or three switches and we would stand up and whip each other. I would go easy on Viney but she would try to cut me to pieces. She hit me so hard I would say, 'Yes suh, massa.'

And she would say, 'Why you sayin' "Yes suh, massa," to me? I ain't doin' nothin' to you.'

"My mother used to say that Lincoln went through the South as a beggar and found out everything. When he got back, he told the North how slavery was ruining the nation. He put different things before the South but they wouldn't listen to him. I heard that the South was the first one to fire a shot.

"Lemme tell you how freedom came. Our master came out where we was grubbing the ground in front of the house. My father was already in Little Rock where they were trying to make a soldier out of him. Master came out and said to mother, 'Martha, they are saying you are free but that ain't goin' to las' long. You better stay here. Reuben is dead.'

"Mother then commenced to fix up a plan to leave. She got the oxen yoked up twice, but when she went to hunt the yoke, she couldn't find it. Negroes were all going through every which way then. Peace was declared before she could get another chance. Word came then that the government would carry all the slaves where they wanted to go. Mother came to Little Rock in a government wagon.

"She left Cordelia. Cordelia was her daughter by Archie Hays. Cordelia was supposed to join us when the government wagon came along but she went to sleep. One colored woman was coming to get in the wagon and her white folks caught her and made her go back. Them Yankees got off their horses and went over there and made them turn the woman loose and let her come on.

They were rough and they took her on to Little Rock in the wagon.

"The Yankees used to come looking for horses. One time Master Archie had sent the horses off by one of the colored slaves who was to stay at his wife's house and hide them in the thicket. During the night, mother heard Archie Hays hollering. She went out to see what was the matter. The Yankees had old Archie Hays out and had guns poked at his breast. He was hollering, 'No sir. I don't.' And mother came and said, 'Reuben, get up and go tell them he don't know where the horses is.' Father got up and did a bold thing. He went out and said, 'Wait, gentlemen, he don't know where the horses is, but if you'll wait till tomorrow morning, he'll send a man to bring them in.' I don't know how they got word to him but he brought them in the next morning and the Yankees taken them off.

"Once a Rebel fired a shot at a Yankee and in a few minutes, our place was alive with them. They were working like ants in a heap all over the place. They took chickens and everything on the place.

Master Archie didn't have no sons large enough for the army. If he had, they would have killed him because they would have thought that he was harboring spies."

Interviewer's Comment

Mrs. A. (Adrianna) W. Kerns is a sister to Charles Green Dortch. Cross reference; see his story.

United States. Work Projects Administration

Interviewer: Miss Irene Robertson
Person interviewed: George Key,
Forrest City, Arkansas
Age: 70 plus

GEORGE KEY

"I was born in Fayette County, Tennessee. My mother was Henrietta Hair. She was owned by David Hair. He had a gang of children. I was her only child. She married just after the surrender she said. She married Henry Key.

"One thing I can tell you she told me so often. The Yankees come by and called her out of the cabin at the quarters. She was a brown girl. They was going out on a scout trip—to hunt and ravage over the country. They told her to get up her clothes, they would be by for her. She was grandma's and grandpa's owners' nurse girl. She told them and they sent her on to tell the white folks. They sent her clear off. She didn't want to leave. She said her master was plumb good to her and them all. They kept her hid out. The Yankees come slipping back to tole her off. They couldn't find her nowhere. They didn't ax about her. They was stealing her for a cook she thought. She couldn't cook to do no good she said. She wasn't married for a long time after then. She said she was scared nearly to death till they took her off and hid her.

"I have voted but not for a long time. I'm too old to

get about and keep too sick to go to the polls to vote. I got high blood pressure.

"Times is fair. If I was a young man I would go to work. I can't grumble. Folks mighty nice to me. I keeps in line with my kin folks and men my age.

"The young age folks don't understand me and I don't know their ways neither. They may be all right, but I don't know."

Interviewer: Miss Irene Robertson
Person interviewed: Lucy Key,
Forrest City, Arkansas
Age: 70 plus

LUCY KEY

"I was born in Marshall County, Mississippi. I seen Yankees go by in droves. I was big enough to recollect that. Old mis', Ellis Marshall's mother, named all the colored children on the place. All the white and colored children was named for somebody else in the family. Aunt Mary Marshall stayed in the house wid old mis'.

"Old mis' had a polly parrot. That thing got bad 'bout telling on us. Old mis' give us a brushing. Her son was a bachelor. He lived there. He married a girl fourteen or fifteen years old and Lawrence Marshall is their son. His sister was in Texas. They said old man Marshall was so stingy he would cut a pea in two. Every time we'd go in the orchard old polly parrot tell on us. We'd eat the turning fruit. One day Aunt Mary (colored) scared polly with her dress and apron till he took bad off sick and died. Mr. Marshall was rough. If he'd found that out he'd 'bout whooped Aunt Mary to death. He didn't find it out. He'd have crazy spells and they couldn't handle him. They would send for Wallace and Tite Marshall (colored men on his place). They was all could do anything wid 'em. He had plenty money and a big room full of meat all the time.

"I recollect what we called after the War a 'Jim Crow.' It was a hairbrush that had brass or steel teeth like pins 'ceptin' it was blunt. It was that long, handle and all (about a foot long). They'd wash me and grease my legs with lard, keep them from looking ashy and rusty. Then they'd come after me with them old brushes and brush my hair. It mortally took skin, hair, and all.

"The first shoe I ever wore had a brass toe. I danced all time when I was a child. We wore cotton dresses so strong. They would hang you if you got caught on 'em. We had one best dress.

"One time I went along wid a colored girl to preaching. Her fellar walked home wid 'er. I was coming 'long behind. He helped her over the rail fence. I wouldn't let him help me. I was sorter bashful. He looked back and I was dangling. I got caught when I jumped. They got me loose. My homespun dress didn't tear.

"I liked my papa the best. He was kind and never whooped us. He belong to Master Stamps on another place. He was seventy-five years old when he died.

"I milked a drove of cows. They raised us on milk and they had a garden. I never et much meat. I went to school and they said meat would make you thick-headed so you couldn't learn.

"I think papa was in the War. We cut sorghum cane with his sword what he fit wid.

"Stamps was a teacher. He started a college before the War. It was a big white house and a boarding house for the scholars. He had a scholar they called Cooperwood. He rode. He would run us children. Mama went to Master

Stamps and he stopped that. He was the teacher. I think that was toreckly after the War. Then we lived in the boarding house. Four or five families lived in that big old house. It had fifteen rooms. That was close to Marshall, Mississippi.

"Me and the Norfleet children drove the old mule gin together. There was Mary, Nell, Grace. Miss Cora was the oldest. Miss Cora Marshall married the old bachelor I told you about. She didn't play much.

"When the first yellow fever broke out, Master George Stamps sent papa to Colliersville from Germantown. The officers stayed there. While he was waiting for meat he would stay in the bottoms. He'd bring meat back. Master George had a great big heavy key to the smokehouse. He'd cut meat and give it out to his Negroes. That meat was smuggled from Memphis. He'd go in a two-horse wagon. I clem up and look through the log cracks at him cutting up the meat fer the hands on his place.

"I had the rheumatism but I cured it. I cupped my knee. Put water in a cup, put a little coal oil (kerosene) on top, strike a match to it and slap the cup to my knee. It drawed a clear blister. I got it well and the rheumatism was gone. I used to rub my legs from my waist down'ards with mule water. They say that is mighty good for rheumatism. I don't have it no more.

"No sir-ree-bob, I ain't never voted and I don't aim to long as I'm in my mind.

"Times ain't hard as they was when I was coming on. (Another Negro woman says Aunt Lucy Key will wash or do lots of things and never take a cent of pay for it—ed.)

Money is scarce but this generation don't know how to work. My husband gets relief 'cause he's sick and wore out. My nephew gives us these rooms to live in. He got money. (We saw a radio in his room and modern up-to-date furnishings—ed.) He is a good boy. I'm good to him as I can be. Seems like some folks getting richer every day, other folks getting worse off every day. Times look dark that way to me.

"I been in Arkansas eight years. I tries to be friendly wid everybody."

Interviewer: Bernice Bowden.
Person interviewed: Anna King (c)
Home: 704 West Fifth, Pine Bluff, Ark.
Age: 80

ANNA KING

"Yes honey, I was here in slavery times. I'se gittin' old too, honey. I was nine years old goin' on ten when the war ceasted. I remember when they was volunteerin'. I remember they said it wasn't goin' to be nothin' but a breakfus' spell.

"My fust marster was Nichols Lee. You see I was born in slavery times—and I was sold away from my mother. My mother never did tell us nothin' 'bout our ages. My white people told me after freedom that I was 'bout nine or ten.

"When the white chillun come of age they drawed for the colored folks. Marse Nichols Lee had a girl named Ann and she drawed me. She didn't keep me no time though, and the man what bought me was named Leo Andrew Whitley. He went to war and died before the war ceasted. Then I fell to his brother Jim Whitley. He was my last marster. I was with him when peace was declared. Yes mam, he was good to me. All my white folks mighty good to me. Co'se Jim Whitley's wife slap my jaws sometimes, but she never did take a stick to me.

"Lord honey, its been so long I just can't remember

much now. I'se gittin' old and forgitful. Heap a things I remember and heap a things slips from me and is gone.

"Well honey, in slavery times, a heap of 'em didn't have good owners. When they wanted to have church services and keep old marster from hearin', they'd go out in the woods and turn the wash-pot upside down. You know that would take up all the sound.

"I remember Adam Heath—he was called the meanest white man. I remember he bought a boy and you know his first marster was good and he wasn't used to bein' treated bad.

One day he asked old Adam Heath for a chew of tobacco, so old Adam whipped him, and the boy ran away. But they caught him and put a bell on him. Yes mam, that was in slavery times. Honey, I had good owners. They didn't believe in beatin' their niggers.

"You know my home was in North Carolina. I was bred and born in Johnson County.

"I remember seein' the soldiers goin' to war, but I never seed no Yankee soldiers till after freedom.

"When folks heard the Yankees was comin' they run and hide their stuff. One time they hide the meat in the attic, but the Yankees found it and loaded it in Everett Whitley's wife's surrey and took it away. She died just 'fore surrender.

"And I remember 'nother time they went to the smokehouse and got something to eat and strewed the rest over the yard. Then they went in the house and jest ramshacked it.

"My second marster never had no wife. He was courtin' a girl, but when the war come, he volunteered. Then he took sick and died at Manassas Gap. Yes'm, that's what they told me.

"My furst marster had a whiskey still. Now let me see, he had three girls and one boy and they each had two slaves apiece. Ann Lee drawed me and my grandmother.

"No mam, I never did go to school. You better not go to school. You better not ever be caught with a book in your hand. Some of 'em slipped off and got a little learnin'. They'd get the old Blue Back book out. Heap of 'em got a little learnin', but I didn't.

"When I fell to Jim Whitley's wife she kept me right in the house with her. Yes mam, she was one good mistis to me when I was a child. She certainly did feed me and clothe me. Yes mam!

"How long I been in Arkansas? Me? Let me see, honey, if I can give you a guess. I been here about forty years. I remember they come to the old country (North Carolina) and say, if you come to Arkansas you wont even have to cook. They say the hogs walkin' round already barbecued. But you know I knowed better than that.

"We come to John M. Gracie's plantation and some to Dr. Blunson (Brunson). I remember when we got off the boat Dr. Blunson was sittin' there and he said "Well, my crowd looks kinda puny and sickly, but I'm a doctor and I'll save 'em." I stayed there eight years. We had to pay our transportation which was fifty dollars, but they sure did give you plenty of somethin' to eat—yes mam!

"No'm my hair ain't much white. My set o'folks don't

get gray much, but I'm old enough to be white. I done a heap a hard work in my life. I hope clean up new ground and I tells folks I done everything 'cept Maul rails.

"Lord honey, I don't know chile. I don't know what to think, about this here younger generation. Now when they raised me up, I took care of myself and the white folks done took care of me.

"Yes mam, honey, I seed the Ku Klux. I remember in North Carolina when the Ku Klux got so bad they had to send and get the United States soldiers. I remember one come and joined in with the Ku Klux till he found out who the head man was and then he turned 'em up and they carried 'em to a prison place called Gethsemane. No mam! They never come back. When they carried you to Gethsemane, you never come back.

"I say the Lord blest me in my old age. Even though I can't see, I set here and praise the Lord and say, Lord, you abled me to walk and hear. Yes, honey, I'm sure glad you come. I'm proud you thought that much of me.

"Good bye, and if you are ever passin' here again, stop and see me."

Interviewer: Mrs. Bernice Bowden
Person interviewed: Anna King
704 W. Fifth (rear), Pine Bluff, Arkansas
Age: 82

ANNA KING

"I used to 'member lots but you know, my remembrance got short.

"I was bred and born in Johnston County, North Carolina. I was sold away from my mother but after freedom I got back. I had a brother was sold just 'fore I was. My mother had two boys and three girls and my oldest sister was sold.

"And then you know, in slavery times, when the white children got grown, their parents give 'em so many darkies. My young Missis drawed me.

"My fust master was such a drinker. Named Lee. Lawd a mercy, I knowed his fust name but I can't think now. Young Lee, that was it.

"He sold me, and Leo Andrew Whitley bought me. Don't know how much—all I know is I was sold.

"After freedom I scrambled back to the old plantation and that's the way I found my mother.

"My last master never married. He had what they called a northern trotter.

"Wish I was able to get back to the old country and find some of my kin folks. If they ain't none of the old head livin', the young folks is. I got oceans of kin folks in Sampson County.

"My husband was a preacher and he come to the old country from this here Arkansas. He always said he was going to bring me out to this country. He was always tellin' me 'bout Little Rock and Hot Springs. So I was anxious to see this country. So after he died and when they was emigratin' the folks here, I come. I 'member Dr. Blunson counted us out after we got off the boat and he said, 'Well, my crowd looks kinda sickly, but I'm a doctor and I'll save you.' Lawd, they certainly come a heap of 'em. When the train uncoupled at Memphis, some went to Texas, some to Mississippi, and some to Louisiana and Arkansas. People hollerin' 'Goodbye' made you feel right sad.

"Some of 'em stayed in Memphis but I wouldn't stay 'cause dat's the meanest place in the world.

"John M. Gracie had paid out his money for us and I believe in doin' what's right. That was a plantation as sure as you bawn."

Interviewer: Miss Irene Robertson
Person interviewed: Mose King,
Lexa, Arkansas
Age: 81

MOSE KING

"I was born in Richmond, Virginia. My master was Ephriam Hester. He had a wife and little boy. We called her mistress. I forgot their names. It's been so long ago.

"My parents named Lizzie Johnson and Andrew Kent. I had seven sisters and there was two of us boys. When mistress died they sold mother and my eldest sister and divided the money. I don't know her master's name in Virginia. Mother was a cook at Ephriam Hester's. Sister died soon as they come 'way from Virginia. I heard her talk like she belong to Nathan Singleterry in Virginia. They put mother and Andrew Kent together. After the surrender she married Johnson. I heard her say my own father was 'cross the river in a free state.

"There was two row of houses on the side of a road a quarter mile long and that is the place all the slaves lived. Ephriam Hester had one hundred acres of wheat. Mother was the head loom. He wasn't cruel but he let the overseers be hard. He said he let the overseers whoop 'em, that what he hired 'em for. They had a whooping stock. It was a table out in the open. They moved it about where they was working. They put the heads and hands and feet in it. I seen a heap of 'em get mighty bad whoopings. I was glad freedom come on fer that one reason. Long as he lived we had plenty to eat, plenty to wear. We had meal, hogs, goat, sheep and cows, molasses, corn hominy, garden stuff. We did have potatoes. I said garden stuff.

"Ephriam Hester come to a hard fate. A crowd of cavalrymen from Vicksburg rode up. He was on his porch. He went in the house to his wife. One of the soldiers retched in his pocket and got something and throwed it up on top of the house. The house burned up and him and her burned up in it. The house was surrounded. That took place three miles this side of Natchez, Mississippi. They took all his fine stock, all the corn. They hauled it off. They took all the wagons. They sot all they didn't take on fire and let it burn up. They burnt the gin and some cotton. They burnt the loom house, the wheat house; they robbed the smokehouse and burned it. We never got nothing. We come purt nigh starving after then. After that round we had no use fer the Yankees. I was learned young two wrongs don't make a right. That was wrong. They done more wrong than that. I heard about it. We stayed till after freedom. It was about a year. It was hard times. Seemed longer. We went to another place after freedom. We never got a chance to get nothing. Nothing to get there.

"In slavery times they had clog dances from one farm to another. Paddyrollers run 'em in, give them whoopings. They had big nigger hounds. They was no more of them after the War. The Ku Klux got to having trouble. They would put vines across the narrow roads. The horses run in and fell flat. The Ku Klux had to quit on that account.

"We didn't know exactly when freedom was. I went to school at Shaffridge, two miles from Clarks store. That was what is Clarksdale, Mississippi now. He had a store, only store in town. Old man Clark run it. He was old bachelor and a all right fellow, I reckon. I thought so. I went to colored teachers five or six months. I learned in the Blue Back books. I stopped at about 'Baker (?)'.

"I farmed all my life. I got my wife and married her in 1883. We got a colored preacher, Parson Ward. I had four children. They all dead but one. I got two lots and a house gone back to the state. I come to see 'bout 'em today. I going to redeem 'em if I can. I made the money to buy it at the round house. I worked there ten or twelve years. I got two dollars ninety-eight cents a day. I hates to loose it. I have a hard time now to live, Miss.

"I votes Republican mostly. I have voted on both sides. I tries to live like this. When in Rome, do as Romans. I want to be peaceable wid everybody.

"The present times is hard. I can't get a bit of work. I tries. Work is hard fer some young folks to get yet.

"I love to be around young folks. Fer as I know they do all right. The world looks nicer 'an it used to look. All I see wrong, times is hard."

United States. Work Projects Administration

Interviewer: Zillah Cross Peel
Information given by: Aunt Susie King, Ex-slave.
Residence: Cane Hill, Arkansas. Washington County.
Age: about 93.

SUSIE KING

Across the Town Branch, in what is dubbed "Tin-cup" lives one of the oldest ex-slaves in Washington county, "Aunt Susie" King, who was born at Cane Hill, Arkansas about 1844.

"Aunt Susie" doesn't know just how old she is, but she thinks she is over ninety, just how much she doesn't know. Perhaps the most accurate way to get near her age would be go to the county records where one can find the following bill of sale:

> "State of Arkansas, County of Washington, for and in consideration of natural affection that I have for my daughter, Rebecca Rich, living in the county aforesaid above mentioned, and I do hereby give and bequath unto her one negro woman named Sally and her children namely Sam, and Fill, her lifetime thence to her children her lawful heirs forever and I do warrant and forever defend said negro girl and her children against all lawful claims whatsoever.
> July, 1840. Tom Hinchea Barker,
>   Witness, J. Funkhouser.
> Filed for record,
>   Feb. 16, 1841.

When this bill of sale was read to "Aunt Susie" she said with great interest,

"Yes'm, yes'm that sure was my Ma and my two brothers, Sam and Fill, then come a 'nother brother, Allan, and then Jack and then I'm next then my baby sister Milly Jane. Yes'm we's come 'bout every two years."

"Yes'm, ole Missy was rich; she had lots of money, lots of lan'. Her girl, she jes' had one, married John Nunley, Mister Ab, he married Miss Ann Darnell, Mister Jack he married Miss Milly Holt, and Mister Calvin he married Miss Lacky Foster. Yes'm they lived all 'round 'bout us. Some at Rhea's Hill and some at Cane Hill," and to prove the keenness of this old slave's mind, as well as her accuracy, one need only to go to the county deed records where in 1849, Rebecca Rich deeded several 40 acres tracts of land to her sons, James, Calvin, William Jackson and Absaolum. This same deed record gives the names of the wives of these sons just as "Aunt Susie" named them. However, Miss Lacky Foster was "Kelika Foster."

Then Aunt Susie started remembering:

"Yes'm, my mother's name was Sally. She'd belonged to Mister Tom H. Barker and he gived her to Miss Becky, his daughter. I think of them all lots of days. I know a heap of folks that some times I forgot. When the War came, we lived in a big log house. We had a loom room back of the kitchen. I had a good mother. She wove some. We all wove mos' all of the blankets and carpets and counterpans and Old Missey she loved to sit down at the loom and weave some", with a gay chuckle Aunty Susie said, "then she'd let me weave an' Old Missey she'd say I takes her work and the loom away from her. I did love to weave, all them bright colores, blue and red and green and yellow. They made all the colors in the back yard in a big kettle, my mother, Sally did the colorin'".

"We had a heap of company. The preacher came a lot of times and when the War come Ole Missey she say if we all go with her, she'd take us all to Texas. We's 'fraid of the Yankees; 'fraid they get us.

"We went in wagons. Ole Missey in the carriage. We never took nothin' but a bed stead for Ole Missey. They was a great drove of we darkies. Part time we walked, part time we rode. We was on the road a long time. First place we stopped was Collins County, and stayed awhile I recollect. We had lots of horses too. Some white folks drove 'long and offered to take us away from Ole Missey but we wouldn't go. We didn't want to leave Ole Missey, she's good to us. Oh Lord, it would a nearly kilt her effen any body'd hit one of her darkies; I'd always stay in the house and took care of Ole Miss. She was pretty woman, had light hair. She was kinda punny tho, somethin' matter with her mos' all the time, headache or toothache or something'."

"Mister Rich went down to the river swimmin' one time I heard, and got drowned."

"Yes'm, they was good days fo' the War."

"Yes'm we stayed in Texas until Peace was made. We was then at Sherman, Texas. Peace didn't make no difference with us. We was glad to be free, and we com'd back to Arkansas with Ole Missey. We didn't want to live down there. Me and my man, Charlie King, was married after the War, and we went to live on Mister Jim Moores place. Ole Miss giv'd my ma a cow. I made my first money in Texas, workin' for a woman and she giv'd me five dollars."

"Yes'm after Peace the slaves all scattered 'bout."

"The colored folks today lak a whole heap bein' like they was fo' the War. They's good darkies, and some aint so good." Me and my man had seven children all dead but two, Bob lives with me. I don't worry 'bout food. We ain't come no ways starvin'. I have all I want to eat. Bob he works for Missus Wade every mornin' tendin' to her flowers and afternoons works for him self. She owns this house, lets us live in it. She's good all right, good woman."

"I like flowers too, but ain't got no water, no more. Water's scarce. Someone turned off the hydrant."

"I belong to the Baptist church a long while."

"Do you know Gate-eye Fisher?" When I said "yes, I went down to talk to him last week," she said, "well, law me, Gate-eye ain't no fool. He's the best cook as ever struck a stove. He married my baby sister, Milly Jane's child. Harriet Lee Ann, she's my niece. She left him, said she'd never go back no more to him. She's somewhere over in Oklahoma."

"And did you see Doc Flowers? Yes'm, I was mos' a mother to him.

"One time my man and me heard a peckin' at the do'. We's eatin' supper. I went to the do' and there was Doc. He and his step-pa, Ole Uncle Ike, had a fight and

Doc come to us and stayed 'bout three years. He started cryin'."

"Yes'm my Pa and Ma had belonged to Mister John Barker, before he giv'd my Ma to Miss Becky, my Pa was a leather worker. He could make shoes, and boots and slippers."

"Yes'm, Good bye. Come back again honey. Yes'm I'd like a little snuff—not the sweet kind. It makes my teeth feel better to have snuff. I ain't got much but snags, and snuff, a little mite helps them."

United States. Work Projects Administration

Interviewer: Mrs. Bernice Bowden
Person interviewed: William Kirk
1910 W. Sixth Street, Pine Bluff, Arkansas
Age: 84

WILLIAM KIRK

"I been here ever since 1853—yes ma'm! Cose I 'member the war! I tell you I've seen them cannon balls goin' up just like a balloon. I wasn't big enough to work till peace was declared but they had my mammy and daddy under the lash. One good thing 'bout my white folks, they give the hands three months' schoolin' every year. My mammy and daddy got three months' schoolin' in the old country. Some said that was General Washington's proclamation, but some of 'em wouldn't hear to it. When peace was declared, some of the niggers had as good education as the white man. That was cause their owners had 'lowed it to 'em.

"They used to put us in cells under the house so the Yankees couldn't get us. Old master's name was Sam Kirk and he had overseers and nigger dogs (bloodhounds) that didn't do nothin' but run them niggers.

"I 'member one time when they say the Yankees was comin' all us chillun, boys and girls, white and black, got upon the fence and old master come out and say 'Get in your holes!'

"The war went on four years. Them was turrible times. I don't never want to see no more war. Them that had plenty, time the regiment went by they didn't have nothin'. Old mistress had lots a turkeys and hogs and the Yankees just cleaned 'em out. Didn't have time to pick 'em—just skinned 'em. They had a big camp 'bout as long as from here to town.

"They burned up the big house as flat as this floor. They wasn't nothin' left but the chimneys. Oh the Yankees burned up plenty. They burned Raleigh and they burned Atlanta—that was the southern capital. I've seen the Yankees go right out in people's fields and make 'em take the horses out. Then they'd saddle 'em and ride right off.

"General Grant had ten thousand nigger soldiers outside of the Irishmen and the Dutchmen. I know General Grant looked fearful when he come by. After surrender he had a corps pass through and notify the people that the war was over.

"Abraham Lincoln was a war captain. He was a man that believed in right. He was seven feet four inches high.

"I was born in North Carolina and I come here in 'sixty seven. I worked too!"

Interviewer: Miss Irene Robertson
Person interviewed: Betty Krump,
Helena, Arkansas
Age: —
[Date Stamp: MAY 31 1938]

BETTY KRUMP

"Mother come to Helena, Arkansas from Lake Charles, Louisiana. I was born here since freedom. She had twelve children, raised us two. She jus' raised me en my sister. She lives down the street on the corner. She was a teacher here in Helena years and years. I married a doctor. I never had to teach long as he lived, then I was too old. I never keered 'bout readin' and books. I rather tomboy about. Then I set up housekeepin'. I don't know nothin' 'bout slavery. I know how they come here. Two boats named Tyler and Bragg. The Yankees took 'em up and brought 'em up to their camps to pay them to wait on them. They come. Before 'mancipation my mammy and daddy owned by the very same old fellar, Thomas Henry McNeil. He had a big two-story stone house and big plantation. Mother said she was a field hand. She ploughed. He treated 'em awful bad. He overworked 'em. Mother said she had to work when she was pregnant same as other times. She said the Yankees took the pantry house and cleaned it up. They broke in it. I'm so glad the Yankees come. They so pretty. I love 'em. Whah me? I can tell 'em by the way they talk and acts. You ain't none. You don't talk like 'em. You don't act like 'em. I watched you yeste'd'y. You don't walk like 'em. You act like the rest of these southern women to me.

"Mother said a gang of Yankees came to the quarters to haul the children off and they said, 'We are going to free you all. Come on.' She said, 'My husband in the field.' They sent for 'im. He come hard as he could. They loaded men and all on them two gunboats. The boat was anchored south of Tom Henry McNeill's plantation. He didn't know they was gone. When they got here old General Hindman had forty thousand back here in the hills. They fired in. The Yankees fired! The Yankees said they was goin' to drive 'em back and they scared 'em out of here and give folks that brought in them gunboat houses to live in. Mammy went to helping the Yankees. They paid her. That was 'fore freedom. I loves the Yankees. General Hindman's house was tore down up there to build that schoolhouse (high school). The Yankees said they was goin' to water their horses in the Mississippi River by twelve o'clock or take hell. I know my mammy and daddy wasn't skeered 'cause the Yankees taking keer of 'em and they was the ones had the cannons and gunboats too. I jus' love the Yankees fer freeing us. They run white folks outer the houses and put colored folks in 'em. Yankees had tents here. They fed the colored folks till little after 'mancipation. When the Yankees went off they been left to root hog er die. White folks been free all der lives. They got no need to be poor. I went to school to white teachers. They left here, folks didn't do 'em right. They set 'em off to theirselves. Wouldn't keep 'em, wouldn't walk 'bout wid 'em. They wouldn't talk to 'em. The Yankees sont 'em down here to egercate us up wid you white folks. Colored folks do best anyhow wid black folks' children. I went to Miss Carted and to Mrs. Mason. They was a gang of 'em. They bo'ded at the hotel, one of the hotels kept 'em all. They stayed 'bout to theirselves. 'Course the white folks had schools, their own schools.

"Ku Klux—They dressed up and come in at night, beat up the men 'bout here in Helena. Mammy washed and ironed here in Helena till she died. I never did do much of that kinder work. I been housekeeping purty near all my days.

"Mammy was Fannie Thompson in Richmond, Virginia. She was took to New Orleans on a boat and sold. Sold in New Orleans. She took up wid Edmond Clark. Long as you been going to school don't you know folks didn't have no marryin' in slavery times? I knowed that. They never did marry and lived together all their lives. Preacher married me—colored preacher. My daddy, Edmond Clark, said McNeil got him at Kentucky.

"I done told you 'nough. Now what are you going to give me? The gover'ment got so many folks doin' so much you can't tell what they after. Wish I was one of 'em.

"The present times is tough. We ain't had no good times since dem banks broke her. Three of 'em. Folks can't get no credit. Times ain't lack dey used to be. No use talking 'bout this young generation. One day I come in my house from out of my flower garden. I fell to sleep an' I had $17.50 in little glass on the table to pay my insurance. It was gone when I got up. I put it in there when I lay down. I know it was there. It was broad open daytime. Folks steals and drinks whiskey and lives from hand to mouth now all the time. I sports my own self. Ain't nobody give me nothin' since the day I come here. I rents my houses and sells flowers."

Interviewer's Comment

This old woman lives in among the white population and rents the house next to her own to a white family. The lady down at the corner store said she tells white people, the younger ones, to call her Mrs. Krump. She didn't pull that on me. She once told this white lady storekeeper to call her Mrs. No one told me about her, because the lady said they all know she is impudent talking. She is old, black, wealthy, and arrogant. I passed her house and spied her.

FOLKLORE SUBJECTS
[HW: Ex-slave, Texarkans Dist.]
Name of Interviewer: Mrs. W. M. Ball
Subject: Folk Tales.

Information given by: Preston Kyles
Place of Residence: 800 Block. Laurel St., Texarkana, Ark.
Occupation: Minister. (Age) 81

PRESTON KYLES

[TR: Personal information moved from bottom of form.]

One of the favorite folk songs sung to the children of a half century ago was "Run Nigger Run, or the Patty Roll Will Get You." Few of the children of today have ever heard this humorous ditty, and would, perhaps, be ignorant of its meaning. To the errant negro youths of slave times, however, this tune had a significant, and sometimes tragic, meaning. The "patty rolls" were guards hired by the plantations to keep the slaves from running away. The following story is told by an ex-slave:

"When I wuz a boy, dere wuz lotsa Indians livin' about six miles frum de plantation on which I wuz a slave. De Indians allus held a big dance ever' few months, an' all de niggers would try to attend. On one ob dese osten'tious occasions about 50 of us niggers conceived de idea of goin', without gettin' permits frum de Mahster. As soon as it gets dark, we quietly slips outen de quarters, one by one, so as not to disturb de guards. Arrivin' at de dance, we jined de festivities wid a will. Late dat nite one ob de boys wuz goin' down to de spring fo' to get a drink ob water when he notice somethin' movin' in de bushes. Gettin' up closah, he look' again when—Lawd hab mersy! Patty rollers! A whole bunch ob 'em! Breathless, de nigger comes rushin' back, and broke de sad news. Dem niggers wuz scared 'mos' to death, 'cause dey knew it would mean 100 lashes for evah las' one ob dem effen dey got caught. After a hasty consultation, Sammy, de leader, suggested a plan which wuz agreed on. Goin' into de woods, we cuts several pieces of grape vine, and stretches it across de pathway, where we knowed de patty rollers would hab to come, tien' it to trees on both sides. One ob de niggers den starts down de trail whistlin' so as to 'tract de patty rollers 'tention, which he sho did, fo' here dey all cum, runnin' jus' as hard as dey could to keep dem niggers frum gettin' away. As de patty rollers hit de grape vine, stretched across de trail, dey jus' piles up in one big heap. While all dis commotion wuz goin' on, us niggers makes fo' de cotton fiel' nearby, and wends our way home. We hadn' no more'n got in bed, when de mahster begin knockin' on de door. "Jim", he yell, "Jim, open up de doah!" Jim gets up, and opens de doah, an de mahster, wid several more men, comes in de house. "Wheres all de niggers?" he asks. "Dey's all heah," Jim says. De boss walks slowly through de house, countin' de niggers, an' sho' nuf dey wuz all dere. "Mus' hab been Jim Dixon's negroes," he says finally.

"Yes, suh, Cap'n, dey wuz a lot happen in dem times dat de mahsters didn't know nuthin' about."

Slave Narratives

FOLKLORE SUBJECTS
[HW: Ex-slave, Texarkana Dist., 9/5/31]
Name of Interviewer: Cecil Copeland
Subject: Apparition and Will-o'-the-Wisp.
Story—Information:

Information given by: Preston Kyles / Occupation: Minister
Place of Residence: 800 Block, Laurel St., Texarkana, Ark. (Age) 81

PRESTON KYLES

[TR: Personal information moved from bottom of form.]

The negro race is peculiarly susceptible to hallucinations. Most any old negro can recall having had several experiences with "de spirits." Some of these apparitions were doubtless real, as the citizens during Reconstruction Days employed various methods in keeping the negro in subjection. The organizers of the Ku Klux Klan, shortly after the Civil War, recognized and capitalized on the superstitious nature of the negro. This weakness in their character doubtless prevented much bloodshed during this hectic period.

The following is a story as told by a venerable ex-slave in regard to the "spirits":

"One day, when I wuz a young man, me an' a nigger, by de name ov Henry, wuz huntin' in an' old field. In dem days bear, deer, turkey, and squirrels wuz plentiful an' 'twant long befo' we had kilt all we could carry. As we wuz startin' home some monstrous thing riz up right smack dab in front ov us, not more'n 100 feet away. I asked

Henry: "Black Boy, does yo' see whut I see?" an' Henry say, "Nigger I hopes yo' don't see whut I see, 'cause dey ain't no such man." But dere it stood, wid its sleeves gently flappin' in de wind. Ovah 8 feet tall, it wuz, an' all dressed in white. I yells at it, "Whut does yo' want?" but it didn't say nuthin'. I yells some mo' but it jus' stands there, not movin' a finger. Grabbin' de gun, I takes careful aim an' cracks down on 'em, but still he don't move. Henry, thinkin' maybe I wuz too scared to shoot straight, say: "Nigger, gib me dat gun!" I gibs Henry de gun but it don't take but one shot to convince him dat he ain't shootin' at any mortal bein'. Throwin' down de gun, Henry say, "Nigger, lets get away frum dis place," which it sho' didn't take us long to do."

Interviewer: Mrs. Bernice Bowden
Person interviewed: Susa Lagrone
25th and Texas Streets, Pine Bluff, Ark.
Age: 79

SUSA LAGRONE

"I don't know exactly how old I am but I know I was here at surrender. I was born in Mississippi. I seen the soldiers after they come home. They camped right there at our gate.

"I think—now I don't know, but I think I was bout six or seven when they surrendered. I went down to the gate with Miss Sally and the children. Old mistress' name was Sally Stanton. She was a widow woman.

"I learned to knit durin' the war. They'd give me a task to do, so much to do a day, and then I'd have all evenin' to play.

"My father was a mechanic. He laid brick and plaster. You know in them days they plastered the houses. He belonged to old man Frank Scott. He was such a good worker Mr. Scott would give him all the work he could after he was free. That was in Mississippi.

"I went to school right smart after freedom. Fore freedom the white folks learned me my ABC's. My mistress was good and kind to me.

"When we went down to the gate to see the soldiers, I heard Miss Judy say (she was old mistress' sister), I heard her say, 'Well, you let em beat you' and started cryin'. I cried too and mama said, 'What you cryin' for?' I said, 'Miss Judy's cryin'.' Mama said, 'You fool, you is free!' I didn't know what freedom was, but I know the soldiers did a lot of devilment. Had guards but they just run over them guards.

"I think Abraham Lincoln wanted to give the people some land after they was free, but they didn't give em nothin'—just turned em loose.

"Course we ought to be free—you know privilege is worth everything.

"After surrender my mother stayed with old mistress till next year. She thought there wasn't nobody like my mother. When she got sick old mistress come six miles every day to see her and brought her things till she died.

"My mother learned to weave and spin and after we was free the white folks give her the loom. I know I made a many a yard of cloth after surrender. My mother was a seamstress and she learned me how to sew.

"I never did hire out—just worked at home. My mother had six boys and six girls and they're all dead but me and my sister.

"Somebody told me I was twenty-five when I married. Had three children—all livin'.

"I used to see the white folks lookin' at a map to see where the soldiers was fightin' and I used to wonder how they could tell just lookin' at that paper.

"Old mistress said after freedom, 'Now, Susa, I don't

want you to suffer for nothin.' I used to go up there and stay for weeks at a time.

"I just got down with rheumatism here bout three or four years ago, and you know it goes hard with me—I always been used to workin' all my life."

United States. Work Projects Administration

Interviewer: Miss Irene Robertson
Person interviewed: Barney A. Laird
Brinkley, (near Moroe) Arkansas
Age: 79

BARNEY A. LAIRD

"I was born in Pinola County, Mississippi. I remembers one time soldiers come by on all black horses and had a bundle on one shoulder strapped around under the other arm. They wore blue jackets. Their horses was trained so they marched good as soldiers. They camped not far from our house. There was a long string of soldiers. It took them a long time to go by.

"One time they had a dinner in a sorter grove on a neighbor's farm. All us children went up there to see if they left anything. We et up the scraps. I say it was good eating. The fust Yankee crackers I ever et was there that day. They was fine for a fact.

"Our owner was Dr. Laird. When I come to know anything his wife was dead but his married daughter lived with him. Her husband's name was John Balentine. My parents worked in the field and I stayed up at the house with my old grandpa and grandma. Their house was close to the white folks. Our houses was about on the farm. Some of the houses was pole houses, some hewed out. The fireplace in our house burned long wood and the room what had the fireplace was a great big room. We had shutters at the windows. The houses was open but pretty stout and good. We had plenty wood.

"My parents both lived on the same farm. They had seven children. My mother's name was Caroline and my father's name was Ware A. Laird. Mother never told us if she was ever sold. Father never was sold. He never talked much.

"One thing I know is: My wife's pa was sold, Squire Lester, so him and Adeline could be on the same farm. Them my wife's parents. They never put him on no block, jes' told him to get his belongings and where to go. I never seen nobody sold.

"Dr. Laird was good to his darkies. My whole family stayed on his place till he died. I don't know how long. I don't know if I ever knowed when freedom come on. We had a hard time durin' the Civil War. That why I hate to hear about war. The soldiers tore down houses, burnt houses. They burnt up Dr. Laird's gin. I think it burned some cotton. They tore down fences and hauled em off to make fires at their camps. That let the stock out what they maybe did leave an old snag. Fust cussin' I ever heard done was one of them soldiers. I don't know what about but he was going at it. I stopped to hear what he saying. I never heard nobody cuss so much over nothing as ever I found out. They had cleaned us out. We didn't have much to eat nor wear then. We did have foe then from what they told us. The old folks got took care of. That don't happen no more.

"I never seen a Ku Klux. I heard tell of them all my life.

"Dr. Laird was old man and John Balentine was a

peaceable man. He wanted his farm run peaceable. He was kind as could be.

"I been farming all my life. I still be doing it. I do all I can. It is the young boys' place to take the plough handle—the making a man out of their young strength. They don't want to do it. Some do and some won't stay on the farm. Go to town is the cry. I got a wife and two boys. They got families. They are on the farm. I tell them to stay.

"I get help from the Welfare if I'm able to come get what they give me.

"I used to pay my taxes and vote. Now if I have a dollar I have to buy something to eat. Us darkies satisfied with the best the white folks can do. Darkies good workers but poor managers is been the way I seen it all my life. One thing we don't want no wars."

United States. Work Projects Administration

Interviewer: Mrs. Bernice Bowden
Person interviewed: Arey Lamar
612 E. 14th Avenue, Pine Bluff, Arkansas
Age: 78
[Date Stamp: MAY 31 1938]

AREY LAMAR

"Yes'm, I was born in slavery days but I don't know what day. But you know I been hustlin' 'round here a long time.

"My mother said I was a great big girl when surrender come.

"I was born in Greenville, Mississippi but I was raised down at Lake Dick.

"I was a servant in Captain Will Nichols' house. I got a cup here now that was Captain Nichols' cup. Now that was away back there. That's a slavery time cup. After the handle got broke my mother used it for her coffee cup.

"My mother's name was Jane Condray. After everything was free, a lot of us emigrated from the old country to Arkansas. When we come here we come through Memphis and I know I saw a pair of red shoes and cried for mama to buy 'em for me, but she wouldn't do it.

"After I was grown and livin' in Little Rock, I bought me a pair of red shoes. I know I wore 'em once and I got ashamed of 'em and blacked 'em.

"My brother run away when they was goin' to have that Baxter-Brooks War and ain't been seen since.

"I was the oldest girl and never did get a education, and I hate it. I learned to work though.

"I don't know 'bout this younger generation. It looks like they're puttin' the old folks in the background. But I think it's the old christian people is holdin' the world together today."

Name of Interviewer: Irene Robertson.
Person interviewed: Solomon Lambert,
Holly Grove, Ark., R.F.D.
Age: 89
Subject: EX-SLAVERY
Story:

SOLOMON LAMBERT

"My parents belong to Jordon and Judy Lambert. They (the Jordon family) had a big family. They never was sold. I heard 'em say that. They hired their slaves out. Some was hired fer a year. From New Year day to next New Year day. That was a busy day. That was the day to set in workin' overseers and ridin' bosses set in on New Year day. My parents' name was Fannie and Ben Lambert. They had eight children.

"How did they marry? They say they jump the broomstick together! But they had brush brooms so I reckon that whut they jumped. Think the moster and mistress jes havin' a little fun outen it then. The brooms the sweep the floor was sage grass cured like hay. It grows four or five feet tall. They wrap it with string and use that for a handle. (Illustration— [TR: not finished] The way they married the man ask his moster then ask her moster. If they agree it be all right. One of 'em would 'nounce it 'fore all the rest of the folks up at the house and some times they have ale and cake. If the man want a girl and ther be another man on that place wanted a wife the mosters would swop the women mostly. Then one announce they married. That what they call a double weddin'. Some got passes go see their wife and family 'bout every Sunday and some other times like Fourth er July. They have a week ob rest when they lay by the crops and have some time not so busy to visit Christmas.

"I never seen no Ku Klux. There was Jay Hawkers. They was folks on neither side jess goin' round, robbin' and stealin', money, silver, stock or anything else they wanted. We had a prutty good time we have all the hands on our place at some house and dance. We made our music. Music is natur'l wid our color. They most all had a juice (Jew's) harp. They make the fiddle and banjo. White folks had big times too. They had mo big gatherins than they have now. They send me to Indian Bay once or twice a week to get the mail. I had no money. They give my father little money long and give him some 'bout Christmas. White folks send their darkies wid a order to buy things. I never seen a big town till I started on that run to Texas. They took the men 450 miles to Indian Nation to make a crop. We went in May and came back in October. They hired us out. Mr. Jo Lambert and Mr. Beasley took us. One of 'em come back and got us. That kept us from goin' to war. They left the women, children and old men, too old fer war.

"How'd I know 'bout war? That was the big thing they talk 'bout. See 'em. The first I seen was when I was shuckin' corn at the corn pin (crib) a man come up in gray clothes. (He was a spy). The way he talk you think he a southern man 'cept his speech was hard and short. I noticed that to begin wid. They thought other rebels in the corn pin but they wasn't. Wasn't nobody out there but me. Then here come a man in blue uniform. After while here come the regiment. It did scare me. Bob and Tom (white boys) Lambert gone to war then. They fooled round a while then they galloped off. I show was glad when the last man rid off!

Moster Lambert then hid the slaves in the bottoms. We carried provisions and they sent more'long. We stay two or three days or a week when they hear a regiment comin' through or hear 'bout a scoutin gang comin' through. They would come one road and go back another road. We didn't care if they hid us. We hear the guns. We didn't wanter go down there. That was white man's war. In 1862 and 1863 they slipped off every man and one woman to Helena. I was yokin' up oxen. Man come up in rebel clothes. He was a spy. I thought I was gone then but and a guard whut I didn't see till he left went on. I dodged round till one day I had to get off to mill. The Yankees run up on me and took me on. I was fifteen years old. I was mustered in August and let out in 1864 when it was over. I was in the Yankee army 14 months. They told me when I left I made a good soldier. I was with the standing army at Helena. They had a battle before I went in. I heard them say. You could tell that from the roar and cannons. They had it when I was in Texas. I wasn't in a battle. The Yankees begin to get slim then they made the darkies fill up and put them in front. I heard 'em say they had one mighty big battle at Helena. I had to drill and guard the camps and guard at the pickets (roads into Helena). They never let me go scoutin'. I walked home from the army. I was glad to get out. I expected to get shot 'bout all the time. I aint seen but mighty little difference since freedom. I went back and stayed 45 years on the Lambert place. I moved to Duncan. Moster died foe the Civil War. Some men raised dogs-hounds. If something got wrong they go get the dogs and use 'em. If some of the slaves try to run off they hunt them with the dogs. It was a big loss when a hand run off they couldn't ford that thing. They whoop 'em mostly fer stealin'. They trust 'em in everything then they whoop 'em if they steal. They know it wrong. Course they did. The worse thing I ever seen in slavery was when we went to Texas we camped close to Camden. Camden, Arkansas! On the way down there we passed by a big house, some kind. I seen mighty little of it but a big yard was pailened in. It was tall and fixed so they couldn't get out. They opened the big gate and let us see. It was full of darkies. All sizes. All ages. That was a Nigger Trader Yard the worst thing I ever seen or heard tell of in my life. I heard 'em say they would cry 'em off certain times but you could buy one or two any time jes by agreement. I nearly fell out wid slavery then. I studied 'bout that heap since then. I never seen no cruelty if a man work and do right on my moster's place he be honored by both black and white. Foe moster died I was 9 year old, I heard him say I valued at $900.00. I never was sold.

"When I was small I minded the calves when they milk, pick up chips to dry fer to start fires, then I picked up nuts, helped feed the stock, learned all I could how to do things 'bout the place. We thought we owned the place. I was happy as a bird. I didn't know no better than it was mine. All the home I ever knowed. I tell you it was a good home. Good as ever had since. It was thiser way yo mama's home is your home. Well my moster's home was my home like dat.

"We et up at the house in the kitchen. We eat at the darkey houses. It make no diffurence—one house clean as the other. It haft to be so. They would whoop you foe your nasty habits quick as anything and quicker. Had plenty clothes and plenty to eat. Folk's clothes made outer more lastin' cloth than now. They last longer and didn't always be gettin' more new ones. They washed down at the spring. The little darkies get in (tubs) soon as they hang out the clothes on the ropes and bushes. The suds be warm, little darkies race to get washed. Folks raced to get through jobs then and have fun all time.

"Foe I jined the Yankees I had hoed and I had picked cotton. Moster Lambert didn't work the little darkies hard to to stunt them. See how big I am? I been well cared fur and done a sight er work if it piled up so it could be seen.

(Solomon Lambert is a large well proportioned negro.) In 1870 the railroad come in here by Holly Grove. That the first I ever seen. The first cars. They was small.

"I never knowd I oughter recollect what all they talked but she said they both (mother and father) come from Kentucky to Tennessee, then to Arkansas in wagons and on boats too I recken. The Lamberts brought them from Kentucky. For show I can't tell you no more 'bout them. I heard 'em say they landed at the Bay (Indian Bay).

"Fine reports went out if you jin the army whut all you would get. I didn't want to be there. I know whut I get soon as ever I got way from them. Course I was goin' back. I had no other place to go. The government give out rations at Indian Bay after the war. I didn't need none. I got plenty to eat. Two or three of us colored folks paid Mr. Lowe $1.00 a month to teach us at night. We learned to read and calculate better. I learned to write. We stuck to it right smart while.

"I been married twice. Joe Yancey (white) married me to my first wife at the white folks house. The last time Joe Lambert (white) married me in the church. I had 2 boys they dead now and 1 girl. She is living.

During slavery I had a cart I drove a little mule to. I took a barrel of water to the field. I got it at the well. I put it close by in the shade of a tree. Trees was plentiful! Then I took the breakfast and dinner in my cart. I done whatever come to my lot in Indian Nation. After the war I made a plowhand. "Say there, from 1864 to 1937 Sol Lambert farmed." Course I hauled and cut wood, but my job is farmin'. I share croppe. I worked fer 1/3 and 1/4 and I have rented. Farmin' is my talent. That whar all the darkey belong. He is made so. He can stand the sun and he needs meat to eat. That is where the meat grows.

"I got chickens and a garden. I didn't get the pigs I spoke fer. I got a fine cow. I got a house—10-1/2 acres of ground. That is all I can look after. I caint get 'bout much. I rid on a wagon (to town) my mare is sick I wouldn't work her. I got a buggy. Good nough fer my ridin' I don't come to town much. I never did.

I get a Federal soldier's pension. I tell you 'bout it. White folks tole me 'bout it and hope me see 'bout gettin' it. I'm mighty proud of it. It is a good support for me in my old helpless days. I'm mighty thankful for it. I'm glad you sent me word to come here I love to help folks. They so good to me.

"I vote a Republican ticket. I don't vote. I did vote when I was 21 years old. It was stylish then and I voted some since then along. I don't bother with votin' and I don't know nuthin 'bout how it is done now. I tried to run my farm and let them hired run the governmint. I knowed my job like he knowed his job.

I come back to tell you one other thing. My Captain was Edward Boncrow.

"I told you all I know 'bout slavery less you ask me 'bout somethin' I might answer: We ask if we could go to white church and they tell us they wanted certain ones to go today so they could fix up. It was after the war new churches and schools sprung up. Not fast then.

Prices of slaves run from $1600 to $2000 fer grown to middle age. Old ones sold low, so did young ones. $1600 was a slow bid. That is whut I heard.

United States. Work Projects Administration

Name of Interviewer: Martin-Barker
Subject: Ex-Slave
Story—Information (If not enough space on this page add page)

This information given by: Frank Larkin
Place of Residence: RFD #1—Bx. 73
Age —

FRANK LARKIN

[TR: Personal information moved from bottom of form.]

I was born a slave, my owner was Mr. Rhodes of Virginia. On a large plantation, my white folks gave a big to do, and served wine. Had corn shuckings. Swapped help around harvesting time. I was sold when 6 or 7 years old. Sold to highest bidder. First marster gave my mother to his white daughter and let her keep me.

I was raised as a house boy. I was always a mean boy. When I was sold I split another boys head open with an axe. Then I runned off. They caught me with blood hounds. My master whipped me with a cowhide whip. He made me take my clothes off and tied me to a tree. He would use the whip and then take a drink out of a jug and rest awhile, then he would whip me again.

Sometimes we would set up until midnight pickin' wool. I would get so sleepy, couldn't hardly pick de wool.

I hung up my stocking at Christmas to get gifts.

When we left de plantation, we had to get a pass to go from one plantation to another.

We went to church, sat on de back seat of the white folks church. It was a Baptist. Baptized in pool. White preacher said: "Obey your master."

When I came to Arkanansas, I was sold to Mr. Larkin.

Interviewer: Mrs. Bernice Bowden
Person interviewed: Frank Larkin
1126 W. Second Avenue, Pine Bluff, Arkansas
Age: 77

FRANK LARKIN

"Yes ma'm, I was born in slavery times, right about 1860. I was bred and born in Virginia—belonged to a man named Rhodes. When I was a little fellow, me and my mother was sold separate. My mother was sent to Texas and a man named Larkin bought me.

"I member when people was put upon the block and sold. Man and wife might go together and might not. Yes ma'm, they sho did separate mother and childen.

"Take a little chile, they would be worth a thousand dollars. Why old master would just go crazy over a little boy. They knowed what they would be worth when they was grown, and then they kept em busy.

"I can't remember no big sight in Virginia but I remember when the hounds would run em. Some of the colored folks had mighty rough owners.

"I remember when the Yankees come and took the best hoss my old boss had and left old crippled hoss with the foot evil.

"And they'd get up in a tree with a spyglass and find where old boss had his cotton hid, come down and go straight and burn it and the corn crib and take what meat they wanted and then burn the smoke house. Yes'm, I remember all that. I tell you them Yankees was mean. Used to shake old mistress and try to make her tell where the money was hid. If you had a fat cow, just shoot her down and cook what they wanted. My old boss went to the bottoms and hid. Tried to make old mistress tell where he was.

"Not all the old bosses was alike. Some fed good and some didn't. But they clothed em good—heavy cloth. Old man Larkin was pretty good man. We got biscuits every Sunday morning, other times got shorts. People was really healthier then.

"I was brought up to work. The biggest trainin' we got was the boss told us to go there and come here and we learned to do as we was told. People worked in them days. A deal of em that won't work now.

"During slavery days, colored folks had to go to the same church as the white folks and sit in the back.

"My father died a long time ago. I don't remember anything bout him and I never did see my mother any more after she was sold.

"After the war, old boss brought me to Arkansas when I was bout twelve years old. Biggest education I got, sit down with my old boss and he'd make me learn the alphabet. In those times they used the old Blue Back Speller.

"After we come to Arkansas I worked a great deal on the farm. Farmin'—that was my trade. I staid with him four or five years. He paid me for my work.

"Well, I hope we'll never have another war, we don't need it.

"I never had trouble votin' but one time. They was havin' a big row between the parties and didn't want us to vote unless we voted democratic, but I voted all right. I believe every citizen ought to have the right to vote. I believe in people havin' the right what belongs to em.

"I'm the father of thirteen childen by one woman— seven living somewhere, but they ain't no service to me.

"Younger people not takin' time to study things. They get a little education and think they can do anything and get by with it. And there's a lot of em down here on this Cummins farm now."

United States. Work Projects Administration

Interviewer: Mrs. Bernice Bowden
Person interviewed: Frank Larkin
618 E. Fifteenth, Pine Bluff, Arkansas
Age: 85

FRANK LARKIN

"I was somewhere 'bout twelve years old when the Civil War ended. I was the carriage driver, fire maker, and worked in the field some.

"I was bred and born in Virginia and I was sold; I was sold. My first old boss was a Rhodes and he sold me to a man named Larkin. See, we had to take our names from our boss. Me and my mother both was sold. I was somewhere between seven and eight years old.

"Then old boss give my mother to his daughter and she carried her to Texas and he kept me. Never have seen her since.

"He was good to me sometimes but he worked us night and day. Had a pile of wool as big as this room and we had to pick it and card it 'fore we went to bed. Old boss was sittin' right there by us. Oh, yes'm.

"Old boss was better to me than old missis. She'd want to whip me and he'd say he'd do it; and he'd take me down to the quarters and have a cow-hide whip and he would whip a tree and say, 'Now you holler like I'm whippin' you.' I'd just be a bawlin' too I'm tellin' you but he never hit me nary a lick.

"All the chillun, when they was clearin' up new ground, had to pick up brush and pile it up. Ever'body knowed how much he had to do. Ever' woman knowed how much she had to weave. They made ever'thing—shoes and all.

"Them Yankees sure did bad—burned up the cotton and the corn. I seen one of 'em get up in a tree and take his spyglass and look all around; directly he'd come down and went just as straight to that cotton as a bird to its nest. Oh, yes ma'am, they burned up everything. I was a little scared of 'em but they said they wasn't goin' to hurt us. Old master had done left home and gone to the woods. It was enough to scare you—all them guns stacked up and bayonets that long and just as keen. Come in and have old missis cook for 'em. Sometimes they'd go and leave lots to eat for the colored folks and maybe give 'em a blanket. Wouldn't give old missis anything; try to make her tell where the money was though.

"When they said Vicksburg was captured, old master come out hollerin' and cryin' and said they taken Vicksburg and we was free. Some of 'em stayed and some of 'em left. Me and my grandma and my aunt stayed there after we was freed 'bout two years. They took care of me; I was raised motherless.

"I farmed all my life. Never done public work two weeks in my life. Don't know what it is.

"Old master had them blue back spellers and 'fore freedom sometimes he'd make us learn our ABC's.

"And he'd let you go to church too. He'd ask if you got 'ligion and say, 'Now, when the preacher ask you, go up and give him your hand and then go to the back.' In them days, didn't have any but the white folks' church. But I was pretty rough in them days and I didn't j'ine.

"But I tell you, you'd better not leave the plantation without a pass or them paddyrollers would make you shout. If they kotch you and you didn't have a pass, a whippin' took place right there.

"Oh Lord, that's been a long time. I sits here sometimes and looks back and think it's been a long time, but I'm still livin'.

"I've always tried to keep out of trouble. 'Co'se I've had some pretty tough times. I ain't never been 'rested fer nothin'. I ain't never been inside of a jail house. I've had some kin folks in there though.

"I've been a preacher forty years. Don't preach much now. My lungs done got decayed and I can't hold up. Some people thinks preachin' is an easy thing but it's not.

"Prettiest thing I ever saw when the Yankees was travelin' was the drums and kettledrums and them horses. It was the prettiest sight I ever saw. Them horses knowed their business, too. You couldn't go up to 'em either. They had gold bits in their mouths and looked like their bridles was covered with gold. And Yankees sittin' up there with a sword.

"Old boss had a fine saddle horse and you know the Yankees had a old horse with the footevil and you know they turned him loose and took old boss's saddle horse. He didn't know it though; he was in the woods.

"I believe there is people that can give you good luck. I

know a woman that told me that I was goin' to have some good luck and it worked just like she said. She told us I would be the onliest man on the place that would pay out my mule and sure 'nough I was. I cleared forty dollars outside my mule and my corn. She said I was born to be lucky. Told me they would be lots of people work agin me but it wouldn't do no good."

Interviewer: Mrs. Bernice Bowden
Person interviewed: William Lattimore
606 West Pullen Street, Pine Bluff, Arkansas
Age: 78

WILLIAM LATTIMORE

"Yes'm I was a slave—I was born in 1859 in Mississippi. During the war I wasn't grown but I can remember when the Yankee soldiers come to Canton, Mississippi. We was sittin' out in the yard and the white folks was on the porch when they was bombardin' Jackson. We could hear the cannons. The white people said the Yankees was tryin' to whip the rebellion and set the niggers free. When they got done I didn't know what had happened but I remember the colored people packed up and we all went to Vicksburg. My father ran off and jined the Yankee army. He was in Colonel Zeigler's regiment in the infantry. I knowed General Grant when I seed him. I know when Abraham Lincoln died the soldiers (Yankees) all wore that black band around their arms.

"After my father was mustered out we went to Warren County, Mississippi to live. He worked on the halves with a schoolteacher named Mr. Hannum. He said he was my godfather.

"One time after the war Mr. Lattimore came and wanted my father to live with him but I didn't want him to because before the surrender old master whipped my father over the head with a walking stick 'cause he stayed too long and I was afraid he would whip him again.

"'Did you ever vote?' Me? Yes ma'm I voted. I don't remember who I voted for first—my 'membrance don't serve me—I ain't got that fresh enough in my memory. I served eight years as Justice of the Peace after I come to Arkansas. I remember one time they put one colored man in office and I said that's pluckin' before it is ripe. We elected a colored sheriff in Warren County once. The white men went on his bond, but after awhile the Ku Klux compelled them to get off and then he couldn't make bond. He appealed to the citizens to let him stay in office without bond but they wouldn't do it. When a man is trying to get elected they promise a lot of things but afterwards they is just like a duck—they swim off on the other side.

"I went to school after freedom and kept a goin' till I was married. I was a school director when I was eighteen. I didn't have any children and the superintendent who was very rigid and strict said 'Boy you is not even a patron of the school.' But he let me serve. I used to visit the school 'bout twice a week and if the teacher was not doin' right, I sure did lift my voice against it.

"I lived in Chicot County when I first come to Arkansas and when I moved to Jefferson County, Judge Harry E. Cook sent my reputation up here. I ain't never peeped into a jailhouse or had handcuffs on these hands.

"We've got to do something 'bout this younger generation. You never saw anything sicker. They is degenerating.

"I hold up my right hand, swear to uphold the Constitution and preserve the flag and I don't think justice is being done when they won't let the colored folks vote. We'd like to harmonize things here. God made us all and said 'You is my chillun.'"

United States. Work Projects Administration

Interviewer: Miss Irene Robertson
Person interviewed: Bessie Lawsom,
Helena, Arkansas
Age: 76
[Date Stamp: MAY 31 1938]

BESSIE LAWSOM

"I was born in Georgia. My mama was brought from Virginia to one of the Carolina states, then to Georgia. She was sold twice. I don't recollect but one of her masters. I heard her speak of Master Bracknell. His wife, now I remember her well. She nursed me. I was sickly and they needed her to work in the crop so bad. She done had a baby leetle older than I was, so I nursed one breast and Jim the other. She raised me and Jim together. Mama was name Sallie and papa Mathew Bracknell. They called him Mat Bracknell. I don't know my master's name. They had other children.

"Me and Jim dug wells out in the yard and buried all the little ducks and chickens and made graves. We had a regular burying ground we made. They treated us pretty good as fur as I knowed. I never heard mama complain. She lived till I was forty years old. Papa died a few years after freedom. He had typhoid fever. He was great to fish. I believe now he got some bad water to drink out fishing. There was six of us and three half children. I'm the onliest one living as I knows of. One sister died in 1923 in Atlanta. She come to see me. She lived with big rich folks there. She was a white man's girl. She never had so much bad luck as we dark skin children the way it was. My papa had to go to war with some of Master Bracknell's kin folks, maybe his wife's kin folks, and they took him to wait on them at the battle-fields. Some soldiers camped by at the last of the war. They stole her out. She went to take something to a sick widow woman for old mistress. She never got back for a week. She said she was so scared and one day when her man, the man that claimed her, went off on a scout trip she asked a man, seemed to be a big boss, could she go to that thicket and get some black gum toothbrushes. He let her ride a little old broken down horse out there. She had a bridle but she was bare back. She come home through the pasture and one of the colored boys took the horse back nearly to the camps and turned him loose. 'Fo'e my own papa got back she had a white chile. Master Bracknell was proud of her. Papa didn't make no difference in her and his children. After the War he bought a whole bolt of cloth when he went to town. Mama would make us all a dress alike. The Yankees whooped mama at their camp. She said she was afraid to try to get away and that come in her mind. Old mistress thought that widow woman was keeping her to wait on her and take care of her small children. She wasn't uneasy and they took care of me.

"I don't recollect freedom. I heard mama say a drove come by and ask her to come go to Atlanta; they said Yankees give 'em Atlanta. She said she knowed if she went off papa wouldn't know where she was. She told 'em she had two young children she couldn't leave. They went on. She told old mistress and she said she done right not to go.

"The Yankees stole mama's feather bed. Old mistress had great big high feather beds and big pillows. Mama had a bed in a shed room open out on the back piazza. They put them big beds across their horses and some took pillows and down the road they went. It was cold and the ground froze. They made cotton beds then and the Yankees done got all the geese and chickens. They nearly starved. The Yankees took all the cows and stock.

"Master Bracknell was cripple. He had a store at Cross Roads. It was twenty-five miles from Marietta, Georgia. They never troubled him like they did old mistress. She was scared of them. She knowed if they come and caught her gone they would set fire to the house. No, they never burned nothing on our place but they did some in sight. I can remember seeing big fires about at night and day time too.

"We lived on Master Bracknell's place till I was eight years old and my sister five. We come to South, Alabama, then to Mississippi and then up the river to Helena. I married in Jackson, Mississippi. A white boy married us. We lived on his place and he was going to preach. He wasn't a preacher then. Richard Moore was his name. It took him several weeks to learn what to say. He practiced on us. He thought a heap of me and he ask Jesse if he could marry us. He brought us a big fine cake his mother cooked for us when he come. My husband named Jesse Lawsom. He was raised in Louisiana. We lived together till he died. My mother went blind before she died. His mother lived there, then we took care of them and after he died his mother lived with me. Now I lives with this niece here some and my daughter in Jackson. I had fourteen children. I just got one left and grandchildren I go to see. I make the rounds. Some of 'em good and some of them ain't no account at tall.

"I used to take advice. They get up and leave the place. They don't want old folks to advise 'em. If they can't get their price they sit around and go hungry. They won't work for what I used to be glad to get. I keep my girl on the right path and that is all I can do. My niece don't work out but her husband works on the farm all the time. She helps him. They go out and live till the work is done. He is off now ploughing. Times is fast sure as you born, girl. Faster 'an ever I seen."

Interviewer: Miss Irene Robertson
Person interviewed: Henry Lee
R.F.D., two and one-half miles, Palestine, Arkansas
Age: 87

HENRY LEE

"I was born close to Huntsville, Alabama during slavery. My master was Tom Laughinghouse and Miss Fannie, his wife. They had two children, Jarman and Mattie. He was Dr. George Laughinghouse's brother. Dr. George lived at Forrest City.

"He brung us to the old Pope place close to Forrest City after 'mancipation. We didn't know we was free. Finally we kept hearing folks talk, then Master Tom told us we was free. We cleared land right on after freedom like we was slaves.

"General Lee, a white man, owned a boat on the Mississippi River. He owned my father. We took on his name way after freedom. Mother was Becky Laughinghouse and father was Willis Lee. They had six children.

"After I come to Arkansas I went to school three days to a white man. He was sont here from the North somewhere.

"My folks was all black pure stock niggers and field folks same as I is.

"Mother's owners was good to her. They give them all day Saturday to wash and iron and cook for her folks. They got a whooping if they went to the field Monday morning dirty. They was very good to us. I can recollect that. They was a reasonable set of white folks. They weighed out everything. They whooped their hands. They had a white overseer but he wasn't hired to whoop Laughinghouse's slaves.

"They 'lowed mother to weave at her home at night. He had seven or eight families on his farm.

"The well was a curiosity to me then and would sure be one now. We had a walled and curbed well. A long forked pole, a short chain and a long rope. We pulled up the water by the long forked pole. Cold! It was good cold water. Beats our water all to pieces.

"The soldiers come up in a drove one day and ask mother for me. She didn't let any of us go.

"Our master got killed over here close to Forrest City. We all picked cotton, then we all went to gin. A coupling pin broke and let a wooden block come down on him. It weighed one thousand pounds I expect. He was spreading a sheet and smoothing the cotton. It mashed and smothered him both. That was first of our scattering.

"The colored folks raised gardens in the fence corners. They raised a heap of stuff that way. We lived a heap better then than now.

"My father died and mother started sharecropping. First, one-half and then, one-third went to us. Things went on very well till the commissary come about. The nigger got figured clean out.

"Nearly all the women of them days wore bonnets

or what they called hoods one the other. Boys wore long shirts to calf of their legs.

"We rode oxen to church. Many time rode to church and home in ox wagon.

"Ku Kluxes followed Pattyrollers, then come on White Caps. If the Pattyrollers kilt a slave he had to pay the master the price. The Ku Kluxes rode at night. All of 'em's main business was to keep the slaves at their own places and at work. Iffen the master instructed them to keep offen his place they kept off. They never come on our place. But though I was feared of 'em.

"I needs help and I don't git it. I applied. 'Cause a grandson helps us a little I don't git the welfare pension. I need it and I think I ought to git it. I worked hard, bought this house, paid my taxes—still trying. Still they don't aid me now and I passed aiding my own self. I think I oughten to git lef' out 'cause I help myself when I could. I sure is left out. Been left out.

"A part of the people is accountable for the way the times is going on. Some of them is getting it all and don't give the others no show a tall. Times is powerful hard for some and too easy for others. Some is turned mean and some cowed down and times hard for them what can't work hard."

United States. Work Projects Administration

Interviewer: Miss Sallie C. Miller
Person interviewed: Mandy Lee,
Coal Hill, Arkansas
Age: 85

MANDY LEE

"Yes'm I was a slave. I been here. I heard the bugles blowing, the fife beat, the drums beat, and the cannons roar. We started to Texas but never got across the river. I don't know what town it was but it was just across the river from Texas. My white folks was good to me. I staid with them till they died. Missy died first, then master died. I never was away from them. They was both good. My mammy was sold but I never was. They said they was surrendered when we come back from Texas. I heard the drums beat at Ft. Smith when we come back but I don't know what they was doing. I worked in the house with the children and in the field too. I help herd the horses. I would card and spin and eat peaches. No, that wasn't all I had to eat. I didn't have enough meat but I had plenty of milk and potatoes. I was born right here in Coal Hill. I ain't never lived anywhere else except when we went South during the war.

"Law woman I can't tell you what I think of the present generation. They are good in their way but they don't do like we did. I never did go naked. I don't see how they stand it.

"I could sing when I was young. We sang everything, the good and bad."

Interviewer: Mrs. Bernice Bowden
Person interviewed: Mary Lee
1308 Texas Street, Pine Bluff, Arkansas
Age: 74
[Date Stamp: MAY 31 1938]

MARY LEE

"I was born in 1864, March the fourth, the year before the Civil War ended. All I know is what they told me and what I read.

"Born in Texas, but my mother and father was both born in Georgia.

"My mother said her white folks was good to her. She was the house girl, she didn't have to work in no field.

"I went to school when I was six or eight. I don't remember which. I had right smart schooling.

"I remember my mother's young missis run off and got married. She was just a young girl, 'bout seventeen. That's been a long time.

"I got a book sent to me a while back. It's a Catholic book—'History of Church and State.' Yes'm, I'm a Catholic. Used to belong to the Methodist church, but I wouldn't be a Methodist no more. I like the Catholics. You would too if you was one of 'em.

"I been here in Arkansas since 1891. That's goin' right on up the road.

"I can't do much work now, my breath gets short.

"I used to make thirty-five dollars a month washin' and ironin'. Oh, that was a long time 'fore the depression.

"I don't think nothin' of this younger generation. All goin' the same way. Oh lord, you better let 'em alone, they won't take no foolishness."

Interviewer: Mrs. Bernice Bowden
Person interviewed: Talitha Lewis
300 E. 21st Avenue, Pine Bluff, Arkansas
Age: 86
[Date Stamp: MAY 31 1938]

TALITHA LEWIS

"I should say I was born in slavery times! Now if you ask me something I don't know, I couldn't tell you, honey, 'cause I believe in people tellin' the truth.

"In a way I know how old I is. I give what my white folks give me. They told me I was born in 1852. Yes ma'am, my young missis used to set down and work on me. She'd say, 'Get it in your head' 'cause I ain't got no education.

"I 'member my old missis. Know her name as good as I do mine. Name was Maria Whitley. After old master died, his property was divided and Jim Whitley drawed me and my mother and my sister. Yes ma'am, it was my sister.

"Goldsboro, North Carolina is where I was born, in Johnston County.

"Do I 'member anything 'bout peace declared? I should say I do—'member long time 'fore it come.

"I seed so many different regiments of people I didn't know which was which. I know the Yankees called ever'body Dinah. They'd say to me, 'Dinah, hold my horse,' and my hands would be full of bridles. And they'd say, 'You got anything buried?' The white folks had done buried the meat under my mother's house. And say, 'Is they good to you?' If they hadn't a been we wouldn't a known any better than to tell it.

"I 'member they found where the meat was buried and they ripped up my mother's feather bed and filled it full of hams and shoulders, and there wasn't a middlin' in the lot. And kill chickens and geese! They got ever'thing and anything they wanted.

"There was a battle-field about four miles from us where they fit at.

"Honey, I can't tell it like I know it, but I know it.

"Old master was a good man. You had plenty to eat and plenty to wear. And on Monday morning all his colored folks had clean clothes. I wish I could tell it like I know. He was a good man but he had as mean a wife as I ever saw. She used to be Nettie Sherrod and she did not like a black face. Yes ma'am, Jim Whitley was a good man but his father was a devil.

"If Massa Jim had a hand he couldn't control, he sold him. He said he wasn't goin' to beat 'em or have 'em run off and stay in the woods. Yes'm, that was my master, Jim Whitley.

"His overseer was Zack Hill when peace declared.

"How long I been in Arkansas? Me? We landed at Marianna, Arkansas in 1889. They emigranted us here. They sure said they had fritter trees and a molasses pond. They said to just shake the tree and the fritters would fall in the pond. You know anybody that had any sense wouldn't believe that. Yes ma'am, they sure told that lie. 'Course there was times when you could make good money here.

"I know I is a slave time chile. I fared well but I sure did see some that didn't.

"Our white folks had hands that didn't do nothin' but make clothes and sheets and kivers.

"Baby, them Ku Klux was a pain. The paddyrollers was bad enough but them Ku Klux done lots of devilment. Yes ma'am, they done some devilment.

"I worked for a white man once was a Ku Klux, but I didn't know it for a long time. One time he said, 'Now when you're foolin' around in my closet cleanin' up, I want you to be pertickler.' I seed them rubber pants what they filled with water. I reckon he had enough things for a hundred men. His wife say, 'Now, Talitha, don't let on you know what them things is.'

"Now my father belonged to the Adkins. He and my mother was married with a stiffcate 'fore peace declared and after peace declared they got a license and was married just like they marry now.

"My master used to ask us chillun, 'Do your folks pray at night?' We said 'no' 'cause our folks had told us what to say. But the Lawd have mercy, there was plenty of that goin' on. They'd pray, 'Lawd, deliver us from under bondage.'

"Colored folks used to go to the white folks' church. I was raised up under the old Primitive Baptist feet washin' church. Oh, that's a time, baby!

"What I think of the younger generation? I don't know what to think of 'em. I don't think—I know they is goin' too fast.

"I learned how to read the Bible after I 'fessed religion. Yes ma'am, I can read the Bible, praise the Lawd!"

Interviewer: Samuel S. Taylor
Person interviewed: Abbie Lindsay
914 W. Tenth Street, Little Rock, Arkansas
Age: 84

ABBIE LINDSAY

[HW: cf. Will Glass' story, No. ——?]

"I was born June 1, 1856; the place at that time was called Lynngrove, Louisiana. It was just about a mile from the post office, and was in Morehouse Parish in the first ward—in the tenth ward I mean.

Relatives

"My father was named Alec Summerville. He named himself after the Civil War. They were going around letting the people choose their names. He had belonged to Alec Watts; but when they allowed him to select his own name after the war, he called himself Summerville after the town Summerville (Somerville), Alabama. His mother was named Charlotte Dantzler. She was born in North Carolina. John Haynes bought her and brought her to Arkansas. My father was an overseer's child. You know they whipped people in those days and forced them. That is why he didn't go by the name of Watts after he got free and could select his own name.

"The name of my mother's mother was Celia Watts.

I don't know my grandfather's first name. Old man Alec Watts' father gave my mother to him. I didn't know anything about that except what was told to me. They bought her from South Carolina. They came to Louisiana. My father was bought in South Carolina too. After the Haynes met the Watts, Watts married old man Haynes' daughter. He gave my father to his daughter, Mary Watts. She was Mary Watts after she was married. She was Mary Haynes before. Watts' father gave my mother to Alec Watts. That is just the way it was.

"My mother and father had three children to live. I think there were about thirteen in all. There are just two of us living now. I couldn't tell you where Jeffrey Summerville, my living brother, is living now.

Slave Houses

"The slaves lived in hewed-log houses. I have often seen hewed-log houses. Have you ever seen one? You cut big logs and split them open with a maul and a wedge. Then you take a pole ax and hack it on both sides. Then you notch it—cut it into a sort of tongue and groove joint in each end. Before you cut the notches in the end, you take a broad ax and hew it on both sides. The notch holds the corners of the house-ties every corner. You put the rafters up just like you do now. Then you lathe the rafters and then put boards on top of the rafters. Sometimes shingles were used on the rafters instead of boards.

"You would finish off the outside of the walls by making clay cakes out of mud and filling up the cracks with them. When that clay got hard, nothing could go through the walls. Sometimes thin boards were nailed on the inside to finish the interior.

Furniture and Food

"They had planks—homemade wooden beds. They made tables and chairs. They caned the chairs. They made the tables with four legs. You made it just like you would make a box, adding the legs.

"A little house called the smokehouse was built in one of the corners of the yard. They would weigh out to each one so much food for the week's supply—mostly meat and meal, sometimes rice. They'd give you parched meal and rye too.

"Sometimes they had the slaves cook their food in the cabins. Mostly all the time. My people ate in the kitchen because my mother was the cook and my father was the yard man. The others mostly cooked at home—in their cabins.

Work

"My mother and father worked around the house and yard. Slaves in the field had to pick a certain amount of cotton. The man had to pick from two to three hundred pounds of cotton a day if he wasn't sick, and the woman had to pick about one hundred fifty. Of course some of them could pick more. They worked in a way of speaking from can till can't, from the time they could see until the time they couldn't. They do about the same thing now.

Recreation

"I remember the time the white folks used to make the slaves all come around in the yard and sing every Sunday evening. I can't remember any of the songs straight through. I can just remember them in spots.

>'Give me Jesus, you can have all the world
>In the morning when I arise, Give me Jesus.'
>
>(Fragment)
>
>'Lie on him if you sing right
>Lie on him if you pray right
>God knows that your heart is not right
>Come, let us go to heaven anyhow.'
>
>(Fragment)
>
>'The ark was seen at rest upon the hill
>On the hills of Calvary
>And Great Jehovah spoke
>Sanctify to God upon the hill.'
>
>(First verse)
>
>'Peter spied the promised land
>On the hill of Calvary
>And Great Jehovah spoke
>Sanctify to God upon the hill.'
>
>(Second verse)

There was lots more that they sung.

"They could go to parties too, but when they went to them or to anything else, they had to have a pass. When they went to a party the most they did was to play the fiddle and dance. They had corn huskings every Friday night, and they ground the meal every Saturday. The corn husking was the same as fun. They didn't serve anything on the place where I was. I never knew them to serve anything at the corn shuckings or at the parties. Sometimes they would give a picnic, and they would kill a hog for that.

Life Since Freedom

"Right after the war, my father hired me out to nurse. Then I stayed around the house and helped my stepmother, and the white girls taught me a little until I got to be thirteen years old. Then I got three months' schooling in a regular school. I came here in 1915. I had been living in Newport before that. Yes, I been married, and that's all you need to know about that. I got two children: one fifty-three years old, and the other sixty.

Opinions

"I don't have much thinking to do about the young people. It's a lost race without a change."

Interviewer's Comment

"Mother" Lindsay is a Bible-reading, neat and clean-appearing, pleasant-mannered business woman, a little bulky, but carrying herself like a woman thirty years. She runs a cafe on Ninth Street and manages her own business competently. She refers to it as "Hole in the Wall." I had been trying for sometime to catch her away from her home. It was almost impossible for me to get a story from her at her restaurant or at her home.

She doesn't like to sit long at a time and doesn't like to tell too much. When she feels quarters are a little close and that she is telling more than she wants to, she says, "Honey, I ain't got no more time to talk to you; I got to get back to the cafe and get me a cup of coffee."

Will Glass, who has a story of his own, collaborated with her on her story. He has an accurate and detailed memory of many things. He is too young to have any personal memories. But he remembers everything he has been told by his grandparents and parents, and they seem to have talked freely to him unlike the usual parents of that period.

Interviewer: Mrs. Bernice Bowden
Person interviewed: Rosa Lindsey
302 S. Miller Street, Pine Bluff, Arkansas
Age: 83

ROSA LINDSEY

"I was born in Georgia and I'm 83.

"My white folks was named Abercrombie.

"I don't remember my mother and I hardly remember my father. My white folks raised me up. I 'member my missis had me bound to her when I was twelve. I know when my grandma come to take me home with her, I run away from her and went back to my white folks.

"My white folks was rich. I belonged to my young missis. She didn't 'low nobody to hit me. When she went to school she had me straddle the horse behind her. The first readin' I ever learned was from the white folks.

"I think the Yankees took Columbus, Georgia on a Sunday morning. I know they just come through there and tore up things and did as they pleased.

"I stayed there a long time after the Yankees went back.

"Old master wasn't too old to go to war but he didn't go. I think he had to dodge around to keep the Yankees from gettin' him. I think he went to Texas but we didn't go.

"I loved my white folks 'cause I knowed more about them than anybody else.

"I come here to Arkansas with a young white lady just married. She 'suaded me to come with her and I just stayed.

"Biggest thing I have did is washin' and ironin'. But now I am doing missionary work in the Sanctified church.

"I don't know 'bout the younger generation. Looks like 'bout near ever'body lost now. There's some few young people is saved now but they ain't many."

Interviewer: Thomas Elmore Lucy
Person interviewed: William Little,
Atkins, Arkansas
Age: 83

WILLIAM LITTLE

"I was born on the plantation of Dr. Andrew Scott, but my old ma'ster was Col. Ben T. Embry. The 14th of March, in the year 1855, was my birthday. Yes suh, I was born right here at old Galla Rock! My old Ma'ster Embry had a good many slaves. He went to Texas and stayed about three years. Took a lot of us along, and de first work I ever done after I was set free was pickin' cotton at $2 a hundred pounds. Dere was seventy-five or a hundred of us freed at once. Yes suh! Den we drove five hundred miles back here from Texas, and drove five hundred head of stock. We was refigees—dat's de reason we had to go to Texas.

"Father and mother both passed away a good many years ago. Oh, yes, dey was mighty well treated while dey was in slavery; never was a kinder mas'r anywhere dan my old mas'r. And he was wealthy, too—had lots of land, and a store, and plenty of other property. Many of the slaves stayed on as servants long after the War, and lived right around here at old Galla Rock.

"No suh, I never belonged to no chu'ch; dey thought I done too much of the devil's work—playin' the fiddle. Used to play the fiddle for dances all around the neighborhood. One white man gave me $10 once for playin' at a dance. Played lots of the old-time pieces like 'Turkey in the Straw', 'Dixie', and so on.

"We owns our home here, and I has another one. Been married twice and raised eighteen chillun. Yes suh, we've lived here eighteen years, and had fine health till last few years, but my health is sorter po'ly now. Got a swellin' in my laigs.

"(Chuckling) I sure remembers lots of happy occasions down here in days before the War. One day the steamboat come up to the landin'. It was named the Maumelle—yes suh, Maumelle, and lots of hosses and cattle was unloaded from the steamer. Sure was busy days then. And our old mas'r was mighty kind to us."

NOTE: "Uncle Bill" did not know how he came about the name "Little." Perhaps it was a nickname bestowed upon him to distinguish him from some other William of larger stature. However, he stands fully six feet in height, and has a strong, vigorous voice. He is the sole surveying ex-slave of the Galla Rock community.

Interviewer: Thomas Elmore Lucy
Person interviewed: "Aunt Minerva" Lofton
Russellville, Arkansas
Age: 69

MINERVA LOFTON

"Come in! Yes, my name's Minerva Lofton—at least it was yistiddy. Now, whatcha gonna ask me? Hope you ain't saying something that'll git me in bad. Don't want to git in any more trouble. Hard times' bad enough.

"I was born in the country nine miles from Clarendon, Monroe County, December 3, 1869. Father died before I was born. My mother came from Virginia, and her mistress' name was Bettie Clark. They lived close to Richmond, and people used to say 'Blue Ridge,' so I think it was Blue Ridge County, Virginia. Mother was sold to Henry Cargile—C-a-r-g-i-l-e.

"When they were expecting peace to be declared soon a lot of the colored people named Parks took many of the slaves to Texas to escape from the Yankees, but when they got to Corpus Christi they found the Yankee soldiers there just the same, so they came back to Arkansas. I sure used to laugh at my dear old mother when she'd tell about the long trip to Corpus Christi, and things that happened on the way. They stopped over at Camden as they went through, and one of the colored gals who hated her played a prank on her to take out her spite on mother:

They had stopped at a dairyman's home near Camden, and she sent my mother in to get a gallon of buttermilk. After drinking all she could hold she grabbed mother by the hair of the head and churned her up and down in the buttermilk till it streamed down her face, and on her clothes—a sight to behold. I laughed and laughed until my sides ached when mother told me about this.

"Old mistis' name (that is, one of the old mistis') was Bettie Young, and my mother was named Bettie for her; she was a namesake—sort of a wedding present, I think.

"I've been a member of the Pentecostal church for nineteen years.

"No sir, I never have voted and never expect to. Why? Because I have a religious opinion about votin'. I think a woman should not vote; her place is in the home raising her family and attending to the household duties. We have raised only two boys (stepchildren)—had no children of our own—but I have decided ideas about women runnin' around among and votin'. When I see em settin' around the ballot box at the polls, sometimes with a cigarette in their mouths, and again slingin' out a 'damn' or two, I want to slap em good and hard.

"Yes, the old time religious songs—I sure remember some of them! Used to be able to sing lots of em, but have forgotten the words of many. Let's see:

> 'I'm a-goin' to tell my Lord, Daniel in de lion's den;
> I'm a-goin' to tell my Lord, I'm a-goin' to tell my Lord,
>
> Daniel in de lion's den.'

Here's another:

> 'Big bells a-ringin' in de army of de Lord;
> Big bells a-ringin' in de army.
> I'm so glad I'm in de army of de Lord;
> My soul's a-shoutin' in de army.'

"Modern youth? Humph! I think they are just a fulfilling of what Christ said: 'They shall grow wiser as they grow older, but weaker.' Where is it in the Scripture? Wait a minute and I'll look it up. Now, let's see—where was that passage? It says 'weaker' here and 'weaken'. Never mind—wait—I'll find it. Well, anyway, I don't know jest how to describe this generation. I heard a white woman once say that she had to do a little cussin' to make herself understood. 'Cussin'?' Why, 'cussin'' is jist a polite word for it.

"Good-bye, mister. You oughta thank the Lawd you've got a job!"

United States. Work Projects Administration

FOLKLORE SUBJECTS

Name of Interviewer: S. S. Taylor
Subject: Biographical Sketch of Robert Lofton
Story—Information (If not enough space on this page add page)

This information given by: Robert Lofton
Place of Residence: 1904 Cross Street, Little Rock, Arkansas
Occupation: Farmer (no longer able to work)
Age: 82

ROBERT LOFTON

[TR: Personal information moved from bottom of form.]

Robert Lofton was born March 11, 1855 in McDonogh, Georgia. His master lived in town and owned two Negro women and their children. One of these was Lofton's mother.

His father was a Negro who lived back of him and belonged to the local postmaster. He had a wagon and did public hauling for his master, Dr. Tie. He was allowed to visit his wife and children at nights, and was kept plentifully supplied with money by his master.

Lofton's master, Asa Brown, bought, or acquired from time to time in payment of debts, other slaves. These he hired out to farmers, collecting the wages for their labor.

After the war, the Lofton family came to Arkansas and lived in Lee County just outside of Oak Forest. They were share croppers and farmers throughout their lives. He has a son, however, a war veteran and unusually intelligent.

Robert Lofton is a fine looking old man, with silky white hair and an octoroon appearance, although the son of two colored persons.

He remembers scarcely anything because of fading mental powers, but he is able to take long walks and contends that only in that way can he keep free from rheumatic pains. He speaks of having died recently and come back to life, is extremely religious, and is fearful of saying something that he should not.

"I was in McDonogh, Georgia when the surrender came. [HW: That is where I was born on March 11, 1855.] There was plenty of soldiers in that little town—Yankees and Rebels. And they was sending mail out through the whole country. The Rebels had as good chance to know what was in the mail as the Yanks (his mother's husband's master was postmaster) did.

How Freedom Came

"The slaves learned through their masters that they were free. The Yankees never told the niggers anything. They could tell those who were with them that they were free. And they notified the people to notify their niggers that they were free. 'Release him. If he wants to stay with you yet, he may. We don't require him to go away but you must let him know he is free.'

"The masters said, 'You are free now, Johnnie, just as free as I am.' Many of them put their things in a little wagon and moved to some other plantation or town or house. But a heap of them stayed right where they were.

"My father found out before my mother did. He was living across town behind us about one-fourth of a mile. Dr. Tie, his master, had a post office, and that post office was where they got the news. My father got the news before my master did. He got on to it through being on with Dr. Tie. So my father got the news before my master, Asa Brown, did and he come over and told my mother before my master did. But my master came out the next thing and told her she could go or come as she pleased. She said she'd stay right along. And we got along just as we always did—until my father came and told us he was going to Atlanta with a crew of Yankees.

Employment and Post-War Changes in Residence

"He got a wagon and a team and run us off to the railroad. He got a job at Atlanta directly. After he made a year in Atlanta, he got dissatisfied. He had two girls who were big enough to cut cotton. So he decided to go farm. He went to Tennessee and we made a crop there. Then he heard about Arkansas and came here.

"When he came here, somehow or other, he got in a fight with a colored man. He got the advantage of that man and killed him. The officers came after him, but he left and I ain't never seen nor heard of him since. He went and left my poor mother and her five children alone. But I was getting big enough to be some help. And we made crops and got along somehow.

"I don't know what we expected. I never heerd anyone

say a word. I was children you know, and it was mighty little that children knew because the old folks did not talk with them much.

What They Got

"I never heerd of anything any of them got. I never heerd of any of them getting anything except work. I don't recollect any pension or anything being given them—nothing but work.

Folks on this place would leave and go over on that place, and folks on that place would come over here. They ate as long as the white folks ate. We stayed with our old master and mistress, (Mr. Asa Brown and Mrs. Sallie Brown).

Good Master and Mistress

"They did not whip us. They didn't whip nobody they had. They were good white folks. My mother never was whipped. She was not whipped after the surrender and she wasn't whipped before. [We lived in the same house as our master] [HW: (in margin) see p. 6] and we ate what he ate.

Wives and Husbands

"There was another woman my master owned. Her husband belonged to another white man. My father also belonged to another white man. Both of them would come and stay with their wives at night and go back to work with their masters during the day. My mother had her kin folks who lived down in the country and my mother used to go out and visit them. I had a grandmother way out in the country. My mother used to take me and go out and stay a day or so. She would arrange with mistress and master and go down Saturday and she would take me along and leave her other children with this other woman. Sunday night she would make it back. Sometimes she wouldn't come back until Monday.

"It didn't look like she was any freer after freedom than she was before. She was free all the time she was a slave. They never whipped her. Asa Brown never whipped his niggers.

Letting Out Slaves

"Asa Brown used to rent out his niggers, sometimes. You know, they used to rent them. But he never rented my mother though. He needed her all the time. She was the cook. He needed her all the time and he kept her all the time. He let her go to see grandmother and he let her go to church.

"Sometimes my mother went to the white church and sometimes she went to the colored folks church. When we went to the white folks church, we took and sat down in the back and behaved ourselves and that was all there was to it. When they'd have these here big meetings—revivals or protracted meetings they call them—she'd go to the white and black. They wouldn't have them all at the same time and everybody would have a chance to go to all of them.

"They wouldn't allow the colored to preach and they

wouldn't even call on them to pray but he could sing as good as any of them.

"Generally all colored preachers that I knowed of was slaves. The slaves attended the churches all right enough—Methodists and Baptists both white and black. I never heard of the preachers saying anything the white folks did not like.

"The Methodists' church started in the North. There was fourteen or fifteen members that got dissatisfied with the Baptist church and went over to the Methodist church. The trouble was that they weren't satisfied with our Baptism. The Baptists were here before the Methodists were thought of. These here fourteen or fifteen members came out of the North and started the Methodist church going.

Share Cropping

"Share cropping has been ever since I knowed anything. It was the way I started. I was working the white man's land and stock and living in his house and getting half of the cotton and corn. We had a garden and raised potatoes and greens and so on, but cotton and corn was our crop. Of course we had them little patches and raised watermelon and such like.

Food and Quarters

"We ate whatever the white man ate. My mother was the cook. She had a cook-room joined to her room [which reached clear over to the white folks' house.] [HW: see

p. 4] Everything she cooked on that stove, we all ate it, white and black—some of the putting, [HW: pudding] some of the cakes, some of the pies, some of the custard, some of the biscuits, some of the corn bread—we all had it, white and black. I don't know no difference at all. Asa Brown was a good old man. There was some mean slave owners, but he wasn't one.

Whippings

"You could hear of some mean slave owners taking switches and beating their niggers nearly to death. But I never heard of my old master doing that. Slaves would run away and it would be a year or two before they would be caught. Sometimes they would take him and strip him naked and whip him till he wasn't able to stand for running away. But I never heard of nothing like that happening with Asa Brown. But he sometimes would sell a hand or buy one sometimes. He'd take a nigger in exchange for a debt and rent him out.

Voting

"There wasn't any voting by the slaves. But ever since freedom they have been voting. None of my friends ever held any office. I don't know anything about the niggers not voting now. Don't they vote?

Patter Rollers, K. K. K., White Carmelias, Etc.

"My mother and father knowed about Patter Rollers, but I don't know nothing about them. But they are dead and gone. I have heard of the Ku Klux but I don't know nothing about it. I don't know what I used to know. No sir, I am out of the question now.

"There is one thing I keep straight. When I wants to drink or when I wants to eat—oh yes, I know how to go to bed.

"You know I have seen the time when they would get in a close place and they would make me preach, but it's all gone from me now. I can't recollect."

Mary D. Hudgins
107 Palm Street,
Hot Springs, Ark.

Interviewer: Mary D. Hudgins
Person interviewed: John H. Logan
Aged: c. 89
Home: 449 Gaines Avenue.
[Date Stamp: MAY 11 1938]

JOHN H. LOGAN

Gaines Avenue was once a "Quality Street". It runs on a diagonal from Malvern Avenue, a one-time first class residential thorofare to the Missouri Pacific Tracks. Time was when Gaines led almost to the gates of the fashionable Combes Racetrack.

Built up during the days of bay windows Gaines Avenue has preserved half a dozen land marks of former genteelity. Long stretches between are filled "shot gun" houses, unaquainted for many years with a paintbrush.

Within half a block of the streetcar line on Malvern an early spring had encouraged plowing of a 200 foot square garden. Signs such as "Hand Laundry" appear frequently. But by far the most frequent placard is "FOR SALE" a study in black and white, the insignia of a local real estate firm specializing in foreclosures.

The street number sought proved to be two doors beyond the red brick church. A third knock brought a slight, wrinkled face to the door, its features aquiline, in coloring only the mildest of mocha. Its owner Laura Burton Logan, after satisfying herself that the visitor wasn't just an intruder, opened the door wide and invited her to come inside.

"Logan, oh Logan, come on here, come on in here," she called to an old man in the next room. "Law, I don't know whether he can tell you anything or not. He's getting pretty feeble. Now five or six years ago he could have told you lots of things. But now——I don't know."

Into the "front room" hobbled the old fellow. His back was bent, his eyes dimmed with age. His face was the sort often called "good"—not good in the sense stupid acquiescence—but rather evidence of an intelligent, non-preditory meeting of the problems of life.

A quarter, handed the old fellow at the beginning of the interview remained clutched in his hand throughout the entire conversation. Because of events during the talk the interviewer reached for her change purse to find and offer another quarter. It was not in her purse. Getting up from her chair she looked on the floor about her. It wasn't there. Mrs. Logan, who had gone back to bed, wanted to know what the trouble was, and was worried when she found what was missing. By manner the interviewer put over the idea that she wasn't suspecting either of the two. But Logan, not having heard the entire conversation got to his feet and extended his hand—the one holding the quarter, offering it back to the interviewer.

When he rose, there was the purse as it had slipped down on the seat of the rocker which the interviewer had almost taken and in which she had probably carelessly tossed her purse. A second quarter, added to his first, brought a beaming smile from the old man. But for the rest of the afternoon there was a lump in the interviewer's throat. Here was a man, evidently terribly in need of money, ready, without even a tiny protest, to return a gift of cash which must have meant so much to him—on the barest notion in his mind that the interviewer wanted it back.

"Be patient with me ma'am," Logan began, "I can't remember so good. And I want to get it all right. I don't want to spoil my record now. I been honest all my life, always stood up and told the truth, done what was right. I don't want to spoil things and lie in my mouth now. Give me time to think.

I was born, on——December——December 15. It was in 1848——I think. I was born in the house of Mrs. Cozine. She was living on Third Street in Little Rock. It was near the old Catholic Church. Was only a little ways from the State House. Mrs. Cozine, she was my first mistress. Then she sold me, me and my mother and a couple of brothers.

It was Governor Roane she sold me to. Don't know just how old I was——good sized boy, though. Guess I was five—maybe six years old. He was a fine man, Governor Roane was—a mighty fine man. He always treated me good. Raised me up to be a good man.

I remember when he gives us a free-pass. That was during the war. He said, 'Now boys, you be good. You stand for what is right, and don't you tell any stories. I've raised you up to do right.'

When he wasn't governor any more he went back to

Pine Bluff. We lived there a long time. I was with Governor Roane right up until I was grown. I can't right correct things in my mind altogether, but I think I was with him until I was about 20.

When the war come on, Governor Roane helped to gather up troops. He called us in out of the fields and asked us if we wanted to go. I did. Right today I should be getting a pension. I was truly in the army. Ought to be getting a pension. Once a white man, Mr. Williams, I believe his name was, tried to get me to go with him to Little Rock. Getting me a pension would be easy he said. But somehow we never did go.

I worked in the powder factory for a while. Then they set me to hauling things— —mostly food from the Brazos river to Tyler, Texas. We had hard times then— —we had a time— —and don't you let anybody tell you we didn't. Sometimes we didn't have any bread. And even sometimes we didn't have any water. I wasn't so old, but I was a pretty good man— —pretty well grown up.

After the war I went back with my pappy. While I'd belonged to Governor Roane, Roane was my name. But when I went back with father, I took his name. We farmed for a while and later I went to Little Rock.

I did lots of things there. Worked in a cabinet maker's shop for one thing. Was classed as a good workman, too. I worked the lathes. Did a good job of it. I never was the sort that had to walk around looking for work. Folks used to come and get me and ask me to work for them.

How'd I happen to come to Hot Springs? They got me to come to work on the water mains. Worked for the water works a long time. Then I worked for a Mr. Smith in the bath house. I fired the furnace for him. Then for about 15 years I kept the yard at the Kingsway— —the Eastman it was then. I kept the lawn clean at the Eastman Hotel. That was about the last steady work I did.

Yes and in between I used to haul things. Had me an express wagon. Used to build rock walls too. Built good walls.

Who did you say you was, Miss? Your father was Jack Hudgins—Law, child, law— —"

A feeble hand reached for the hand of the white woman and took it. The old eyes filled with tears and the face distorted in weaping. For a few minutes he sat, then he rose, and the young woman rose with him. For a moment she put a comforting arm around him and soon he was quieter.

"Law, so your father was Jack Hudgins. How well I does remember him. Whatever did become of that fine boy? Dead did you say? I remembers now. He was a fine man, a mighty—mighty fine man. Jack Hudgins girl!

Yes, Miss, I guess you has seen me around a lot. Lots of folks know me. They'll come along the street and they'll say, 'Hello Logan!' and sometimes I won't know who they are, but they'll know me.

I remember once, it's been years and years ago, a man come along Central Avenue—a white man. I was going along the street and suddenly he grabbed me and hugged me. It scared me at first. 'Logan,' he says, 'Logan' he says again. 'Logan, I'd know you anywhere. How glad I am to see you.' But I didn't recognize him. 'Wife,' he says 'wife, come on over and speak to Logan, he saved my life once.' Invited me to come and see him too, he did.

Things have been mighty hard for the last few years. Seems like we could get the pension. First they had a rule that we'd have to sign away the home if we got $9.00 a month. Well, my wife's daughter was taking care of us. Even if we got the $9 she'd still have to help. She wasn't making much, but she was dividing everything—going without shoes and everything. So we thought it wasn't fair to her to sign away our home after all she'd done for us——so that they'd just kick her out when we was dead—she'd been too good to us. So we says 'No!' We been told that they done changed that rule, but we can't seem to get help at all. Maybe, Miss, there's somthing you can do. We sure would be thankful, if you could help us get on.

All my folks is dead, my mother and my father and all my brothers, my first and my second wives and both my children. My wife's daughter helps us all she can. She's mighty good to us. Don't know what we'd do without her. Thank you, glad you come to see us. Glad to know you. If you can talk to them over at the Court House, we'd be glad. Good-bye. Come to see us ag in."

Interviewer: Mrs. Bernice Bowden
Person interviewed: Elvie Lomack
Residence: Foot of King Street on river bank, no number; Pine Bluff, Arkansas
Age: 78

ELVIE LOMACK

"Come right in and I'll tell you what I know. I was born in Tennessee in slavery days. No ma'm I do not know what year, because I can't read or write.

"I know who my mistress was. She was Miss Lucy Ann Dillard. She come from Virginia. She was an old maid and she was very nice. Some very good blooded people come from Virginia. She brought my mother with her from Virginia before I was born.

"My father belonged to the Crowders and mammy belonged to Miss Lucy Ann Dillard. They wouldn't sell pappy to Miss Lucy and she wouldn't sell mammy to the Crowders, so mammy lost sight of him and never married again. She just married that time by the consent of the white folks. In them times they wasn't no such thing as a license for the colored folks.

"I remember my mother milked and tended to the cows and issued out the milk to the colored folks.

"Miss Lucy lived in town and come out once a week to see to us. When the overseer was there she come out oftener. We stayed right on there after the war, till we come to Arkansas. I was betwixt eleven and twelve years old.

"And we was fooled in this place. A man my mother knowed had been here two years. He come back to Tennessee and, oh Lord, you could do this and do that, so we come here.

"First year we come here we all got down sick. When we got well we had to go to work and I didn't have a chance to go to school.

"I've seen my mother wring her hands and cry and say she wished she was back in Tennessee where Lucy Ann Dillard was.

"When I got big enough I went to work for Ben Johnson and stayed there fifteen years. I never knew when my payday was. Mammy come and got my pay and give me just what she wanted me to have. And as for runnin' up and down the streets—why mammy would a died first. She's dead and in her grave but I give her credit—she took the best of care of us. She had three girls and they didn't romp up and down the big road neither.

"I just looks at the young folks now. If they had been comin' along when I was, they'd done been tore all to pieces. They ain't raisin' em now, they're just comin' up like grass and weeds. And as for speakin' to you now—just turn their heads. Now I'm just fogy nuf that if I meet you out, I'll say good mornin' or good evenin'.

"If it hadn't been for the Yankees, we'd have the yoke on our necks right today. The Lord got into their hearts.

"Now I don't feel bitter gainst people. Ain't no use

to hold malice gainst nobody—got to have a clean heart. Folks does things cause they's ignorant and don't know no better and they shouldn't be crowned with it.

"But I'll tell you the truth—I've heard my mother say she was happier in slavery times than after cause she said the Dillards certainly took good care of her. Southerners got a heart in em."

United States. Work Projects Administration

Interviewer: Mary D. Hudgins
Person interviewed: Henry Long
Home: 112 East Grand
Age: c. 71

HENRY LONG

"Yes, 'um, I owns my own home—and what's more it's on the same street with the Mayor's house. Yes 'um, I owns a good home, has my own chickens and my flowers and I has a pension of $50 a month.

"Just the other day I got a letter. It wanted me to join the National Association of Retired Federal Workers. I took the letter to the boss and he told me not to bother. Guess I'd better spend my money on myself.

"I got some oil stock too. Been paying pretty good dividends since I had it. Didn't pay any this year. They are digging a new well. That'll maybe mean more money. It's paid pretty good up to now. Yes, me and my wife, we're getting along pretty good. Nothing to worry about.

"Where was I born—it was in Kentucky, Russellville it was, just a few miles from Bowling Green. Yes, 'um, Kentucky was a regular slave state——a genuine slave state. Lots of 'em there.

"The man we belonged to——his name was Gabe Long. I remember hearin' 'em tell how they put him up on one block and sold him. They put his wife up on another and sold her too. Only they both went in different directions. They didn't see each other again for 30 years. By that time he had married again twice. My mother was his third wife. She lived to be 102 and he lived to be 99. Yes, 'um, I comes from a long lived family. There's four of us still living. I got two brothers and one sister. They all live back in Kentucky——pretty close to where we was all born. One time, when I had a vacation——you know they gives you a vacation with pay——30 days vacation it was. Well one time on my vacation I went back to see my sister. She is living with her daughter. She is 78. One brother is living with his son. He's 73. My youngest brother owns his own farm. He is 64. All of 'em back in Kentucky, they've been farmers. I'm the only one who has worked in town. And I never worked in town until I come to Arkansas.

"Been in Hot Springs for over 50 years. Law, when I first come there wasn't any Eastman hotel. There wasn't any Park hotel. I don't mean that Park Hotel up in Happy Hollow. The one I mean was down on Malvern. It burned in the fire of 1913. Law, when I come there wasn't nothing but mule street cars. Hot Springs has seen lots of changes.

"Back in Kentucky I'd been working around where I was born. Worked around the houses mostly. They paid me wages and wanted me to go on working for them. But I decided I wanted to get away. So I went to Little Rock. But didn't find nothing much to do there. Then I went on up Cedar Glades way. Then I come to Hot Springs.

"First I worked for a man who had a big garden——it's out where South Hot Springs is now——oh you know what the man's name was——he was named——he was named—name was Barker, that's it, Barker." (The "Barker Place" has been divided up into lots and blocks and is one of the more popular residential districts.)

"Then I got a job at the Park hotel. No ma'am. I didn't work in the yard. I worked in the refrigerators and the pantry. Then about meal times I served the fruit. You know how a big, fashionable hotel is—there's lots of things that has to be done around 'em.

"Finally I got rheumatism and I had to quit that kind of work. So I got a job firing the furnace at the electric light plant. It was down on Malvern then. That was before the fire of 1913. I was working right there when the fire come. It was pretty awful. It burned just about everything out there on Malvern——and places on lots of other streets too.

"After that I got a job at the Eastman hotel. I fired the furnace and worked on the boilers. Worked there a long time. Then they sent me to the Arlington. You know at that time the same company owned both the Eastman and the Arlington. It wasn't this new Arlington——it was the second one—the red brick one. Built that second one while I was here. The first one was wood.

"Back in the time when I come, there was a creek running through most of the town. There wasn't any Great Northern hotel. There was just a big creek there.

"But how-some-ever, to go on. After I worked at the Arlington on the boilers and the furnace—I got a job at the Army and Navy Hospital. Now that wasn't the new hospital either. It was the old one—it was red brick too.

"Next, I worked at the LaMar Bath house. I was there

a long time——for years and years. Then they got to building over the bath houses. One by one they tore down the old ones and put new ones up. I worked on at the LaMar until they tore the old one down to build the new one. Then I went up to the Quapaw to work. Worked there for quite some time.

"Finally they sent for me to come on down and work for the government. I's worked under a lot of the Superintendents. I started working for the government when Dr.——Dr.——Dr. Warring——Warring was his name. He was a nice man. Then there was Dr. Bolton. I worked for him too. Then there was——there was——oh, what was his name——De—De—DeValin—that's it. Then there was Dr. Collins. He was the last of the Doctors. Then there was Mr. Allen and now Mr. Libbey.

"Yes, 'um, I worked for a lot of 'em and made a HOME RUN with all of 'em. Every one of 'em liked me. I always did good work. All of 'em liked the way I worked.

"Yes 'um. I been married 41 years——20 years to the first woman——21 to this one. The first one come from Mississippi. Her name was Ula. This one's name is Charlotte. She come from Magnolia—that's in Arkansas.

"You know ma'am, I come from Kentucky where they raise fine race horses. I worked around 'em a lot. But I ain't seen many races. We lived out in the country. We had good horses, but they didn't race 'em. I worked with the horses around the place, but we didn't go in town to see the races. What did we raise? Well tobacco and wheat and the usual things. All my folks, but me is still working on farms.

"No 'um, I didn't rightly know how old I was. I was working along, not thinking much about what I was doing. Then the men down at the office" (Hot Springs National Park) "started asking me how old I was. I couldn't tell 'em. But I thought I was born the year the slaves was freed. They said I ought to be retired.

"So they wrote back——or somebody stopped over while he was on his vacation—can't quite remember which. Anyhow they found I was old enough to retire——ought to have retired several years ago. So now I got my home, got my pension and got my time to do what I wants to do."

United States. Work Projects Administration

Interviewer: Mrs. Bernice Bowden
Person interviewed: Annie Love
1116 E. Twelfth Street, Pine Bluff, Arkansas
Age: 85?

ANNIE LOVE

"I don't know exactly how old I am. I was here when the war was goin' on. I know I used to see the soldiers come by and come in, but I wasn't big enough to work. I was born in Richmond, Virginia.

"My owners moved from Virginia to Mississippi. My mother and I lived on one place and my father lived on another plantation. I remember one Sunday he come to see me and when he started home I know I tried to go with him. He got a little switch and whipped me. That's the onliest thing I can remember bout him.

"Billy Cole was my master and I didn't have any mistress cause he never was married.

"My mother worked in the field and I was out there with her when the cannons commenced shootin' at Helena. We said they was shootin' at us and we went to the house. Oh Lord, we said we could see em, Lord yes!

"After surrender, our owner, Billy Cole, told us we was free and that we could go or stay so we stayed there for four or five years. I don't know whether we was paid anything or not. After that we just went from place to place and worked by the day.

"I never did see any Ku Klux but they come to my mother's house one night and wanted my stepfather to show'em where a man lived. He went down the road with 'em a piece. They wanted a drink and, oh Lord, they'd drink mighty nigh a bucket full.

"Oh Lord, when I was young goin' to parties and dances, that was my rule. Oh Lord, I went to them dances.

"I went to church, too. That was one thing I did do. I ain't able to go now but I'll tell anybody when I could, I sure went.

"I went to school mighty little—off and on bout two years. I never learned nothin' though.

"I lived right in Memphis mighty nigh twenty years then I come to Arkansas bout thirty-two years ago and I'm mighty near right where I come to Pine Bluff.

"I don't know of anything else but all my days I believe I've worked hard, cookin' and washin' and ironin'."

Interviewer: Samuel S. Taylor
Person interviewed: Needham Love
1014 W. Seventeenth Street, Little Rock, Arkansas
Age: 80, or older

NEEDHAM LOVE

"Old Joe Love sold us to old Jim McClain, Meridian, Mississippi, and old McClain brought us down on the Tallahatchie River in Mississippi. That was during the War. It was down there on a big old plantation where the cane was high as this house. I was born in Alabama. When the War started, he brought us all down to Meridian and sold us. He sold me in my mother's arms.

"We cut down all that cane and woods and cleared up the place on the Tallahatchie. We did all that before we learned we was free.

"They built log houses for the white and black. They sealed the white folks' houses and chinked the colored folks'. They didn't have but one house for the white folks. There was only one white person down there and that was old Jim McClain. Just come down there in time of harvest. He lived in Lexington the rest of the time. He told his people, 'When I die, bury me in a bale of cotton.' One time he got sick and they thought he would die. They gathered all the hands up and all the people about the place. There was about three hundred. He come to his senses and said, 'What's all these people doing here?'

"His son said, 'Papa, they thought you was goin' to die and they come up to see you.'

"And he said to his son, 'Well, I ain't dead yet. Tell 'em to git back on the job, and chop that cotton.'

"I did not have any work to do in slavery time. When the War ended I was only five years old. But I played the devil after the War though. When the slaves were freed, I shouted, but I ain't got nothin' yet. I learned a lot though. My father used to make a plow or a harrow. They made cotton in those days. Potatoes ain't no 'count now. In them days, they made potatoes so good and sweet that they would gum up your hands. Mothers used to make good old ash cakes. Used to have pot-liquor with grease standin' up on it. People don't know nothin' now. Don't know how to cook.

"My father's name was Joe Love and my mother's name was Sophia. I don't know any of my grandparents. All of them belonged to old Joe Love. I never did know any of them. I know my father and mother—my mammy and pappy—that's what we called 'em in them days.

"Old man Joe would go out sometimes and come in with a hog way in the night. He was a cooper—made water buckets, pans to make bread up in and things like that. Mammy would make us git up in the night and clean our mouths. If they didn't, children would laugh at them the next day and say the spiders had been biting your mouth, 'cause we were sposed to had so much grease on our mouths that the spiders would swing down and bite them.

"I professed religion when I was sixteen years old. It

was down in the Free Nigger Bend where my father had bought a little place on the public road between Greenwood and Shellmount.

"I married that fall. My father had died and I had got to be a man. Done better then than I do since I got old. I had one cow and my mother let me have another. I made enough money to buy a pair of mules and a wagon. My wife was willing to work. She would go out and git some poke greens and pepper and things and cook them with a little butter. Night would come, we'd go out and cut a cord of wood. Got 'long better then than people do now.

"I began preaching soon as I joined the church. I began at the prayer-meetings. I preached for forty-seven years before I fell. I've had two strokes. It's been twenty-eight years or more since I was able to work for myself.

"I have heard about the pateroles but I never did know much about them. I have heard my father talk about them. He never would get a new suit and go to town but what they would catch him out and say, 'You got a pass?' He would show it to them, and they would sit down and chew old nasty tobacco and spit the juice out on him all over his clothes.

"The Ku Klux never did bother us any. Not after I got the knowledge to know what was what. They was scared to bother people 'cause the niggers had gone and got them some guns and would do them up.

"Old Jim McClain had one son who was bad. He used to jump on the niggers an' 'buse and beat them up. The niggers got tired of it and he started gittin' beat up every time he started anything and they didn't have no more trouble.

"Jim McClain didn't mistreat his niggers. The boys did after he was dead though. He died way after slavery. If a nigger went off his place and stole a cow or a hog or something, you better not come 'round there and try to do nothin' about it. Jim McClain would be right there to protect him.

"When he died, the horses could hardly pull him up the hill. He wanted to stay back down there in the bottoms where that cotton was.

"When I got to realizing, it was after freedom. But they had slavery rules then. There was one old woman who used to take care of the children while their parents were working in the fields. Sometimes it would be a week before I would see my mother and father. Children didn't set up then and look in old folks' faces like they do now. They would go to bed early. Wake up sometimes way in the middle of the night. Old folks would be holding a meeting and singing and praying.

"They used to feed the children pot-liquor and bread and milk. Sometimes a child would find a piece of meat big as your two fingers and he would holler out, 'Oh look, I got some meat.'

"Fourth of July come, everybody would lay by. Niggers all be gathered together dancing and the white folks standin' 'round lookin' at them.

"Right after the surrender, I went to night school a little, but most of my schooling was got by the plow. After I come to be a minister I got a little schooling.

"I can't get about now. I have had two strokes and the doctor says for me not to go about much. I used to be able to go about and speak and the churches would give me something, but since this new 'issue' come out, theology and dogology and all such as that, nobody cares to pay any 'tention to me. Think you are crazy now if you say 'amen.' Don't nobody carry on the church now but three people—the preacher, he preaches a sermon; the choir, he sings a song; and another man, he lifts a collection. People go to church all the years now and never pray once.

"I get some help from the Welfare. They used to pay me ten dollars pension. They cut me down from ten to eight. And now they cut me down to four. They cut the breath out of me this time.

"I got some mighty good young brothers never pass me up without givin' me a dime or fifteen cents. Then I got some that always pass me up and never give me nothing. I have built churches and helped organize churches from here back to Mississippi.

"I don't know what's goin' to become of our folks. All they study is drinking whiskey and gamblin' and runnin' after women. They don't care for nothin'. What's ruinin' this country is women votin'. When a woman comes up to a man and smiles at him, he'll do what she wants him to do whether it's right or wrong.

"The best part of our preachers is got so they are dishonest. Stealing to keep up automobiles. Some of them have churches that ain't no bigger than this room."

Interviewer's Comment

The statements of Needham Love like those of Ella Wilson are not consistent on the subject of age. It is evident, however, that he is eighty years old or older. He thinks so. He has memories of slave times. He has some old friends who think him older.

Interviewer: Samuel S. Taylor
Person interviewed: Louis Lucas
1320 Pulaski Street, Little Rock, Arkansas
Age: 83

LOUIS LUCAS

Masters, Birth, Parents, Grandparents

"I was born in 1855 down on Bayou Bartholomew near Pine Bluff, Jefferson County.

"My mother's name was Louisa. She married a man named Bill Cardrelle after freedom. Her husband in slavery time was Sam Lucas. He belonged to a man by the name of O'Neil. They took him in the War and he never did come back to her. (He didn't much believe he was my father, but I went in his name anyway.)

"My mother's father's name was Jacob Boyd. I was young, but I know that. He was free and didn't belong to nobody. That was right here in Arkansas. He had three other daughters besides my mother, and all of them were slaves because their mother was a slave. His wife was a woman by the name of Barclay. Her master was Antoine Barclay (?). She was a slave woman. She died down there in New Cascogne. That was a good while ago.

"The French were very kind to their slaves. The Americans called all us people that belonged to the Frenchmen free people. They never gave the free Negroes among them any trouble. I mean the Frenchmen didn't give them no trouble.

"The reason we finally left the place after freedom was because of the meanness of a colored woman, Amanda Sanders. I don't know what she had against us. The old mistress raised me right in the house and fed me right at the table. When she died, this woman used to beat the devil out of me. We had had good owners. They never had no overseers until just before the War broke out, and they never beat nobody.

"The first overseer was on a boat named the Quapaw when the mate knocked him in the head and put him in a yawl and took him to the shore. The boss saw it and took four men and went and got him and had the doctor attend to him. It was a year before he could do anything. He didn't stay there long before they had him in the War. He just got to oversee a short time after he got well. He was in the cavalry. The other boys went off later. They took the cavalry first. None of them ever came back. They were lost in the big fight at Vicksburg. My paran, Mark Noble, he was the only one that got back.

"I don't remember my father's father. But I know that his mother went in the name of Rhoda. I don't know her last name. She was my grandma on his side.

"I belonged to a man named Brumbaugh. His first name was Raphael. He was a all right man. He had a colored man for an overseer before this here white man I was tellin' you about came to him. 'Uncle' Jesse was the foreman. He was not my uncle. He was related to my wife though; so I call him uncle now. Of course, I didn't marry till after freedom came. I married in 1875.

Early Days

"When I was a little child, my duty was to clean up the yard and feed the chickens. I cleaned up the yard every Friday.

House, Furniture, and Food

"My mother lived in a cabin—log, two rooms, one window, that is one window in each room.

"They didn't have anything but homemade furniture. We never had no bed bought from the store—nothin' like that. We just had something sticking against the wall. It was built in a corner with one post out. They made their table and used benches—two-legged and sometimes four-legged. The two-legged benches was a long bench with a wide plank at each end for legs.

"For food we got just what the white folks got. We didn't have no quarters. They didn't have enough hands for that. They raised their own meat. They had about seven or eight. There was Dan, Jess, Bill, Steve. They bought Bill and Steve from Kentucky.

"Old 'Free Jack' Jenkins, a colored man, sold them two men to ol' master. Jenkins was the only Negro slave trader I ever knowed. He brought them down one evening and the old man was a long time trading. He made them run and jump and do everything before he would buy them. He paid one thousand five hundred dollars for each one of them. 'Free Jack' made him pay it part in silver and some in gold. He took some Confederate paper. It was circulating then. But he wouldn't take much of that paper money.

"He stole those boys from their parents in Kentucky. The boys said he fooled them away from their homes with candy. Their parents didn't know where they were.

"Then there were my brothers—two of them, John Alexander and William Hamilton. They were half-brothers. That makes six men altogether on the place. I might have made a miscount. There was old man Wash Pearson and his two boys, Joe and Nathan. That made ten persons with myself.

"Brumbaugh didn't have such a large family. I never did know how large it was.

Soldiers

"'The rebel soldiers were often at my place. A bad night the jayhawkers would come and steal stock and the slaves too, if they got a chance. They cleaned the old man's stock out one night. The Yankees captured them and brought them back to the house. They gave him his stallion, a great big fine horse. They offered him five thousand dollars for him but he wouldn't take it. They kept all the other horses and mules for their own use, but they gave the stallion back to the old man. If they hadn't give him back the stallion, the old man would have died. That stallion was his heart. The Yankees didn't do nobody no harm.

"When the soldier wagons came down to get the feed, they would take one crib and leave one. They never bothered the smokehouse. They took all the dry cattle to feed the people that were contrabands. But they left the milk cows. The quartermaster for the contrabands was Captain Mallory. The contrabands were mostly slaves that they kept in camps just below Pine Bluff for their own protection.

How Freedom Came

"It was martial law and twelve men went 'round back and forth through the county. They come down on a Monday, and told the children they were free and told them they had no more master and mistress and told them what to call them. No more master and mistress, but Mr. and Mrs. Brumbaugh. Then they came down and told them that they would have to marry over again. But my ma never had a chance to see the old man any more. She didn't marry him over again because he didn't come back to her. But they advised them to stay with their owners if they wanted to. They didn't say for none of the slaves to leave their old masters and go off. We wouldn't have left but that old colored woman beat me around so all the time, so my mother came after me and took me home since I wanted to go. The Yankees' officer told her it would be good to move me from that place so I wouldn't be so badly treated. The white folks was all right; it was that old colored woman that beat on me all the time.

Right After Freedom

"Right after freedom my mother married Bill Cardrelle. She moved from the O'Neil place and went up to a place called the Dr. Jenkins' place. She kept house for her husband in the new place. I didn't do much there of anything. After they moved away from there when I was twelve years old, they taught me to plow (1867). I went to school in the contraband camp. Mrs. Clay and Mr. Clay, white folks from the North, were my teachers. At that time, the colored people weren't able to teach. I went a while to school with them. I got in the second reader—McGuffy's—that's far as I got.

"I stayed with my mother and stepfather till I was about sixteen years old. She sent me away to come up here to my father, Sam Lucas. My oldest brother brought me here and I worked with him two years. Then I went to a man named Cunningham and stayed with him about six months. He paid me fifteen dollars a month and my board. He was going to raise my wages when his wife decided she wanted women to do the work. The women would slip things away and she wouldn't mention them to her husband till weeks afterwards. Then long after the time, she would accuse me. Those women would have the keys. When they went in to get soap, they would take out a ham and carry it off a little ways and hide. By the time his wife would tell him about it, you wouldn't be able to find it nowhere.

"He owed me for a month's work. She told him not to pay it, but he paid it and told me not to let her know he did it. I didn't either.

"When I left him, I came over the river here down here below Fourche Dam. I stayed there forty or fifty years in that place. When I was between thirty-two and thirty-three years old, I married, and I stayed right on in that same place. I farmed all the time down there. I had to go in a lawsuit about the last crop I made. Then I came here to Little Rock in 1904 and followed ditching with the home water company. Then I did gas ditching with the gas people. Then I worked on the street car line for old man White. I come down then—got broke down, and couldn't do much. The relief folks gave me a labor card; then they took it away from me—said I was too old. I have done a heap of work here in this town. I got old and had to stop.

"I get old age assistance from the Welfare. That is where I get my groceries—through them. I wouldn't be able to live if it wasn't for them.

Opinions

"There is a big difference between the young people now and what they used to be. The old folks ain't the same neither."

Interviewer's Comment

Lucas told his story very fluently but with deliberation and care. The statement about his father on the first page was not a slip. He told what he wanted to tell but he discouraged too much effort to go into detail on those matters. One senses a tragedy in his life and in the life of his mother that is poignant and appealing. Although he states no connection, one will not miss the impression that his stepfather was hostile. Suddenly we find his mother sending him to his father. But after he reached his father, there is little to indicate that his father did anything for him. Then, too, it is evident that his father deliberately neglected to remarry his mother after freedom.

United States. Work Projects Administration

Interviewer: Miss Irene Robertson
Person interviewed: Lizzie Luckado,
Hazen, Ark.
Age: 71

LIZZIE LUCKADO

"I was born at Duck Hill, Mississippi. There was three of us children. All dead now but me. My parents was Molly Louden and Jake Porter. One master my parents talked about was Missis Molly and Dr. McCaskill. I don't think my mother was mixed with Indian. Her father was a white man, but my father said he was Indian and African. My father was in the Civil War.

"When the war was coming on they had the servants dig holes, then put rock on bottom, then planks, then put tin and iron vessels with money and silver, then put plank, then rocks and cover with dirt and plant grass on top. Water it to make it grow. They planted it late in the evening. I don't know what become of it.

"When I was eight or nine years old I went to a tent show with Sam and Hun, my brothers. We was under the tents looking at a little Giraffe; a elephant come up behind me and touched me with its snout. I jumped back and run under it between its legs. That night they found me a mile from the tents asleep under some brush. They woke me up hunting me with pine knot torches. I had cried myself to sleep. The show was "Dan Rice and Coles

Circus" at Dednen, Mississippi. They wasn't as much afraid of snakes as wild hogs, wolves and bears.

"My mother was cooking at the Ozan Hotel at Sardis, Mississippi. I was a nurse for a lady in town. I took the children to the square sometimes. The first hanging I ever seen was on Court Square. One big crowd collected. The men was not kin, they called it "Nathaniel and DeBonepart" hanging. They was colored folks hung. One killed his mother and the other his father. I never slept a wink for two or three nights, I dream and jump up crying. I finally wore it off. I was a girl and I don't know how old I was. Besides the square full of people, Mrs. Hunter's and Mrs. Boo's yards was full of people.

"We cooked for Capt. Salter at Sardis, Mississippi.

"The first school I went to was to Mrs. J. P. Settles. He taught the big scholars. She sent me to him and he whooped me for singing:

> "Cleveland is elected
> No more I expected."

I was a grown woman. They didn't want him elected I recken the reason they didn't want to hear it. Nobody liked em teaching but the last I heard of them he was a lawyer in Memphis. If folks learned to read a little that was all they cared about."

Interviewer: Mrs. Bernice Bowden
Person interviewed: John Luckett
Highway No. 65, Pine Bluff, Arkansas
Age: 83

JOHN LUCKETT

"I was born in Mississippi up above Vicksburg. I 'member the old Civil War but I was just a little boy.

"Oh, I've seen the Yankees in Vicksburg where the battle was.

"I was 'bout ten when freedom come—nothin' but a boy.

"Clara Luckett was my mother. When the War was in Fort Pillow, I was a small boy. I don't know 'bout nothin' else—that's all I know about it.

"I been workin' at these mills ever since surrender. I been firin' for 'em.

"I voted the Republican ticket. I voted for General Grant and Garfield. I was a young man then. I voted for McKinley too. I never did hold no office, I was workin' all the time. I knowed Teddy Roosevelt—I voted for him.

"They wouldn't let me go to school I was so bad. I went one day and whipped the teacher. I didn't try—I whipped him and they 'xpelled me from school.

United States. Work Projects Administration

"Since I been in this country, firin' made me deaf."

Interviewer: Miss Irene Robertson
Person interviewed: John Lynch,
Brinkley, Arkansas
Age: 69

JOHN LYNCH

"My mother was a slave of Buck Lynch. They lived close to Nashville, Tennessee. My father run away from Buck Lynch before the Civil War. He lived in the woods till he nearly went wild. My mother fed him at night. I was twenty-one years old before I ever seen him. My mother worked several years and didn't know she was free. She come with some traders from close to Nashville out here. I was born at Cotton Plant. I got two living brothers in Memphis now.

"I was raised a farmer. The first work I ever done away from home was here in Brinkley. I worked at the sawmill fur Gun and Black. Then I went to Ft. Smith and worked in er oil mill. I come back here and farmed frum 1911 till 1915. Then I worked in the Brinkley oil mill. I cooked the cotton seed meal. One of my bosses had me catch a small cup full fur him every once in awhile. The oil taste something like peanut butter. It taste very well while it is hot and smells fine too. I quit work when they quit the mill here. It burned up. I do like the work. They got some crazy notion and won't hire old fellows like me no more. Jobs are hard to get. Younger men can get something seems like pretty easy. I make a garden. That is 'bout all I can do or get to do.

"My mother's name was Molly Lynch. She cooked some at Cotton Plant and worked in the field. She talked a right smart bout the way she had to do in slavery times but I don't recollect much.

Shes been dead a long time. I heard folks say times was awful hard right after the war, that times was easier in slavery for de reason when they got sick they got the best of care. She said they had all kinds of herbs along the side of the walks in the garden. I don't guess after they got settled times was near as hard. She talked about how hard it was to get clothes and something to eat. Prices seemed like riz like they are now.

"I don't know 'bout my father's votin' cause I didn't know him till after I was grown and not much then. He was down about Marianna when I knowed him. I did vote. I vote the Republican ticket. I like the way we voted the best in 1886 or '87. It was called Fair Divide. Each side put his man and the one got most votes got elected. I don't think it necessary fur the women to vote. Her place is in the home. Seem like the women all going to work and the men quit. About 40 years ago R. P. Polk was justice of the peace here and Clay Holt was the constable. They made very good officers. I don't recollect nothing 'bout them being elected. Brinkley is always been a very peaceable town. The colored folks have to go clear away from town with any rowdiness." (The Negroes live among the whites and at their back doors in every part of town.)

"I live with my son-in-law. He works up at the Gazzola Grocery Company. He owns this house. He is doing very well but he works hard.

"The young generation so far as I knows is getting along fairly well. I don't know if times is harder; they is jes' different. When folks do right seems there's a way provided for 'em.

"I signed up with the PWA. I signed up two or three times but they ain't give us nothing much yet. They wouldn't let me work. They said I was too old. I works if I can get any work to do."

United States. Work Projects Administration

Interviewer: Miss Irene Robertson
Person interviewed: Josephine Scott Lynch,
Brinkley, Arkansas
Age: 69

JOSEPHINE SCOTT LYNCH

"Josephine Scott Lynch is my name and I sho don't know a thing to tell you. I don't remember my father at tall. The first thing I can remember about my mama she was fixing to come to Arkansas. She come as a immigrant. They paid her fare but she had to pay it back. We come on the train to Memphis and on the boat to Gregory Point (Augusta). We left her brother with grandma back in Tennessee. There was three children younger than me. The old folks talked about old times more than they do now but I forgot all she said too much to tell it straight.

"We farmed, cleared land and mama and me washed and ironed and sewed all our lives. I cooked for Mr. Gregory at Augusta for a long time. I married then I cooked and washed and ironed till I got so porely I can't do much no more.

"I never voted and I wouldn't know how so ain't no use to go up there.

"Some of the younger generation is better off than they used to be and some of them not. It depends a whole heap on the way they do. The colored folks tries to do like the white folks far as they's able. Everything is changing so fast. The present conditions is harder for po white folks and colored folks than it been in a long time. Nearly everything is to buy and prices out of sight. Work is so scarce."

Slave Narratives

www.ingramcontent.com/pod-product-compliance
Lightning Source LLC
Chambersburg PA
CBHW071647160426
43195CB00012B/1382